EMPIRES

EMPIRES

The Logic of World Domination from Ancient Rome to the United States

Herfried Münkler

Translated by Patrick Camiller

polity

First published in German in 2005 by Rowohlt as *Imperien* and
© Rowohlt·Berlin Verlag GmbH, Berlin, 2005

This English translation © Polity Press, 2007

Polity Press
65 Bridge Street
Cambridge CB2 1UR, UK

Polity Press
350 Main Street
Malden, MA 02148, USA

ISBN-10: 0-7456-3871-6
ISBN-13: 978-07456-3871-6
ISBN-10: 0-7456-3872-4 (pb)
ISBN-13: 978-07456-3872-4 (pb)

Typeset in 10.5 on 12pt Palatino
by Servis Filmsetting Ltd, Manchester
Printed and bound in Malaysia by Alden Press Malaysia

For further information on Polity, visit our website: www.polity.co.uk

CONTENTS

PREFACE

Since the middle of the twentieth century, scholars have no longer been particularly interested in the theory and history of empires. The collapse of the Soviet Union briefly revived an interest in the subject, sustained by the comforting observation that the history of empires, which goes back to the time of ancient high civilizations, was now definitively over. But, as the new global role of the United States became apparent, all this changed quite abruptly. Suddenly people were talking about American imperialism, and since then criticism of US actions in world politics has taken a strongly anti-imperial turn. It is true that the USA has often been accused of imperialism – during the Vietnam War, for instance, or in relation to military interventions in Latin America or the Persian Gulf – but these charges were directed at specific decisions and actions of the US government. The anti-imperial trend, on the other hand, is directed against US supremacy and claims to dominance as such. It goes decisively beyond earlier criticisms.

Does the world community depend for its security on a supreme imperial power? Or does that imperial power represent a serious threat to world order, and would it be better if it did not exist? The debate leading up to the latest war in the Gulf fundamentally revolved around these questions. The world community assembled in the UN has actually relied again and again on the capabilities of the dominant imperial power. That this reliance has not been selfless, and that the USA could use it to demand special rights, is something people have refused to accept. The resulting irritations also have to do with the fact that it is a long time since the functions and demands of an empire have been systematically thought through.

Empires are more than large states; they move in a world of their own. States are bound together in an order created together with other states, over which they do not have sole control. Empires in contrast see themselves as creators and guarantors of an order that ultimately depends on them and that they must defend against the outbreak of chaos, which they regard as a constant threat. A glance at the history not only of the USA but also of other empires shows that formulations such as 'the axis of evil' or 'outposts of tyranny' are nothing new or extraordinary. They run like a red thread through the history of empire.

Fear of chaos, and the self-appointed role of defender of order against disorder, good against evil, through which the empire sees and legitimizes itself, are corollaries of the imperial mission, which also represents a fundamental justification for world empire – whether it be to spread civilization, establish a worldwide socialist order, defend human rights or promote democracy. While states stop at the borders of other states and permit them to regulate their own internal affairs, empires intervene in the affairs of others in order to fulfil their mission. Empires can therefore set in train much more powerful processes of change, whereas a system of states is marked by structural conservatism.

When we look at things in this perspective, it casts doubt on what has seemed self-evident under the influence of theories of imperialism: that we ought to prefer and strive for a global order of states with equal rights and without an imperial actor. The political order of the European region, after the fall of the Roman empire, developed in such a way that it no longer produced a lasting and effective imperial power, while creating a host of pretenders to that role who soon came to grief. Elsewhere it was different – leaving aside the fact that Europeans certainly built large empires on other continents. Above all in Asia a political order was established in which empires surrounded themselves with a circle of client states. As a result, order in that region was strongly centralized, whereas in Europe there emerged a diverse polycentrism.

Our image of empires is shaped by the idea that the periphery is sucked dry and exploited, that it grows poorer while the centre becomes ever richer. Such empires have indeed existed, but they have been of short duration; after some time, resistance to the centre has grown out of control, and the costs of domination have exceeded the gains derived from the periphery. By contrast, empires have lasted longer when they have invested in their dependencies and taken pains to ensure that the periphery had as much interest as the centre in their continuation.

This book is about the types of imperial domination, the forms of imperial expansion and consolidation and the contexts in which empire-building has occurred. But our concerns are not limited to a distinction between sea and land empires, commercial and military empires, imperial orders that develop by controlling territory and those that essentially depend on controlling flows of human beings, commodities and capital. Our further aim is to consider the rationality of players, as well as the logic of world domination. The book will also offer prognoses on the duration and stability of the American empire, and reflections on how to create a Europe that can both establish itself as a political power independent of the USA and stabilize its unsettled or disintegrating neighbours and influence them in a positive way. That kind of Europe can hardly avoid developing its own imperial characteristics and capabilities – and, on closer inspection, this process has already begun. The precondition, of course, is that imperial activity is not considered a priori to be bad and reprehensible but rather is seen as a mode of problem-solving alongside the state and other forms of political organization.

This is not to be confused with rehabilitation of the old colonial empires. A war of independence against such a colonial empire is the founding myth of the USA; Europeans see themselves as having once exercised and then relinquished such domination over non-European regions. Yet it is doubtful that the model of equality and reciprocity among states will in the coming decades be able to withstand a number of already discernible challenges. The failure of states, and especially their collapse, is more likely to prompt the intervention or creation of empires.

Many will object that this opposition of state and empire does not exhaust all possibilities, and will instead outline their own conception of a good and desirable political order. But this will take them ever further away from existing reality. A glance at history shows that, when all is said and done, political models have come down to a choice between state and empire – if we understand both these concepts broadly and inclusively, without creating a generic term to cover every special case of statehood or imperiality. In exploring what is entailed in the concept of empire, in considering how empires came into being and how they collapsed, we will enter a field of knowledge that has lain waste for too long a time.

Berlin, February 2005

ACKNOWLEDGEMENTS

In the early stages of this book, I had a number of long conversations with colleagues at Humboldt University and the Berlin-Brandenburg Academy of Sciences on such questions as what empires are, whether they are a significant quantity for political analysis, and how recent empires differ from earlier ones. A further stimulus for these conversations originated in a request by Dr Ulrich Speck, at the height of European–American tensions before and during the Iraq War, that I write a contribution for a book *Empire Amerika* that he was then editing. In the framework of various lectures, including one I gave at the Goethe Institute in Boston and another at the 2004 conference of ambassadors at the German Foreign Office, I was able to develop my thoughts on the subject of empire and to present them for discussion. More than once, Dr Karsten Fischer, Dr Harald Bluhm, Dr Hans Grünberger, Dr Gerald Hubmann and Nicolas Stockhammer read and commented on sections of text, raised objections and, above all, gave me continual suggestions. In these ways the book finally began to take shape.

My secretary Karina Hoffmann once again put the text into finished form, copying out my handwritten notes and making the necessary corrections to the typescript. In the final stages, Anna Arndt and Samuel Müller gave me valuable help in ordering the notes and completing the bibliography – a possibility for which I have to thank the Wissenschaftszentrum Berlin, and especially its president Prof. Dr Jürgen Kocka, who played host to me for a year in the quiet and agreeable atmosphere of the centre.

During the whole period of work on the book, Gunnar Schmidt at Rowohlt-Berlin Verlag encouraged me to follow through the original idea and to base it on historically grounded comparative research. Bernd Klöckener, who had already worked with me on *Die neuen Kriege* (published by Polity as *The New Wars*), was again a thoughtful but also decisive editor, who made a crucial contribution to the final draft of the book. As always in the last two decades, my wife, Dr Marina Münkler, attentively accompanied me throughout the project and read the manuscript with great care. Her objections and advice once again grew out of a deep intellectual closeness. To all the above I express my heartfelt thanks.

1

WHAT IS AN EMPIRE?

Debates on the latest war in Iraq, the possible causes and hidden goals of renewed US military intervention in the oil-rich Gulf region, and the general role of the United States in the Gulf and Central Asia, together with deep rifts in transatlantic relations, have focused attention in Europe on the emergence of a new world order since the end of the East–West conflict. With Washington's notorious refusal to join international agreements, from the Kyoto Protocol to the International Criminal Court in The Hague, we have been seeing a redefinition of the American position in world politics. Relations between the USA and the UN, never unproblematic in recent decades, are now fundamentally in question after President George W. Bush, in a keynote speech at the General Assembly on 12 September 2002, threatened that the United States would solve some of the most pressing security problems on its own, if the international organization proved itself incapable of dealing with them.

In the spring of 2003, the third Gulf war demonstrated that this was no empty threat. One possible interpretation was that Washington was seeking to use the Security Council as a submissive source of legitimacy. Another was that it was beginning to free itself from demands that it act as the military arm of the international organization: it would no longer place its highly developed and costly military apparatus at the service of the international community but would deploy it in pursuit of its own interests and objectives. The conflicts in the run-up to the Iraq War were – also – a controversy about who would use whom as an instrument: whether the United States would use the United Nations or the United Nations the United States.[1]

The European security architecture, on which Germany had until then depended, seemed also to be crumbling. Largely unnoticed, NATO had in the 1990s transformed itself from an alliance based on consultation into an instrument of US control over Europe. And where it seemed too unmanageable, it was quickly replaced with a 'coalition of the willing'. In comparison with the Cold War era, the dependence of Europeans on the United States had grown rather than diminished: whoever failed to comply with US demands should expect political and economic pressure or an onslaught of derision. By contrast, anyone who wished to engage on the American side could do so any time – to be sure, on American terms and without influence on fundamental political decisions, as even Britain, the USA's principal ally, more than once discovered. In principle, then, the problems encountered by the United States in Iraq changed nothing. The era of reciprocal consultative obligations in the North Atlantic alliance was over, and NATO's eastward expansion was proving, on reflection, to be a step that significantly reduced the influence of those who had been America's allies in the East–West confrontation.[2]

In this situation, there were mounting appeals for the United States not to strive for imperial power but to content itself with its longstanding role of beneficent hegemon. To lend force to these warnings, references were made to the uncontrollable risks of empire, to the dangers of overextension and to the inevitable collapse of all previous empires. 'Whereas in the recent past', wrote Michael Mann, a Briton teaching in America, 'American power was hegemonic – routinely accepted and often considered legitimate abroad – now it is imposed at the barrel of a gun. This undermines hegemony and the claim to be a benevolent Empire.'[3] Anyone who sought to replace hegemony with an imperial position, it was argued, not only risked failing in that project but ran the danger of losing hegemony too. Hegemony and empire were thus played against each other in endless variations, almost always accompanied with advice that it was better to remain a hegemon than to strive for empire.

All at once the debate, having started as an argument about US interests and intentions in the Gulf, was being conducted with a wealth of historical arguments and comparisons, all of which, by means of analogies with earlier developments, served to turn what was disturbingly new in US policy, as well as in the shape of world politics, into something familiar and manageable. The history of the *Imperium Romanum* was held up as a foil against which to judge the prospects and risks of American policy; the structure of the *British empire* served as a model against which to measure the challenges facing the United States and its capacities to overcome them; and finally the collapse of the Soviet Union, already a good decade in the past, was cited as an example of the consequences of imperial over-stretch, which would also threaten the United States if it continued on its present course.[4] But the historical references and examples were proposed more associatively than systematically, and they were used almost entirely to support positions already adopted long before. They served to illustrate an argument rather than as empiri-cally fruitful verifications of what can be learned from the historical formation of earlier world empires.

Now, the parallel between American and Roman history arises because the United States has since its foundation invoked the Roman Republic and placed itself in that tradition.[5] What has to be critically examined, therefore, is a parallel that long ago assumed a central position in the self-consciousness and self-understanding of the American political elite. The comparison with the British world empire also arises because the United States has succeeded Britain in all those places where the British were pushed out after the Second World War – not least in the Middle East, recently a major focus of US political attention and military potential. The compari-son with the Soviet Union, finally, is unavoidable because the USA and the Soviet Union were for a good four decades rivals for supremacy in world politics, until the Russians under Gorbachev – drained by the arms race and weakened by the costs incurred in the maintenance of empire – were eliminated from the contest.[6]

The range offered by these three imperial forms is, however, too narrow for a sound analysis of the prospects and risks of the American empire. Certainly the empire of the Russian tsars and the Ottoman and Chinese empires – imperial powers of by far the longest duration – must be included in a comparative analysis. Nor should the Mongol empire of the thirteenth century be overlooked in an investigation of the logic and imperatives of empire. It fell quickly, but its territorial expanse made it among the largest in history: with an area of 25 million square kilometres it was sur-passed only by the British empire, which at its height encompassed 38 million square kilometres but stretched over five continents. The Mongol empire embraced almost the whole of Eurasia as a closed territorial unit. At the height of its power it reached from the Yellow Sea in the east to the edges of the Baltic in the west; only the Indian subcontinent and the Southeast Asian peninsula, including Burma and Indochina, as well as Western, Central and Southern Europe remained free from Mongol occupation.[7] As to the ancient world, the

Hellenistic empire in the East must also be considered alongside the Roman; and among the seaborne empires, the Portuguese must be taken into account alongside the British and Spanish, especially as it was the first European colonial empire and the last to disappear from the political map – although, since the eighteenth century, it had existed more as a protégé of the British empire than as a world power in its own right.[8]

This overview exposes a fundamental problem for any comparative investigation of the logic of empire: namely, we must first establish what we mean by empire – a task that becomes even more complicated if we further distinguish between *great* empires and *world* empires. It might have been easier to find an answer if, in recent decades, serious work in the social sciences had already developed reliable critical criteria of imperiality. But this is not the case. There is an abundance of historical accounts of individual empires, as well as important comparative studies of imperialism;[9] but the question of what an empire is and how it differs from the political order of the territorial state that evolved in Europe has remained virtually unexamined. This also explains why, in most recent debate on US policy, the concept of empire has had an arbitrary, often simply denunciatory, meaning. Political science has not provided solid definitions and backed them up with examples, but has rather left the field to the whimsical operations of everyday journalism.

What has not been achieved through prolonged scholarly work cannot be supplied all at once. In any event, so long as it is unclear what empires are and what they are not, what they must accomplish and how they differ from other structures of political order, it is impossible to derive anything from comparative scrutiny of world empires that would be significant for analysis of the new world order and the role of the United States. The logic of how empires act can be understood only if it is quite clear what distinguishes an empire.

A brief sketch of the characteristics of empires

To begin, what an empire is needs to be carefully delineated in contrast to what it evidently is not.

First, an empire must be distinguished from a state, or, more precisely, from an institutional territorial state, which operates according to completely different imperatives and a completely different action logic. This begins with the way the population is internally integrated and extends to how boundaries are conceived. The boundary line typical of states is sharp and clearly demarcated; it indicates the transition from one state to another. Such precise dividing-lines are exceptional in the case of empires. To be sure, the boundaries of an empire are no longer lost in those wide expanses in which tribes and nomadic peoples sometimes obeyed imperial requirements and sometimes resisted them; but, even since the disappearance of those unruled spaces into which the classical empires were able to expand, imperial boundaries have remained different from state borders.

Imperial boundaries do not divide political units possessing equal rights; instead they involve gradations of power and influence. Moreover, in contrast to state boundaries, they are not equally permeable in both directions: those who wish to enter an imperial space must satisfy different conditions from those who leave it. This is connected to the economic as well as the cultural attraction of imperial powers; more want to enter than to leave, and this has consequences for the border regime. US-Americans travel and work throughout the world. But anyone who does not have US citizenship cannot simply enter the United States. This points to another difference from states: communities bordering on the imperial power do not have the same dignity as that power itself.

Radically different conditions of intervention follow from the unequal permeability of imperial boundaries. Since the nineteenth century, the United States has repeatedly intervened in the politics of other states in Central America and the Caribbean, without having to consider the possibility that these will intervene in the sphere of the US state, either economically or politically and certainly not militarily. This asymmetry above all distinguishes imperial from state boundaries. Empires have no neighbours which they recognize as equals, that is, as *possessing equal rights*; with states, by contrast, this is the rule. In other words, states are always in the plural, empires mostly in the singular. This actual, or even simply asserted, peculiarity of empires affects the manner of their internal integration: whereas states, not least as a result of direct competition with neighbouring states, integrate their populations equally – above all, grant them equal rights whether they live at the core of the state or in its border regions – this is not the case with empires: there is almost always a scale of integration descending from centre to periphery, which usually corresponds to decreasing rights and an increasingly limited capacity to determine the politics of the centre.

In the case of the United States, this is true in all regions under American influence that have never had the chance to be incorporated as US federal states. There are several examples of this in the Caribbean.

Imperial borders may be alternatives to state borders. The European colonial powers were separated from one another within Europe by state borders, whereas in Africa and Asia they had imperial borders with their neighbours, within what were in most cases loose imperial condominia. These two types of border differ significantly; they made it apparent whether what lay beyond them was a state or an empire. Imperial borders may also be superimposed on, and thereby reinforce, state borders: between the Federal Republic of Germany and the German Democratic Republic, for example, there was a state border that was at the same time the outer boundary of the Soviet empire; this combination gave it the particular character with which it entered history. Since the whole habitable surface of the earth has been organized in the form of states, there remains only a complementary, not an alternative, relation between the two types of border: imperial structures are superimposed on the state order, but they no longer replace it. This sometimes makes it difficult to identify an empire. Whoever thinks of imperiality as simply an alternative to statehood will come to the conclusion that no empires exist today. Whoever, on the contrary, proceeds from the superimposition of imperial structures on the state order will encounter structures of power and influence not identical to those of the state. The fact that imperial structures are more likely to be observed in the informal sphere also follows from the particularity of imperial borders. State borders often represent overlapping political and economic, linguistic and cultural borders. This gives them their strength and makes them both hard and inflexible. Imperial borders, by contrast, may be described as a tangled web in which political and economic boundaries are separate, cultural differences are unevenly distributed and linguistic differences are quite irrelevant. This detracts from the formality of imperial boundaries and increases their flexibility.

Second, empire must be delineated in contrast to hegemonic structures of dominance. The line between hegemonic supremacy and imperial domination may be fluid, but it is still meaningful to distinguish the two. Hegemony is supremacy within a group of formally equal political players; imperiality, by contrast, dissolves this – at least formal – equality and reduces subordinates to the status of client states or satellites. They stand in a more or less recognizable dependence in relation to the centre.

In the postwar period, the position of the Soviet Union in the Warsaw Pact and that of the United States in NATO were described in terms of the contrast between empire and hegemony: the Soviet Union was supposed to be surrounded by satellite states, whose movements were determined from the centre,[10] while NATO was in principle a system of equal allies, in which the USA, by far the largest and strongest partner, had particular importance – for instance, it generally provided the supreme commander of the military forces, while other members were allowed to hold the post of general secretary. This contrasting perception makes it clear that, within the East–West conflict, the distinction between hegemony and empire was politically and ideologically charged.

Another example of the difference between hegemony and empire, more politically innocuous because of its temporal distance, is the transformation of the Delian League into the Athenian thalassocracy. The original League was an alliance against Persian dominance on the west coast of Asia Minor and the Aegean, in which all partners had the same rights. To be sure, their contributions were always very different: some only supplied money, while others provided ships, but the main contingent of the fleet always came from Athens.[11]

This inequality of contributions and capabilities did not fail to affect the inner constitution of the League, which increasingly changed from a *hegemonia* into an *archē*: supremacy turned into domination.[12] Athens provided the commander of the fighting forces and the treasurer of the League, determined the size of contributions, dominated commercial jurisdiction and ensured that its own weights and measures were binding throughout the League. It maintained garrisons in the cities of its partners and thus wielded influence over their internal affairs. And finally it moved the League's treasury from Delos to Athens, changed the object of the League's oath of allegiance from 'Athens and its allies' to 'the people of Athens', and moved decisions on war and peace from the League assembly to the Athenian popular assembly. A hegemon had turned into a despot, as the Corinthians explained when they incited the Peloponnesian League to war against Athens.[13]

The repositioning of the United States within 'the West' may be described against this background of the transformation of the Delian League into the Athenian thalassocracy. To be sure, the League was not a true empire in either its scope or its duration, but many elements of imperial politics may be seen in it as through a magnifying glass – not least because Thucydides himself established a precedent for this soon after the events. In what follows, reference will therefore often be made to Athenian maritime supremacy, even if it can be subsumed under the generic concept of empire only in a limited sense.

Third, and lastly, empire may be delineated in contrast to what has since the nineteenth century been called imperialism. A distinction between theories of empire and theories of imperialism makes it possible to disregard the normative perspective of nearly all theories of imperialism and to sharpen our descriptive-analytic focus on the imperatives of empire. The concept of imperialism also includes theories of empire-formation as a unilateral process running from centre to periphery, which proves to be rather a hindrance in the observation of real empires.

'Imperialism' means that there is a will to empire. Whether from political or economic motives, this is seen as the decisive, if not the only, cause of world empire-building. Against such an assumption is the *bon mot* of the English historian John Robert Seeley, who once said that the British empire was created 'in a fit of absence of mind'.[14] Precisely in its strategic one-sidedness – Seeley was calling for a conscious imperialist policy, because he feared that the British empire might be crushed between the great powers of the USA and Russia – his formulation underlines the extent to which theories of imperialism exaggerate the consciously purposive deliberation of those who in one way or another were drawn into the history of empire. Hardly a single empire has been founded on a *grand strategy*. Most empires have owed their existence to a mixture of chance and contingency, often taken up by individuals who were in no way legitimately authorized to do so. In that sense, almost all empires have been created 'in a fit of absence of mind'.

A focus on the centre, characteristic of imperialism theory, must be supplemented with a focus on the periphery – on power vacuums and economic dynamics, requests for intervention by losers in regional conflicts, and decisions made by local authorities. The formula 'empire by invitation', recently coined to describe the expansion of American power and influence,[15] above all expresses the initiating function of the periphery in the emergence of empire. There is, no doubt, an imperial dynamic that presses from the centre to the periphery and expands its sphere of power ever more widely; however, at the same time a current running out from the periphery also serves to expand the sphere of domination. Which of the two is stronger can be determined only in each individual case. Whereas theories of imperialism assume that the dynamic of the centre is decisive,[16] our starting point here is that a more precise observation of the periphery is important not only in relation to past empires but also for the analysis of US policy in the last decades.

World empires and great empires

Our attempt to delineate the contours of 'empire' by contrasting it with other political orders will be continued in the following chapters. First, however, we must establish some heuristic criteria to distinguish world empires from regional empires or short-lived imperial formations.

There is, to begin with, the *temporal* duration of an empire, which must have gone through at least one cycle of rise and decline and have begun a new one.[17] The criterion of long existence thus refers to the capacity for reform and regeneration that makes an empire independent of the charismatic qualities of its founder (or founding generation). We shall accordingly pay little attention to Napoleonic empire-building, or the projects of Italian fascism and German National Socialism, or the Japanese attempt to construct an 'East Asian Co-prosperity Sphere'.

It is harder to decide in the case of the Wilhelmine empire, which – even if we place the beginnings of its imperial politics not at its founding in 1871 in the Hall of Mirrors at Versailles but only at the dismissal of Bismarck by Wilhelm II – lasted somewhat longer than the imperial projects of Mussolini and Hitler, both of which were whittled down after the early successes of the war. If we take Wilhelmine and Nazi imperial politics together as, in the end, two successive cycles only separated by the defeat of the First World War, there is something to be said for the inclusion of Germany in the list of empires, since the changeover of elites would allow the criterion of regeneration to be met. A similar point might be made about Japanese empire-building, if its onset is pushed back to the Russo-Japanese War of 1905. In both cases, however, we would have to enter the reservation that a true world empire began to take shape very late and lasted for a relatively short time. The early collapse of Germany and Japan makes it hard to say for sure whether we are dealing here with the formation of world empires or great regional empires. In contrast to Michael Doyle, who gives Germany and France a central place in his comparative analysis of the formation of great empires, we shall treat both of them here as examples of *failed empires*.[18]

Besides the temporal criterion, spatial reach is also important: a power that does not dominate a significant area cannot be seriously described as an empire. Thus the Habsburg monarchy may unquestionably be called an imperial power on the grounds of duration but hardly on the grounds of spatial extent. It was much more a Central

European empire, which in the so-called Concert of Europe was on a par with states like France but exercised no hegemony within Europe as a whole. Its supremacy – even at the time when the Habsburgs held the German imperial crown – was limited to Central Europe. An exception is Emperor Charles V, who was both king of Spain and ruler of the Netherlands and commanded substantially greater resources than the later emperors resident in Vienna. With the separation of the Spanish and German lines of the Habsburgs in 1556, the marks of empire were transferred to Madrid.[19] After that, the famous 'AEIOU', the imperial formula *Austriae est imperare orbi universo*, or its German version, 'Alles Erdreich ist Österreich untertan' ('The whole world is subject to Austria'),[20] was just a historical memory.[21]

The criterion of spatial reach is much easier to apply to continental empires than to maritime empires, whose power and influence manifest themselves less in the square kilometres they dominate than in the control of commodity, capital and information flows, as well as economic nodal points.[22] Deep sea harbours and secure trade routes, available resources, and the trust of commercial partners in a currency accepted throughout the world are much more important for the development of maritime power than is the physical control of territory.[23] We shall return to a more detailed consideration of this central difference between land and sea empires; the point for the moment is simply that the formation of imperial power is not independent of geo-economic factors. Control of trade can be a source of imperial power no less than is command over territory and space. Spain in the late sixteenth century had no internationally significant commercial or banking city and was therefore not in a position to control European world trade, or to prevent the rise of England's rival and finally superior empire.

But the beginning of Spain's fall and England's rise demonstrates that it is not so easy to separate the control of commodity and capital flows from the command of territories. When Spain failed in its efforts to win back domination of the Netherlands, or (in places where it did regain control) trade came to a standstill and economic flows made a detour around the territories under their rule, the Spanish lost economic control of Europe and with it their international creditworthiness. The result was a series of state bankruptcies. A victory for the Armada in 1588 and an invasion of England would have given Spain one last chance to recapture control of economic flows via the detour of territorial domination. But its failure to achieve these objectives indicated that Spanish imperial power had passed its peak.

Geopolitical and geo-economic factors are even more closely intertwined in the formation of imperial power than state power. Because they work together time and time again, they must also be examined together. What is more, minor elements of military superiority, such as England's better metallurgy in the casting of cannons, may then tip the scales in the rise and decline of empires.[24] But this example shows that the criterion of spatial reach in the designation of world empires is not limited to physical control of territory but may also involve near-total control of commodity and capital flows. The criterion of spatial reach is therefore at least as complex as that of temporal duration.

This leads to one of the most difficult problems in the identification of world empires: what we understand by 'world'. It seems obvious that the term should denote the whole terrestrial globe, and that in this sense, since the end of the Soviet Union, only the United States can qualify as a world empire. At most, the British empire might then be added as a predecessor. What this means, however, is that a comparative examination of world empires would become impossible. In principle, this is the argument of those who insist on the historical uniqueness of the USA as the first power to span the whole earth, even if by methods of informal dominance rather than formal domination – so that any further attention to the history of world empires becomes meaningless for an understanding of the contemporary situation. In a sense, Michael Hardt and Antonio Negri in their book *Empire* (2002) follow this model of argumentation, though admittedly the new empire identified by them does not coincide with American power but has constituted itself as a network structure transcending political borders and sovereignty.

Today, we can see somewhat more clearly that US power grows out of control not only over the earth but also over outer space. Satellite-guided cruise missiles enable the US military to reach any place on earth, while America also has the capacity to bundle and channel all of man's technological visions and fantasies of expansion – from the moon landing to the colonization of Mars. As a result, the concept of the world has been acquiring truly transglobal characteristics.[25] Transglobality is an essential source of power for the American empire. But this is no reason to maintain that there are no comparisons with earlier empires.

'World' is a relative and variable quantity, which cannot be tied down by means of invariants such as the geographical outline of continents or the physical dimensions of the globe. The world community is always determined by the current field of vision and the horizon of civilizations, and therefore more by cultural and techno-logical than by geographic factors.[26] What the 'world' is today has to do with the extent of commercial relations, the density of informa-tion flows, the state of knowledge, navigational capacities and much more. The claim of empires to world domination has thus acquired an ever wider reach from antiquity to the present, so that there is now indeed room on the globe for only one empire – in accordance with the feature of uniqueness and distinctiveness on which empires must always insist.

From antiquity to the modern era there was room for several empires, but this did not negate each one's claim to imperiality. The Chinese and Roman empires existed side by side for centuries as 'parallel empires',[27] without this in any way restricting their claims to legitimacy. The 'worlds' ruled by the two empires did not impinge upon each other. By contrast, the coexistence of the Byzantine and Carolingian or Ottoman and Salic emperors placed their legitimacy in question: they belonged to the same 'world', and there could be only one imperial overlord. This meant that, at least on the ceremonial level, they denied each other's claims to equality.[28]

Until the early twentieth century the British and Russian empires could coexist relatively unproblematically. The 'worlds' they ruled were separate from each other, and above all sufficiently different. This applied not only to the areas dominated by the British and the Russians – which involved a division of Asia into northern and southern halves along the mountain ranges from the Caucasus to the Himalayas[29] – but even more to the ways in which they exercised their domination. The land empire of the Russians, integrated by administrative, and when necessary military, control, and the British empire of the seas, essentially held together by commercial exchange, did not threaten each other or place each other's legiti-macy in question – at least as long as the Russians held back their 'thrust towards the sea' and warm water ports.

This was no longer the case in the US and Soviet empires that took over from the British and Russians: even in their most basic assump-tions, in their *mission*, each denied the other's right to exist. Moreover, they contested the same spaces and spheres: from the Soviet Union's push into the oceans with a sizeable navy, to the com-petition for supremacy in space. For the United States and the Soviet Union, unlike the British and Tsarist empires, the existence of the other was a limitation on its own imperial claims to leadership. They divided a common 'world', whereas the Tsarist and British empires had each ruled in its own world.

What was not acceptable in the coexisting 'worlds' of the British maritime empire and the continental Russian empire was any attempt by a third empire to establish itself in the space remaining between them. It would inevitably come into conflict with one of the empires, and that would regularly grow into a larger war in which the other empire would also enter against it. We may say that the logic of both empires, each confined to its own 'world', was to work together in the observation and assessment of the third and to prevent the deployment of its power. This was so from Napoleon through Wilhelm II to Hitler and Emperor Hirohito, and it made no difference which of the two empires the third chose to confront strategically. For Napoleon it was from the beginning the British empire, while Wilhelm II and Hitler tried as much as possible to avoid a conflict with Britain, either confining their imperial claims to continental Europe or directing them towards the east. Napoleon and Hitler came unstuck essentially in the East, whereas Wilhelm II lost throne and empire in conflict with the West. Finally, Japan, having successfully asserted itself against Russia in the early twentieth century, was defeated in the Second World War by the United States, which in East Asia too pursued strategic cooperation with the Soviet Union. In all cases, the imperatives of maritime and continental empire gave rise to cooperation against the third, and the imperatives emanating from the respective imperial 'worlds' asserted themselves against all opposing objectives and plans.[30]

How can these imperial 'worlds', whose external boundaries are fairly easily recognizable, be described from within? What characterizes them internally, and how do they differ from non-imperial worlds? And, not least, do the internal spaces of continental and maritime empires have any characteristics in common?

The centre–periphery contrast characteristic of imperial spaces has already been mentioned; it is clearly visible in empires based on the domination of space and in those whose power depends mainly on the control of various flows. Furthermore, the specialist literature again and again shows evidence of the multi-ethnic or multinational character of empires. This characterization is nevertheless problematic, both because it is trivial – large empires necessarily embrace several ethnic or national communities – and because it is politically defined, given that the imperial centre ultimately operates on the 'divide and rule' principle to decide which differences are national and whether they are to be accepted or suppressed.[31]

Above all in the European context, in relations between West European national states and Central and East European empires, the issue has also been where their strengths and weaknesses have lain at a particular time: in national exclusiveness or ethnic diversity. The notorious weakness of the Ottoman empire, as well as the centrifugal tendencies of the Habsburg monarchy and the Tsarist empire, gave rise to a conviction in the early twentieth century that the nation-state was superior to a multi-ethnic formation in cases of conflict – a conviction that seemed to be confirmed by the outcome of the First World War – but then the rise of the United States and the Soviet Union, together with the marginalization of European states in world politics, helped to swing the pendulum the other way. Obviously, we are dealing here with impressions and assumptions for which the conditions of the time were responsible, and not with empirically robust criteria of scholarly analysis.

A look at the percentage share of dominant peoples within an empire tells us nothing about its spatial extent or temporal duration: the share of the Han Chinese in the Chinese empire amounted to over 90 per cent for the longest time; the share of Russians within the Tsarist empire in 1897 was about 44 per cent; that of German-Austrians in the Danubian monarchy during the last census in 1910 was about 24 per cent; and that of the British in their world empire in 1925 about 10 per cent.[32] At least in the short to medium term, these figures allow no further conclusions to be drawn. They offer no general criterion of empire.

The compulsion to intervene, neutrality options and the Melian dialogue in Thucydides

In contrast, a number of conclusions may be drawn from the fact that the central power is under an evident compulsion to intervene politically and militarily *within* the imperial 'world' it dominates – a compulsion it cannot resist without endangering its position. In other words, an empire cannot remain neutral in relation to the powers in its sphere of influence, and accordingly it has a strong inclination not to allow them the possibility of neutrality either. Only within a 'world' order shaped by the state model is there such an option. An imperial power that remains neutral in relation to conflicts within its 'world' or periphery inevitably loses its imperial status. This also distinguishes empires from states. Many of the recent irritations in American–European relations arise from a failure duly to acknowledge this difference.

That imperial, and to a somewhat lesser degree hegemonic, powers are under constant pressure to intervene essentially has to do with the credibility problem, to which they are subject in very different ways from non-imperial powers. A famous example is the conflict between the Athenians and Melians portrayed by Thucydides in his *History of the Peloponnesian War*.[33] Wishing to stay out of the war with Sparta, the Melians maintained that Athens could easily accept the neutrality of a small island in the Aegean, a territory it dominated, that neither political nor military participation by the Melians would make any difference, and that magnanimity on the part of the Athenians – if they did not force the Melians into the war – would be celebrated everywhere. The Athenians countered that, if they yielded in this case, other allies would want the same freedom to decide; the power of Athens would quickly crumble, or it would be obliged on countless occasions to re-establish its political authority by force. The Melians must therefore obey its orders, or their city would be destroyed. Athens might perhaps have been able to tolerate Melian neutrality if it had not appeared before Melos with a massive fleet. But, under the circumstances, a climb-down was no longer possible without causing considerable damage to Athens's authority. Any compromise with the Melians would have meant a loss of prestige, and Athens would have suffered in terms of its power and influence.

It has been said of the Melian dialogue that the two sides were fundamentally talking past each other.[34] That is certainly an accurate observation, but the apparent misunderstandings were essentially due to the incompatibility of an imperial logic with the expectations of a small power in its relations with a larger power. Athens did not accept the wish of the Melians to be acknowledged as an equal partner.

In the literature on Thucydides, as in histories of the Athenian maritime empire, there are two contrary verdicts on the outcome of the conflict. One says that Thucydides' account judges in favour of Athens: Melos fell, its men were killed, its women and children were dragged into slavery. In the face of the reality principle represented by Athens, the Melians based themselves essentially on hopes and wishes, and this led them to a faulty judgement of the situation that proved to be their undoing. This interpretation is not content to express the pathos of actuality in the Athenian argument. It is much more a judgement that, in the difficult situation of war with Sparta, Athens was right to deal as it did with the vacillation of allies and the example that refractory behaviour on their part might give to others; there was nothing to be done but force Melos into a decision for or against the imperial power in the Aegean. Even the smallest concession would have been a mistake with great consequences.

Empires lack a neutrality option when seriously challenged, since they must impose on their 'world' the alternative of being for or against the dominant power and must treat neutrality as concealed enmity. In this view, then, President Bush's declaration that 'Who's not for us is against us' is a frank expression of the imperial logic.

The contrary interpretation of the Athenian–Melian dialogue derives its meaning not directly from the events surrounding Melos but from how they are inserted into Thucydides' whole account of the war. For he immediately follows the section on Melos with a crucial report on the Athenian expedition against Syracuse, which marked the beginning of the end of Athenian power. With a grossly inflated opinion of itself, Athens overextended its capacities and powers with a naval enterprise that led to its own collapse.[35]

But how could such a disastrous deviation from Pericles' original war plan have occurred? He had intelligently weighed up the capabilities of Athens and Sparta and adopted a defensive strategy whereby the Athenians would refrain from any wider conquests and provisionally satisfy themselves with the status quo.[36] If they held to this, their victory in the struggle against Sparta would in the end be assured. According to this interpretation, Athens was defeated by hubris – 'the arrogance of power', to use William Fulbright's much-quoted phrase[37] – which was already at work in the Melian dialogue. The Athenian argument against the Melians was determined not by the pathos of actuality but by blindness, which could lead only to political-military catastrophe: the Athenians spoke of political credibility, but their words and deeds suggested a loss of any sense of obligation to their allies, on which the unity of the maritime alliance depended more than on military might. With its disappearance, Athenian hegemony turned into empire; only then did the allies of Athens try to free themselves from the burdensome force of the dominant power.

The two interpretations of Thucydides express quite precisely the contradictory judgements of US policy in recent years: either it has been driven by imperatives bound up with the logic of empire; or the US has been destroying its own moral credibility by reckless power politics, and American influence in the world would be much more secure if grounded on moral credibility rather than on the deployment of aircraft carriers, cruise missiles and ground troops. Jürgen Habermas, above all, has expressed this latter view in a number of articles.[38] It of course assumes that a wide range of decisions is possible, so that responsible politicians can choose to respond to a challenge in various ways. It is on the basis of this assumption that most critics hold particular individuals responsible for US policy.

Habermas thus also assumes that after the end of the East–West conflict the USA had the choice 'whether the one remaining superpower would resume the road to a cosmopolitan legal order or revert to the imperial role of a good hegemon beyond international law',[39] and above all he blames the influence of Bush's neoconservative advisers for the decision to take the second course.

A contrasting approach, which looks at the logic of empire and the imperatives arising from it, ascribes a more limited significance to the influences and decisions of individuals. It concerns itself much more with structures and guidelines that define the scope for action. It does not, therefore, ask what relevance Christian revivalism has for George Bush's policies, nor does it examine the role of Paul Wolfowitz, deputy defense secretary in the Bush administration, nor does it assume that the influence of neoconservatism is decisive in US policy. It is also not particularly interested in the psychological condition of the United States after the attacks of 11 September 2001.[40] Instead, it seeks out the logic of imperial power.

Of course such imperatives never operate on their own, and they can be missed or misunderstood by political players. Moral credibility, for example, is undoubtedly among the resources of imperial power. In this perspective, however, it is not the standard of policy but one of its instruments: the logic of empire knows very well how to deploy moral credibility as an element of power, but it would never allow itself to be measured by that standard.

What constitutes the imperial logic, what its requirements are and what scope it allows for resistance – all this will now be investigated and discussed in relation to past empires.

2

EMPIRE, IMPERIALISM AND HEGEMONY: A NECESSARY DISTINCTION

Ways of seeing empires are still subject to the claims of imperialism theory, for which the formation of great empires is attributable only to the actions of expansionist elites. Whether out of a need for prestige, a striving to become more powerful or a thirst for ever greater profit, a few large states are supposed to have pursued a policy of economic penetration or political annexation of foreign lands, which resulted in the formation of Europe's colonial empires. As these experiences remain central in most discussions of empire, we should now take a closer look at them.

If we were to consider only the political journalism of the late nineteenth and early twentieth centuries, we might indeed gain the impression that empire-building was purely a matter of elite imperialist ambitions.[1] In this view, rivalry among European powers was decisive, since the fear was that any country which fell behind in the race to expand political and economic power would not only lose ground to others but enter the path of general decline.[2] Only those who stayed in the fight for the lion's share of global dominance and the most important resources and markets of the world economy could survive as independent political powers. Nationalism, social Darwinism and a general jitteriness were pushing Europe, with Russia and America on the wings, into a state of feverish excitement,[3] so that suddenly the future of the continent seemed to depend upon the division into spheres of power and influence outside Europe.

In retrospect, it is hardly possible to see the phase of wild, hectic competition as a consequence of rational, well-considered decisions, and in the end European colonialism did not at all yield what had been expected of it. This contradicts the analyses one finds in economic theories of imperialism. Colonial imperialism may well have been, as they argue, one of the most brutal forms of exploitation and repression ever seen in history, yet as a rule it tended to cost as much as it brought in. From the point of view of economics, it was a great political and economic miscalculation.

The self-destructive dynamic of capitalism: economic theories of imperialism

How can such a miscalculation be explained, especially as it was not limited to one country or the European continent (where the famous, or notorious, 'scramble for Africa' originated) but applied all around the world?[4] Japanese and American politics were gripped by imperialist fever: Japan invaded the East Asian mainland, entering into a conflict with Russia over Manchuria that led to the classical imperialist war of 1905; and the United States, following the Spanish–American war of 1898, not only established itself in the Central American and Caribbean but annexed the Philippines, where it suffered heavy losses in a guerrilla war stretching over several years.[5]

Was the miscalculation due to an epidemic of hysteria that made it impossible for the elites to pursue their interests in a rational manner? Was overaccumulation or underconsumption in the economically advanced countries really the crucial reason why new markets had constantly to be found for commodities and investment capital, as Marxist theorists in particular have argued? Or is it rather the case, as Joseph Schumpeter maintained, that late nineteenth- and early twentieth-century imperialism was a last rebellion by premodern elites against the new spirit of trade and change, setting in train conquests about which it was evident that they would never prove their worth?[6]

There are two possible ways of explaining the rush of empire-building in the nineteenth century and the conflicts associated with it. One starts from the essential irrationality of the enterprise and defines the problem as its breakthrough into a world increasingly based on rational thinking. The other sees imperialism precisely as rational action on the part of the most powerful players in the capitalist world, so that it is competition among national capitals and their amortization requirements which determine the direction of imperialist expansion – hence the relatively little interest of such theories in the rise of empires and their focus instead on whether this will be the age of barbarism (as Rosa Luxemburg predicted) or whether the capitalist dynamic can be checked through social-political reforms (as John Atkinson Hobson believed).

Hobson, writing at the turn of the twentieth century, was the first to develop a purely economic basis for imperialism theory, which was then worked up by later theorists. His idea was that imperialist policies brought no profit to society as a whole but, on the contrary, involved heavy losses. In no case did the proceeds of trade with economically underdeveloped, often only partly accessible regions justify the military and administrative costs of empire, not to speak of investments in infrastructure.

So, who did have an interest in building such unprofitable empires? Neither taxpayers nor merchants nor entrepreneurs, in Hobson's opinion, but only finance capital looking for investment opportunities. Expansionist policies created such opportunities – at least if the state gave appropriate guarantees and was prepared to intervene militarily, and if necessary to assume political control, in order to protect overseas investments amid uprisings or civil wars.[7] Finance capital manipulated public opinion in its efforts to persuade the state to open up safe and lucrative investment opportunities abroad; in particular, it aroused nationalist instincts and stirred up a pro-imperialist mood, so that the interest of a few capitalists in overseas investments could be made to seem a task of the whole nation. For Hobson, then, imperialism was fundamentally a project of internal distribution within economically advanced countries.

Unlike later Marxist theorists of imperialism, Hobson did not hold that capitalism would collapse without overseas expansion and political-military guarantees for the capital invested there. Rather, he was convinced that the underconsumption problem in the capitalist countries could be solved in the medium term through active social policies that raised the purchasing power of the masses. The political domestication of capitalism and the development of effective welfare systems was thus his alternative to the worldwide spread of aggressive imperialism.

John Maynard Keynes, the theoretician of anti-cyclical economic management, was stimulated and influenced in many ways by Hobson's critique of imperialism. Luxemburg and Lenin, on the other hand, in their inner-party disputes with currents geared to trade union action or social reform, categorically rejected a 'social-democratic' perspective of the reformability of capitalism and emphasized its *inherent* drive to imperialist expansion. From the first, their theories of imperialism had the function of directing the whole focus on the overcoming of capitalism by revolutionary means; imperialist competition itself was leading in that direction, since the great powers would weaken themselves in war and place socialist revolution on the agenda.

All these theories and debates did not evince a real interest in empire-building, but turned on the question of whether European societies could or could not be reformed. They therefore paid scant attention to the problems of the periphery into which the empires were expanding. For imperialism theory, these political-economic spaces were literally peripheral to the issue of the reformability of capitalism and the nature of its strengths and weaknesses. Empire-building was conceived as a process inevitably flowing out from the centre to the periphery; only push-factors were taken into account, while pull-factors remained unnoticed. Hence the conclusion reached by imperialism theories was determined in advance by the questions they posed and the cognitive interests they defended.

Lenin was the only one whose theoretical work took up the periphery in a little more detail, but this mainly had to do with the fact that Russia – though itself for centuries an imperial power – belonged to the periphery as this was defined in *economic* imperialism theory. If imperialism was understood as a consequence of the overaccumulation of capital, Russia could have only a walk-on part because of its well-known shortage of capital, especially as this meant that its attempts in the British or American style to complement military imperialism with an economic 'ruble imperialism' were doomed to failure.[8] For Lenin, Russia was the 'weakest link' where the imperialist chain would inevitably break.

The prognosis of Lenin the theoretician came at just the right time for Lenin the politician, for it meant that the socialist revolution would first take place in Russia and only then spread out to the real heartlands of the capitalist-imperialist world. Lenin too was fundamentally indifferent to the periphery: he was interested only in the weakest link of the imperialist chain, where he saw the best opportunities for a revolutionary takeover. How true this was may be gauged from the rigidity of his actions during and after the Civil War: the reconquest of parts of the Tsarist empire that had seceded during the Revolution, and their brutal incorporation into the new Soviet Union. The periphery was for him only a means to the end of winning the battle in the centre.

Economic theories of imperialism, most of them socialist, therefore converted a specific problem of capitalist societies into the key for the interpretation of empire-building. They were – and this is not meant as a reproach – contemporary answers to contemporary questions. As a rule, however, they were not understood in this way, but were presented as *general* explanations of empire-building. Purporting to explain more than they were capable of explaining,[9] they obscured the real factors and dynamics of imperial policy.

What might have been true of Britain, America and even Germany in the late nineteenth or early twentieth century was much less applicable to France, which, though possessing Europe's second largest colonial empire, had a more modest dynamic of capital accumulation than its major rivals. It was applicable even less to Japan and, as we have seen, least of all to Russia. During the period in question, the Tsarist empire had to rely on imports of capital, and its changing alliances – especially the switch from Germany to France at the end of the 1880s, which was to be so important in the run-up to the First World War – were closely bound up with the loan agreements that Russia had to make in order to modernize its infrastructure and army and to build up its industry.[10] Economic dynamics cannot explain the imperialist policies of the Tsarist empire in the second half of the nineteenth century.

The centre–periphery problem

The building of the Tsarist empire involved pressing the Russian people into service and pumping it dry.[11] This has been described as 'internal colonialism', one of whose central components was the (partly forcible) population transfer from European Russia to Siberia.[12] There can be no talk here of corruption of the masses by the 'superprofits' resulting from empire, which Lenin invoked in Western Europe to explain the long absence of revolution. The Russian peasantry, in particular, coughed up for centuries to increase the power of the tsars, and it is more than questionable whether (as imperialism theory supposes) the aristocracy profited so much from empire. The fact that some 90 per cent of the land belonging to the nobility changed hands between 1863 and 1904 would seem to indicate the contrary.[13] Russia's attempt to keep up with the imperial rivalry of the great powers forced changes in its social-economic structures, which further promoted the decay of noble property and the impoverishment of the peasantry. As far as the analyses and prognoses of imperialism theory are concerned, a greater problem is the impoverishment of the aristocracy itself, the social-economic base of the Tsarist empire. It is quite evident that its social interests cut across the political imperatives of empire, and in order to defend them it would actually have had to oppose further expansion. For most of its history, Tsarist Russia constituted a good example of an empire in which scarcely any real profiteers from imperial policy were to be found at the centre of power.

There was another element in Russia which cannot be explained in the terms of imperialism theory: the fact that, since the time of Peter the Great, the tsars largely fell back on non-Russians to administer their huge empire. Germans played a prominent role in this respect: not only the Baltic German nobility, which came under Tsarist rule with the expansion of the early eighteenth century and enjoyed a number of special privileges, but also officers and administrators recruited in Germany itself. In the eighteenth and nineteenth centuries, some 18 per cent of senior officials in Russia were of German origin, and by the turn of the twentieth century the proportion had probably risen even higher.[14] They certainly profited from Russia's imperial expansion, and owed their position and careers to it. The same was true of the Cossacks, who were given an important role in defending the frontiers. The true beneficiaries of the Tsarist empire were thus peripheral groups and national minorities that assumed positions they would not otherwise have had.[15]

This preference for groups and minorities newly settled in the periphery of the empire is explicable in theories of imperial rule, but not in imperialism theory. The latter tries to find links between existing social-political power and imperial expansion, identifying the most powerful players as the forces pulling the strings and benefiting from a policy of expansion, whereas theories of imperial rule develop the idea that certain socially marginal groups are useful for a far-flung empire in which the centre cannot control all events and decisions but must delegate responsibility; the interesting question is then not so much whether the decisions are right or wrong, but how the loyalty of local decision-makers can be ensured. The greater the extent of an empire, the more noticeable centrifugal forces become. Thus, in Russia, governors and military commanders forged links with local populations on the periphery or gained the trust and affection of the troops serving under them, but this increased the danger that they would try to secede from the empire or stage a coup to grab the central power for themselves. The history of the *Imperium Romanum* after the civil wars of the first century BC is marked by a series of rebellions and usurpations that began in the periphery and spread to the centre.[16]

Excessively close ties between a local population and its governor or military personnel can be prevented if top administrators and officers are regularly switched around at short intervals. Empires have not infrequently resorted to this device, but it has the drawback that decision-makers have no time to familiarize themselves with the peculiarities of the region and therefore make mistakes by rigidly applying general principles. A well-known example of the negative consequences of rotation is P. Quinctilius Varus, the Roman governor in Germania, who had previously served in Syria and was insufficiently familiar with the quite different conditions between the Rhine and the Elbe. This was not the least reason why, in AD 9, a conspiracy of German tribal chieftains was able to draw the governor and his legions into an ambush in the Teutoburg Forest, inflicting on them a rout that stopped Rome's push to the northeast.[17] The history of imperial defeats is filled with figures of the same kind as Varus.

The alternative to rapid circulation of office-holders is the elite recruitment of groups or individuals who, since their political and personal fate is tied to that of their sovereign, will be forced to display energy and unconditional loyalty to the imperial centre, even when the sovereign is far away and cannot directly control his representatives.

Another example of the use of minorities to secure imperial power is the Ottoman janissary corps, though admittedly it was stationed not in the periphery but at the heart of imperial power, in and around Constantinople, and could therefore itself present a danger to the sultan's rule. As they were the best-trained and best-equipped troops at his disposal, he would have found it difficult to defeat a janissary uprising; for better or worse he therefore relied upon their loyalty. The unconditional support of these elite units, as well as their high level of combat-readiness, was ensured through the so-called *devshirm* or 'blood tax', the enlistment of children from Christian parts of the Balkans dependent on the Ottoman empire. They had no social ties or political contacts in the centre of power and owed their privileged position entirely to the ruler's goodwill.

This Balkan reservoir, ethnically less Turkish than Albanian, ensured that the sultans would not share the fate of so many Roman emperors and fall victim to an uprising by their praetorian guard. Much the same was true of the Ottoman administrative elite. Its decline began in the late seventeenth century, when more and more free-born Muslims began to rise in its ranks and the centre increasingly lost control of the periphery as tax-farmers set about lining their own pockets.[18]

The rapid growth of centrifugal forces, eventually leading to the secession of whole territories, may also be observed in the decline and fall of the Spanish world empire. In Latin America, the Spanish colonial authorities kept down the numbers of bureaucrats and military officers and were able to operate in a relatively cost-effective manner, but this led to growing creolization both of the administration and of the militia leadership, at a time when a large soldiery was needed to keep order and to repel the nomadically inclined Indian tribes. Trade within Spanish America was already largely in Creole hands.[19] Soon the Creole upper layers, in a region that stretched at its height from California and Texas in the north to the tip of Chile in the south, saw no reason why the riches of Latin America should continue to be sent to the mother country to finance its pursuit of European hegemony.

Things looked very different at the heart of the empire, in Madrid, where the Bourbon reforms sought to contain Creole influence and to increase the weight of European Spaniards in the New World. However, the economic success of these reforms resulted in a growing estrangement of Spanish America from the mother country.[20] When French troops occupied Spain in 1807 and shortly afterwards installed one of Napoleon's brothers on the throne, this was only the occasion, not the deeper cause, of the separation of Central and South America from Spain.

The marginal social and political position of parts of the Tsarist military-administrative elite corresponded, in the case of the Spanish empire, to the longstanding minority position of the white urban upper classes within a mostly Indian environment. The centrifugal tendencies of the imperial order were here offset by the uncertainty of the Creole upper classes as to whether, following a political break with Spain, they would be able to maintain their social position in the New World or would be swept aside by slave or Indian uprisings. It was Spain's guarantees of stability, covering the administration, the justice system and internal and external security, which acted as a centripetal counterforce. Only when the Creoles had to pay ever rising costs for the Bourbon reforms, and when Spain, at war with Britain, was no longer able to deliver the promised stability, did the idea become widely accepted that it would be more advantageous to break with the empire than to remain within it.

The Russian and Spanish examples show that, at least after an empire has been put in place, the structure and dynamic of its political order cannot be understood only from the point of view of the centre. Numerous decisions affecting the very existence of the empire are taken on its periphery, or by individuals or groups of individuals who originated there and whose political perception remains coloured by it. This was true, for example, of Roman emperors after the second century.

A quite different kind of peripheral influence on the centre may be seen in the case of the British empire. In the closing decades of the nineteenth century, the British at least partly gave up the comfortable position of an empire in control of events and burdened themselves, in India and Africa, with the costs and responsibilities of a territorial imperium. At first the tasks of empire-building, spreading free trade and guaranteeing peace through intensive economic links were largely left up to non-state players, especially trading companies, but also individual businessmen and banks, which opened up new markets and made the flow of commerce run deeper and wider. Richard Cobden, founder of the free trade movement, wrote in 1846: 'I see in the free trade principle that which shall act on the moral world as the principle of gravitation in the universe, drawing men together, thrusting aside the antagonisms of race, and creed, and language, and uniting us in the bonds of eternal peace.'[21]

Towards the end of the century, however, things began to develop in ways not foreseen in the free trade theories and liberal internationalism.[22] The economic agreements forced on dependent countries did not lead to a strengthening and liberalization of the political order, but rather to its gradual weakening and eventual breakdown. Rebellions broke out, India's Sepoy Rising of 1857 not being the first, and under their impact the British altered their whole administrative and military structure in the subcontinent. They suspended cost-effective elements of indirect rule and replaced them with more expensive forms of direct rule. This was a decision that came from the centre, essentially prompted by instability on the margins of the empire.

Unrest overseas, together with the rise of politicians less indulgent towards the economic dreams of empire, led to delays in debt repayment and threats to the security of investments in the newly opened regions. The United States faced similar problems – especially in its Central American/Caribbean 'backyard' – and felt compelled to intervene on a number of occasions. Suddenly, a stark choice confronted the very powers which, until then, had refrained with good reason from direct political interference in the regions they had economically penetrated: either to withdraw from them altogether or to take over administrative and political control.[23] The Europeans, especially the British, opted for the latter and established colonies in sub-Saharan Africa and Asia, while the United States limited itself to a policy of ad hoc military intervention in the Caribbean and Central America. Complete withdrawal, on the other hand, would have meant writing off the investments that had already been made, and none of the powers involved in this phase of economic globalization seriously considered such a response to the first signs of resistance or instability.[24]

For the theories of economic imperialism, the decision by the expanding societies of the West to place their state apparatus, armed forces and fiscal revenue in the service of economic interests, in the ways we have just been describing, marked the transition from capitalist to imperialist states.[25] In this approach the changes taking place in the periphery are scarcely visible. Yet there traditional forms of production were breaking down under the pressure of imports from the industrial heartlands, and traditional ways of life were losing their power to bind people together. Not the least important were the effects that early forms of globalization had upon these societies in the second half of the nineteenth century, leading to the great push of the 1880s that ushered in the true age of imperialism. If this process is described as an economically induced erosion of existing orders, which made it necessary to stabilize them from outside through the application of power politics, then some remarkable parallels with the situation at the end of the twentieth century become visible. Thus, the several humanitarian military interventions of the last decade – from the prevention of genocide to the ending of civil wars – appear as aftercare directed at unintended effects of the new globalization process. The humanitarian imperialism of which some authors speak would then be nothing other than political management of the traces that the social-economic process of globalization has left behind.

It is true that voices have often been raised to demand that historians of European imperialism should pay greater attention to the periphery,[26] but they have not found much of an echo. Imperialism theory neglects the periphery simply because its underlying conception and problematic refer essentially to the centre: it designates as imperialist those intellectual currents and political movements which have an interest in empire-building, and therefore inevitably fixes its gaze on the goals of a few players in the centre while downplaying the role that the two-way chain of functional effects between centre and periphery plays in the formation of empires. By contrast, theories of empire have to keep centre and periphery equally in view, both in analysis of the formative period of empires and in relation to the era following their consolidation.

This brings us to another problem of imperialism theory: its concentration on the formative period and its neglect of the later functioning of empire. This one-sidedness is also evidently due to the cognitive interest in the dynamic of capitalism. Writers in this tradition were convinced that imperialism would not produce a stable order but would itself collapse amid the inevitably resulting wars and conflicts. With such expectations, there was clearly no point in making detailed analyses of the functioning of developed empires. During the revival of imperialism theory in the 1960s and 1970s, the main interest was again in ephemeral empire-building ventures, such as those of Bismarck and the Wilhelmine regime, or the Greater Germany conceptions of National Socialism. Perhaps a critical glance was also cast at American and Japanese imperialism, but no major empire, with the exception of the British, was found worthy of intensive discussion.[27] The idea that the end of the imperial age lay just ahead seemed to make such debates irrelevant, and so even in the case of the British empire writers concentrated on its periods of hectic expansion rather than on those when it was functioning smoothly. We should not exclude the possibility that this particular design of imperialism theory laid the ground for today's hasty predictions that the American empire has no future.

Prestige and great power rivalry: political theories of imperialism

Can we expect genuinely political theories of imperialism to give a better account of recent trends in power politics? This is scarcely true with regard to the centre–periphery problematic, since it too focuses attention on the development of the metropolitan countries. The first political theories of imperialism were already concerned to explain the rise of Napoleon III and the genesis of the Second Empire in France, and so they took as their comparative reference the First Empire, constructed by Napoleon I, and showed how both placed themselves in the tradition of the Roman empire. At the source of these theories stands Karl Marx's *Eighteenth Brumaire of Louis Bonaparte* (1852). Here he attributed the political rise of Napoleon III to a 'class equipoise' in mid-nineteenth-century France: the forces of progress and the forces of inertia held each other in a paralysing balance, with the result that the state rose autonomously above them and pursued a policy of its own, not subject to the directive force of a ruling class.

The so-called theory of Bonapartism[28] is not itself a theory of imperialism, but it contains some elements of one, in so far as the army and state elite are no longer subject to the interests and profit calculations of the ruling class but can give free rein to their striving for prestige (to use a Weberian concept). The costs of prestige can be disregarded, since they have to be assumed by a politically power-less society. Marx summed up as follows the events of December 1851: 'France therefore seems to have escaped the despotism of a class only to fall back beneath the despotism of an individual, and indeed beneath the authority of an individual without authority.'[29]

For Marx, Louis Bonaparte was simply the leader of two sections of the lumpenproletariat: the parvenus and the thugs; the army, not the National Assembly, would therefore be the real power in France. Even before the declaration of the Second Empire, he wrote that 'only one thing was needed to complete the true form of this repub-lic: the former's [i.e., parliament's] recess must be made permanent, and the latter's [the republic's] motto, *liberté, égalité, fraternité*, must be replaced with the unambiguous words *infantry, cavalry, artillery!*'[30] Unable, like Napoleon I, to prolong his imperial usurpa-tion of power except through 'periodical wars', Louis Bonaparte built his regime on 'despotism at home and war abroad'.[31] Imperialism and despotism were two sides of the same coin.

If Marx, instead of focusing exclusively on economics and the class struggle, had also built political and psychological aspects into his account, he would soon have encountered that inclination which Max Weber called the 'striving for prestige'. The emperor, the court and the generals made strenuous efforts to achieve recognition of their pre-eminent role, not only in France but also in Europe and the rest of the world, and they could do this only through new imperial adventures, from the consolidation of French rule in the Maghreb to the policy of support for the Habsburg Maximilian in Mexico.

Of course, no one was more aware than Marx of the playful-adventurous side of Louis Bonaparte's endeavours. A policy geared to increasing the international prestige of the French ruler and his empire could not be judged by criteria of economic profitability, and was in any case not guided by them. Rather, it was to be seen in terms of a constant trading of economic capital for political prestige. This might also have an economic pay-off in the medium to longer term, but the idea was that in the short term every Frenchman and Frenchwoman would gain by participating in the glitter of *empire*.[32]

Political theories of imperialism have the advantage over eco-nomic theories that their analysis is based on several kinds of capital, which can be compared and replaced with one another.[33] In fact, the concept of imperialism was tinged with Louis Bonaparte's policies as it gained wider currency,[34] and when Disraeli adopted it in his famous Crystal Palace speech in 1872 to describe the project of an expansionist foreign policy, he was thinking above all of the prestige of the British throne (and the public image of his Conservative Party). Queen Victoria's elevation to empress of India in April 1876 was literally an imperial project, designed to establish a new empire in which economic advantages counted for less than political prestige.

Not least among the reasons for Disraeli's playing of the imperial card was the fact that, on the continent, the title of emperor had meanwhile migrated from Paris to Berlin. In September 1870, following its defeat in the war with Prussia, France had returned to the republican form of state, whereas the various princes and rulers of the German states, now unified under Prussia, had placed themselves in early 1871 under the supreme power of the Kaiser. The major continental powers – first, quite explicitly, the two Napoleonic empires, then in a quite different way the German Reich as the Bismarck era gave way to Wilhelmine rule[35] – sought to increase their prestige by associating themselves with the ancient Roman empire. Disraeli, on the other hand, wagered on Britain's power outside Europe to underline its global significance, its world dominance. By comparison the German empire, which at that time had no colonies, looked decidedly modest. The colonial fever that soon gripped Germany was thus also the expression of a striving for prestige, which would give the Reich too a 'place in the sun'.

The purpose of the imperial claim, then, was not only to dampen internal economic conflicts over distribution by offering every citizen a share in the national glory. It also had an external political function of generating prestige and hence power and influence.[36] In this respect, the striving for prestige is a politically functional business, which cannot be adequately measured through short-term cost–benefit analysis. In the broadest sense, the competitive struggle for prestige may be conceived as productive of international hierarchies that manage without the 'expedient of war' (Clausewitz) – or, in any event, without wars between the direct competitors for supremacy. This is not to say that such rivalries are essentially peaceful. But most accompanying wars unfold on the periphery of the respective realms, and the imperial rivals are usually careful to ensure that they do not get in each other's way.[37] They gain prestige through military victories over politically or economically inferior opponents. Only when the rivalry for power and standing breaks down do these normally asymmetrical imperial wars on the periphery turn into imperialist wars, in which the rivals are directly locked together in a struggle for hegemony.

At the heart of political imperialism theories,[38] then, is a different kind of competition from the one emphasized by economic imperialism theories: not the competition of capital for markets and investment opportunities, but the struggle of states for power and influence. In this, the weighing of costs and benefits in the economic sense has less importance. Of course, the striving for prestige is always a gateway for irrational motives and expectations, but we should be cautious about consigning it to the realm of the irrational *tout court*, in the manner of those approaches which measure costs and benefits only in terms of economic return.

Empires, unlike states, are under an informal pressure to assume primacy in every sphere in which power, prestige and performance can be measured and compared. Nowadays, this compulsion is evident in relation not only to military capabilities or economic performance, but also to scientific and technological development, sporting achievements and the world of entertainment. Nobel prizes, university rankings, Olympic medal tables and Oscar awards are some of the constant tests in which imperial 'soft power' has to prove itself; occasional slipping is immediately seen as a sign of the empire's decline, and reflected in a loss of prestige that has to be made good at the first opportunity. These, however, are only the harmless ways in which the empire is held under observation and must keep asserting its claim to supremacy.

The testing is much harder in the terrain of the natural sciences and advanced technology, since this is the seedbed for control over the world economy as well as political-military power. The history of space travel is one example of this. When the Soviet Union, in the late 1950s, achieved the first spectacular successes in this area, it triggered in the United States not only the 'sputnik shock' but a whole programme to catch up and overtake the Russians in space. Eventually the manned landing on the moon became a symbol of American superiority, and Neil Armstrong's one giant leap for mankind, his pioneering moonwalk, was first and foremost a giant leap for the striving for prestige and claim to supremacy of the United States.

To judge the significance of the striving for political prestige, we need to look at the prevailing structure of the competition for prestige – and here it is important to distinguish between multipolar and bipolar systems of international politics. In fact, in the theory of international relations, it would make more sense to supplement the usual distinction between multipolarity and bipolarity[39] with a third possibility: unipolarity. Here, the striving for power of the undisputed hegemon is of a rather conservative nature, although the only real point is that the various players on the stage should recognize the objective data of the distribution of power for what they are.

The more this is the case, the more stable is the political order; the less it is the case, the more one has to reckon with refusal of allegiance or even open revolt against the prevailing hierarchy. Thus, in the disputes during the run-up to the latest Iraq war, the United States suffered visible damage to its political prestige from the public refusal of some of its allies to toe the line.

Since the 1960s, within the Western community, France has played the role of the country that challenges the superior prestige of the United States and claims an almost equal status for itself. President de Gaulle initiated this policy and made it the distinguishing feature of Gaullism, but the liberal and socialist presidents Valéry Giscard d'Estaing and François Mitterrand continued in the same line. The British, on the other hand, through close support for the USA as the leading power, have sought to share in its prestige and thereby increase their own standing.

The consequences that such second-rank prestige games have for the international order change once they cease to take place within a bipolar order (as they did during the time of the East–West conflict). Bipolarity limits the effects of prestige games, whereas unipolarity or multipolarity strengthens them. In the conditions of the East–West conflict, it was clear that France's occasional acts of rebelliousness would not go so far as to call into question its membership of the West. To allow any doubt about this was never the aim of French policy, and it was here that all manifestations of an independent French foreign policy reached their outer limit. The French striving for prestige served to satisfy national vanities more than actually to change the political configuration. And so, Washington did not think it necessary to underline its hegemony with any great vehemence, while the premium that Britain could extract for its much greater compliance was relatively limited.

All this changed, at first almost imperceptibly, with the end of the bipolar structure.[40] This is the difference between the situation of the United States before and after 1991, although the year 1991 (at the end of which the USSR ceased to exist even formally) is a rather fictitious date in that it took nearly another ten years for the players to understand the consequences of the end of bipolarity. For the hegemon, despite its relative gain in power after the demise of its bipolar rival, 'prestige games in the second rank' represent a real challenge that it regards with much less equanimity than in the days of the bipolar system. For this reason, the premium for unconditional obedience has at least symbolically increased. Since the structural constraints of bipolarity have ceased to apply, the hegemonic power must place its allies under much greater pressure to live up to its expectations of them. With regard to the fault-lines that have recently opened up in transatlantic relations, a number of observers argue that the United States has transformed itself from a 'benevolent hegemon' into a hard imperial power, and attribute this to the plans and objectives of certain neoconservative members and advisers of the Bush administration.[41] It may be, however, that it is simply due to the collapse of bipolar constraints and the resulting exacerbation of the competition for prestige.

The greater the rivalry of the aspiring hegemons, the stronger is the pressure on the pre-eminent power to underline its own claim by adopting an imperial manner. Disraeli was responding to such a situation in his Crystal Palace speech: British influence on the continent had been threatened since German unification; the government felt provoked by Russia's aggressive actions in Central Asia; the meteoric rise of the United States was ever more apparent; and Britain's position as the world's leading industrial power was in danger. The empire was facing a challenge, and Disraeli's imperialist project was his answer. We should therefore see it as much more of a reaction to external problems than economic or political theories of imperialism have assumed. Britain was attempting to defend its position as global political hegemon, which had fallen to it almost without any action on its part and was now being called into question. What most theorists of imperialism interpret as an offensive and predatory posture may thus have had a thoroughly defensive motivation for the political players in question.

In the course of the eighteenth century, Britain came to hold the balance of power in continental Europe. In order to play this role, and to block the rise of any rival hegemon, it was usually enough to motivate the relatively weaker side with subsidies and to strengthen its staying power, without actually sending any British troops. In the conflict with Napoleonic France, however, this highly cost-effective policy of hegemony came up against its limits, and Britain had to commit its own forces to the continent for a long period of time to overthrow the emperor and advance British interests. Napoleon not only put Britain under military pressure – for example, by occupying the Iberian peninsula – but also imposed a trade embargo, the so-called Continental System, which was meant to cut off the British Isles from important markets.

The situation that arose after Napoleon's defeat was entirely in Britain's interests. The old multipolar balance of forces was rebuilt, but at the same time fixed through the development of bipolar arrangements. Thus, facing the Russian-dominated Holy Alliance, a weakened France in the West had to rely upon a policy of alliance with Britain. The British could revert to their classical policy of hege-mony: they controlled the seas with a navy greatly superior to any rival's; they steered affairs on the continent with the help of alliances and subsidies; and they kept markets open for the commodity flows that were continually expanding in the wake of England's industrial revolution. Britain profited from this highly cost-effective hegemony without having to invest much in anything other than its navy. It is therefore readily understandable that Disraeli's liberal counterpart, William Gladstone, firmly rejected his imperial project and gave the term imperialism a fundamentally pejorative sense.[42] Why should Britain have given up its comfortable hegemony, involving a European balance of power, a system of indirect rule in non-European lands and a policy of free trade, and plunged instead into costly imperialist adventures with no certain outcome?

Expansion pressures, marginality advantages and time sovereignty

The British always had to give up much less than did continental countries for the sake of their security and military self-assertion. They could afford to do without a standing army and to invest instead in a powerful navy; when they needed a large land army, they long followed the practice of hiring or recruiting forces on the continent.

The navy was a means of guaranteeing economic prosperity. Whereas the land armies of continental states mostly stayed in their barracks and added to costs, the navy was always in action control-ling and protecting trade routes; it therefore contributed not only political but also economic value-added. For land armies the dis-tinction between war and peace is fundamental: a declaration of war or the conclusion of a peace agreement changes everything. But this is not the case for the navy, especially that of a leading maritime power. If peace ever prevails throughout the world, it continues to exercise a police function by defending shipping from pirates. Navies can pay for themselves both politically and economically, land armies at best only politically. This is one of the most important cost advantages of maritime over land empires, as US Admiral Alfred Thayer Mahan showed in detail in his seminal work *The Influence of Sea Power upon History* (1890). One advantage for Britain in empire-building was its position on the margins of the European centres of power. Whereas France, Prussia and Austria wore one another down in recurrent warfare and blocked the achievement of an imperial position, the rise of Britain took place outside these wars for European hegemony, in which, as we have seen, it was anyway in a position to tip the scales.[43]

Empire-building that spread out from a state system or a pluriverse of equal powers nearly always ended in failure, but similar attempts that originated on the margins of the main world centres were often successful. From the beginning, greater efforts were required in those centres to assert a proto-imperial power against others of equal or only slightly inferior strength, and empire-building projects soon led to *major wars* in which the nascent empire had to confront coalitions that were hard to defeat. In these 'hegemonic wars',[44] either the empire-building project collapsed or (as in Napoleonic France and Wilhelmine Germany) the military apparatus became dominant within the emergent empire, making the costs of the enterprise unsustainable and political action dangerously inflexible. Thus, empire-building based on the key power-centres never managed to enjoy that phase in which imperial supremacy could restrict control over trade flows and bring in more than it cost. A number of temporary hegemonies emerged in Europe after the fall of the Roman empire – but never a lasting empire. Spain in the age of Phillip II to Phillip IV,[45] France under Louis XIV and again under Napoleon, unified Germany under the Hohenzollerns: all had to face long wars that not only hindered empire-building but lost them the hegemony they had previously acquired.

As opponents of equal power are usually lacking on the margins of the main political centres, huge wars do not break out there and the rise to empire can occur through a series of *small wars* in which the resistance of organizationally and technologically inferior opponents is eventually broken.[46] Typically, they are not fought with heavy equipment, large bodies of troops or complex logistics, and are therefore relatively cheap. Most instances of successful empire-building have occurred not in the centre but on the margins of areas disputed in world politics: Britain and Russia, the USA and Rome, Spain and Portugal.[47] Even the Ottoman empire was built from the Anatolian periphery outwards, and only in its expansionist phase pushed into its later heartlands in Asia Minor and Southeast Europe. The only significant empires built from a central position in world politics were those of China and the ancient Persian kings. They are an exception in the imperial typology.

Apart from the lower costs of empire-building than those incurred by rival or enemy powers, the greatest advantage enjoyed by the so-called peripheral powers was the *time sovereignty* that grew out of their position on the margins. Whereas the central powers were involved in constant military or other conflict with rivals that often had superior human and material resources, the peripheral powers could invest the peace dividend from their marginality in the building of an economic and industrial base. In this way, during the eighteenth and nineteenth centuries, Britain gained an economic lead over the continent, and since it could only profit from more intensive trade in this first phase of globalization it championed free trade and opposed any kind of protectionism.[48] The British empire therefore had an interest in peace, and the wars it waged were to secure trade routes or to open up markets – literally profit-making wars. Whenever possible, it avoided conflict with powerful rivals. In any case, since the defeat of Spain in the seventeenth century, the decline of Portugal to the status of a British protégé and the exhaustion of France in a series of hegemonic wars, London had not had to face any enemies equal in power to itself.[49]

The rise of the United States also proceeded from a comfortable position on the margins, which meant that between 1815 (when the British successfully checked its push into Canada) and 1917 (when it entered the First World War) its forces never had to measure up to an equally powerful rival. The conflicts with Mexico and Spain in the middle and late nineteenth century were wars of imperial expansion against greatly inferior enemies. The United States could fight out the war between the northern and southern states without the intervention of foreign powers – an impossibility in continental Europe, where other countries would have tried to make capital out of the uncertainty of power politics.

The advantages of a peripheral location are also apparent in the history of Rome (which expanded over a long period on the margins of the Hellenistic core of the Mediterranean world), as well as of Portugal and Spain, whose economic and political rise took place outside the core European triangle of power roughly formed by Paris, Rome and Vienna. Probably it was Spain's undoing that it allowed the dynastic ties of the House of Aragon with southern Italy and the election of Charles as German emperor in 1519 to draw it so early into the European hegemonic wars that weakened it so much economically and politically. The British, it would seem, learned from Spanish history and managed to stay out of the gruelling continental wars for as long as possible. The War of the Spanish Succession in the early eighteenth century is the great exception, but the objective then was to hinder the formation of an anti-hegemonic bloc that might prove dangerous to British influence on the continent.

And Russia? Evidently a peripheral position on land was not the same as one on the sea. For the rise of the Tsarist empire immediately brought a series of hostile engagements with serious rivals, which were then worn down in protracted confrontations. This process began with the succession of wars against the Golden Horde, whose heritage the tsars took over in southern Russia; it was followed by the confrontation with the Polish–Ukrainian and then Swedish empire, which stood in the way of northeastward expansion; and it ended in the hundred-year conflict with the Ottomans, whose control of the Bosphorus and Dardanelles meant that they could deny Russia access to ice-free sea routes all year round. In Byzantium the Ottomans also held the holy places of Eastern Christendom, from which the political legitimacy of the Russian tsars was derived.[50] In the second half of the nineteenth century, a further protracted conflict developed with the Austro-Hungarian monarchy, as the tsar saw himself as lord protector of the western and southern Slavs. This constant warfare ensured that the construction of the Russian empire was incomparably more expensive than that of the British or American empire, and that the army was much more important in Russia than in the West as a factor in imperial power. Russia was never able to draw the same advantages as Britain or the United States from its peripheral location.

Nevertheless, in comparison with the Central and West European powers, Russia had the advantage of only rarely having to face a grand coalition against it. It could therefore take on and try to defeat its adversaries one by one. In this respect, the Russians were also able to exploit the time sovereignty stemming from their peripheral position: they stretched the process of territorial expansion over a long period made up of several different steps and stages, avoiding the danger of overextending their forces.

One of the most serious dangers was that imperial policy would lose its power to set the pace of expansion and consolidation, its capacity to accelerate or slow down the growth of empire. In fact, imperial time sovereignty can be restricted by external as well as internal factors. The former should be understood to include powerful rivals or coalitions of rivals that stand in the way of the contender for empire or dispute the position it has already achieved. The main advantage of a geographically marginal position is that such a clash is less likely there than in the core area of power politics, where none of the players is master of time unless it has already won undisputed supremacy. The outstanding feature of geographical marginality is that only one strong actor is present who sets the pace. The First

World War, which was essentially an intra-European conflict, is an example of the loss of control over sequential time that affected all European powers, including Russia and Britain. The only major power that remained in control of time frames was the United States, and it became the real winner of the war.

Things change with the consolidation of an empire. What used to be periphery becomes centre, and former core areas turn into marginal locations in the reordered 'world'. This also explains why empire-building that starts from the global centres of power is successful only in exceptional cases, whereas marginal geographical positions are often favourable to it. In fact, we may go a little further and say that marginal positions actually bring forth empires, because of the absence of strong rivals and the high degree of time sovereignty that they afford the powers located there. The weak borders displaying no resolute opponent function, so to speak, as openings through which the growing empire rushes to fill a vacuum. This was true both of the American western frontier (which in the eighteenth and nineteenth centuries was pushed ever closer to the Pacific) and of the Russian eastern frontier (which in the same period shifted ever further and for a time even crossed to the American continent). But, whereas Russia's expansion came to an end at the Sea of Japan, where its adversary had to be taken much more seriously,[51] the Pacific coast represented no more than a temporary halt for American expansion; the United States began its rise as a Pacific power at the end of the nineteenth century and entered a collision course with Japan. Similarly, a political vacuum on the periphery led to an ever greater extension of the European colonial empires. We may generally say that, in the formation of territorial empires, the suction effect of the periphery is as important as the expansionist dynamic of the centre.

Of course, the dynamic of the centre remains indispensable to imperial expansion, since the political vacuum in the periphery would not otherwise be perceived as such. Admittedly, the concept of imperial time sovereignty includes the idea that this dynamic does not generate uncontrollable pressure for expansion; it is *internal* factors, then, which counteract imperial time sovereignty. Both economic and political imperialism theories give a central place to such pressure for expansion. In their view, the strongest argument for the impending collapse of imperialism – together with war between the great powers – was that *internal* conditions were eroding the time sovereignty of the empires. Only Mao Zedong's guerrilla-based theory of imperialism and world revolution, where 'the countryside encircles the towns', maintained that the imperial world would collapse because of external rather than internal factors, because of resistance in the periphery rather than developments in the centre. This too contained a concept of the time sovereignty of the imperial centres, which was supposed to be curtailed by means of Mao's 'protracted' guerrilla warfare.[52]

The idea of the erosion of imperial time sovereignty through internal factors was taken further in the theories of overaccumulation or underconsumption, where sales crises in the economic centres *compelled* the opening up of new markets for the export of goods and capital. Theories of social imperialism, for their part, argued that it was becoming ever more necessary for the imperial centres to keep their lower classes quiet by distributing some of the surplus profits of imperialist plunder or by founding new settlement colonies. Competition for prestige, on which theories of political imperialism lay particular stress, was also at bottom nothing other than a pressure for expansion that restricted the politically invaluable time sovereignty.[53]

This handicap was more striking among imperial rivals in the centre of world politics than among those on the margins, where time horizons remained larger. The continental European powers, particularly Germany but also France and even Italy, suddenly had to hurry to take possession of extra-European territories, so as to demonstrate their status as a world power or at least their claim to it. Those of their neighbours which acquired no colonies or failed to expand territorially in other ways came away empty-handed from the distribution of markets and sources of raw materials, and also lost weight and influence within the European system of powers. Political and economic factors worked in harness with each other.

The great nervousness[54] that spread throughout Europe at the end of the nineteenth century was not due only to the shortening of time horizons as a result of intra-European competition. Countries on the margins were also gripped by it, as we can see in the expansionist policies of the United States in the late nineteenth century, but on the whole the competitive pressure was less intense there. Whereas the imperial and proto-imperial powers in the centre were less and less able to set the rules of behaviour,[55] the peripheral powers – with the exception of Russia, still reeling from its showdown with Japan – succeeded much better in keeping control of events and their own decisions. Not only is the distinction between marginal location and power-political centre decisive for the type and the success of empire-building; it is also relevant to the question of whether we are dealing with a hegemon or an empire.

The tricky distinction between hegemony and empire

In a multipolar system, according to the American political scientist John Mearsheimer, all the major participants strive to achieve hegemony because it offers them the greatest security under the circumstances. But the rivalry among them leads to a well-known instability of the system, since each great power feels threatened by the other's striving for hegemony and fights all the harder to establish its own supremacy. Describing this vicious circle as the 'tragedy of great power politics', Mearsheimer assumes that no power which wishes to remain 'great' can lastingly escape it.[56]

In comparson with hegemons, empires are much less open to challenge from other powers and therefore tend to be much more settled. They do not compete in their 'world' with players of approximately equal strength; at most, lesser powers vie with one another for second, third or even fourth place, so that the imperial centre operates as a kind of umpire and ensures that the rivalry does not lead to war. This explains the often observed fact that spaces within are zones of peace, whereas spaces ruled by a hegemon are marked by greater belligerence. Of course, this does not mean that *in principle* military force is never used within imperial orders: anti-imperial wars of liberation certainly do occur there, and they usually last longer than major hegemonial wars. It is true that the latter are considerably more violent and soon lead to high casualty figures. But anti-imperial wars of liberation call the whole imperial order into question, while hegemonial wars tend rather to stabilize it: they involve at most only an exchange of hegemons; the actual model continues to be recognized by all the warring parties.[57] Empire and hegemony differ also in their characteristic kinds of war.

In Europe there is deep and widespread mistrust of international systems that make the struggle for hegemony compulsory. Two huge wars in the twentieth century prevented a hegemonic power from developing a position of imperial supremacy on the continent, and an attempt was later made to devise ways and means of preventing another outbreak of hegemonial competition. As it had become clear that the costs of war were greater than the benefits, and that even military victors stood to lose out politically and economically,[58] the European powers wagered everything on building mutual trust through international treaties, economic links and political democratization that would block the deadly striving for continental hegemony.

What German writers present as a process of learning from the first and second world wars may, of course, be described quite differently: as the creation of an interstate order secure from Germany's repeated attempts to bring the continent under its imperial aegis[59] and also of a bulwark against the threat of a Soviet empire already present in Eastern Europe. In this account, it was not the EU and OSCE but NATO that played the main role in ensuring the peaceful development of Europe after 1945. As its first (British) secretary-general, Hastings Lionel Ismay, tersely put it, the point of NATO was 'to keep the Germans down, the Russians out and the Americans in'; struggles for European hegemony were prevented mainly by the hegemonic role of the United States. The implication here is that the European postwar order, rather than resulting from a learning process that might serve as a model for other crisis regions, depended on the luxury of handing over the region's security to the Americans.

In this view of things, the security guarantees of a great power to medium powers are not only an aid in the creation and consolidation of empire, but also a means of ending struggles for hegemony, pacifying war-torn regions and establishing long-term peace. This assumes, however, that a sufficiently strong external power has an interest in giving such guarantees to ensure the peaceful stability of an area repeatedly shaken by hegemonial wars. Whereas the United States shied away from this task after 1918, it was prepared to take it on after 1945.[60] Whatever benefits the Americans may have expected from this, it was first of all a political investment in Western Europe that cost them quite a lot.

The associated idea of US 'benevolent hegemony' seems hardly appropriate to refer to a state that has emerged victorious from great power rivalry. The latter suggests a harsh competitive struggle with approximate equals, while the former evokes a good shepherd protecting his flock from enemy attack and forgoing any self-interested exploitation of superiority, as if his main concern were to serve others rather than to assert his own interests against them. In this conception of the US role, hegemony is *potential imperiality* that is not fully actualized, whether out of respect for the legal order or the moral sensitivities of the American population, out of political astuteness, or from another, anyway benevolent motive; the leading power decides alone between hegemony and imperiality, and so it makes sense to use wooing appeals or allusive warnings to convince it of the benefits of hegemony and the disadvantages of an imperial role. Since there is a real choice to be made, it falls within the province of political morality or prudence and not, if we may put it so, political physics. To be sure, it is an open question whether the number one power and its leading politicians will see things in this way, or whether political physics will determine their perception. It may anyway be assumed that the constraints will seem more important in the eyes of the leading power, while the smaller powers will tend to emphasize the scope for decision on the part of the great powers.

Michael Mann conceives hegemony as a rule-bound form of supremacy – in contrast to empire, in which the dominant power does not feel bound by any rules. The central issue for American foreign policy is therefore as follows: 'The Americans must themselves decide whether they wish to resume hegemony and then stick by its rules. But if they go for Empire and fail, they lose hegemony too. The world would not much care. It could live with the multilateral consequences.'[61] On the other hand, the US political theorist Chalmers Johnson, who first made a name for himself as an East Asia expert, doubts that the distinction between hegemony and empire corresponds to anything substantive; it ultimately involves a rhetorical strategy either to highlight the exercise of power or to leave it in the shadows. 'Some writers have employed the term hegemony as a substitute for imperialism without colonies, and in the post-World War II era of superpowers, hegemonism became coterminous with the idea of Eastern and Western "camps". Always complicating matters has been a longstanding American urge to find euphemisms for imperialism that soften and disguise the U.S. version of it, at least from other Americans.'[62] For Chalmers Johnson, then, 'hegemony' is just a euphemism for 'empire': the distinction between the two has little factual justification but simply reflects the differing judgements of those who describe the international order. Rather than scientific categories, they are labels used in the language of politicians.

Henry Kissinger, a man with a reputation for cynical frankness, has recently added to the confusion by treating the terms 'hegemonial' and 'imperial' as synonymous. The central message of his *Does America Need a Foreign Policy?* (2002) is that, by taking on a hegemonial role, the United States may very quickly have to shoulder such a weighty burden that American society will not be prepared to accept it. Thus, even without any talk of empire, the US will already come unstuck as a result of its quest for hegemony.[63]

It is possible to turn the problem around, however, by seeing the creation of empire as an assurance against the collapse of an ever precarious hegemony. If hegemony means that the number one power bears the essential responsibility for certain collective goods (security from external threats, curbs on the arms programmes of smaller powers, well-ordered economic spaces, and so on) while its subordinates simply take advantage of them, it is easy to understand why its citizens should be dissatisfied with such a distribution of costs and benefits. The situation is very different in an empire which brings in more than it costs for the population in the metropolis, or which passes on some of the costs of the collective goods to the countries under its protection. Such an empire would certainly enjoy greater approval among its citizens than would a merely hegemonic power. Many politicians and intellectuals who, in a rather un-American manner, have recently spoken of an 'American empire', or called for one to be created and consolidated,[64] have clearly been concerned about the dangers and costs of a hegemony that must continually be reaffirmed. Setting little store by clear-cut conceptual distinctions, they have understood by 'empire' simply a permanent, consolidated form of 'hegemony'.

Perhaps no one in recent years has given more thought to the relationship between imperiality and hegemony than the German legal historian Heinrich Triepel, whose great work on hegemony was first published in 1938. He too doubted that there was any *category distinction* between empire and hegemony, seeing the latter as simply 'one of the forms in which imperialist politics may express itself'.[65] Triepel thought he could discern a secular tendency towards greater respect for the autonomy of territories that are placed under imperial domination without participating in it; he referred to this as 'the law of diminishing force'.[66] What Triepel had in mind was a process of 'self-limitation' or 'self-control' of power [*Selbstbändigung der Macht*],[67] whereby imperiality had increasingly assumed the form of hegemony. 'It is safe to say that, in the politics of modern imperialism, the gaining of hegemony is more and more the typical way in which power is extended.'[68]

For Triepel, empire and hegemony coincide 'where imperialism deliberately forgoes the incorporation of foreign lands into the framework of an old state'.[69] The tendency for imperial politics to turn into hegemonial politics is especially strong where the empire-building process is marked by federative elements, but Triebel doubts whether it will prevail everywhere and at all times. This note of caution was more than appropriate in the mid-1930s when he composed his reflections on the matter.

In his search for the earliest thinking on hegemony as a form of imperial domination marked by greater self-restraint, Triepel came across the ancient Greek historians and rhetoricians who had concerned themselves with the rise and fall of the Athenian thalassocracy. He noted their graduated use of the terms *archē, dynamis* and *hegemonia*: the first expresses power relations in a strong and intensive sense; the second too is often used in this sense; whereas the third denotes a weaker power relation that Triepel would like to see translated as 'supremacy' [*Vorherrschaft*].[70]

Michael Doyle, in his comparative study of empires, notes certain differences between Athenian and Spartan alliance policy in the fifth century BC, and develops from them a category distinction between empire and hegemony. Whereas the Athenian-dominated Delian–Attic maritime league was an empire, the Peloponnesian League, in which Sparta was the leading power, was an instance of hegemony.[71] For Doyle, the characteristic feature of hegemony is that its claim to dominance is restricted to the 'external policy' of its alliance partners and refrains from interference in their internal development; it does not affect – still less seek to change – either their political or their economic order, either constitutional issues or the regulation of markets.

This self-limitation with regard to allies does not, in Doyle's view, happen in an empire. Rather, imperial rule is characterized by a lack of clear boundaries between what is internal and what is external, so that interference in the internal affairs of alliance partners is a constant occurrence.[72] Precisely this was what distinguished Sparta from Athens: it limited itself to control over its allies' external policy, in order that the Peloponnesian League should have a united position vis-à-vis the other two great powers in the Aegean: the Persians and the Athenians.[73] Athens, on the other hand, constantly intervened in the affairs of its allies: it took steps to ensure that democratic forces kept the upper hand; it had a monopoly in legal proceedings where the death penalty could be pronounced; it enforced a single currency in the area of the alliance; and it compelled allied states to hand over land occupied by Athenian settlers.[74] Evidently people in Athens thought that the allies could be relied upon only if they were kept under suitable control. And, of course, Athenian citizens also wanted to profit from the burden of the maritime alliance: the invocation of long-term interests was never sure to win popular support for any measure; only short-term benefits made that possible. For Doyle, whereas the Spartan aristocracy was capable of a politics of hegemony, the Athenian democracy had a plain inclination to empire.[75]

Of course, Doyle is aware that the structural premises of the Spartan and Athenian alliance systems were so different from each other that it is scarcely possible to speak of a free political choice between empire and hegemony. Rather, hegemony was the only way in which Sparta could organize an alliance, given its fundamentally conservative political and social orientation. In the case of Athens, where alliance-building went hand in hand with radical internal democracy, it had to pass on the dynamic of its own development to the alliance structures and thus set in train, throughout the Aegean, a process that led to dramatic social-economic transformation and the supplanting of the traditional layer of landowners by a much more mobile layer of merchants and traders.[76] Athens therefore had no choice but constantly to intervene in the internal affairs of its allies – not only to create a unified economic space, to control sea routes in the Black Sea and the Aegean and to keep within limits the permanent threat from pirates, but also to safeguard politically the development of society and economy in the allied cities, with their inevitable winners and losers. This was possible only in so far as the rule of the democratic party was ensured. Sparta's traditional social structure meant that it could only establish a system of hegemony; Athens's economic, social and ultimately political dynamic drove it to establish an empire.

Triepel himself made a similar argument.[77] For him, however, the formation of hegemonies and empires as well as transitions between the two were essentially determined by social-economic and political configurations in the centre of power, whereas Doyle summarized his thoughts on Spartan hegemony and Athenian empire in a political-structural distinction: it was appropriate to speak of empire when a network of relations joined together centre and periphery through trans-state social structures, and of hegemony when there was a system of relations between centres of clearly unequal strength.[78]

Whether a political order should be classified as imperial or hege-monial therefore depends on the level of social-economic develop-ment and the relative strength of the subordinate allies and powers. If the gap is considerable, perhaps growing wider as a result of the dynamic in the centre, the inevitable result is an 'imperialization' of the structures of domination. But if the gap is narrow, and if relations between the participant countries are stable over time, there is more likely to be a 'hegemonialization' of the power system. At least as important for the development of hegemony, however, is a lack of interest or effort on the part of the subordinate powers to supplant the existing hegemonic power. Only if the hegemonic power can count on this will it limit its claim to supremacy and refrain from trying to convert hegemonial into imperial relations.

Basing itself on an excellent military apparatus, Sparta evidently regarded its superiority over its allies as beyond danger. Yet the dynamic of the alliance system among adjoining powers appeared so threatening that the Spartans decided to wage a preventive war against the further rise of Athens.

In view of the political dynamics that have taken root since the late eighteenth century, hegemonial orders have been able to exist only temporarily and have had either to transform themselves into imperial structures or to go under in self-destructive wars. Probably there has also been a third option: namely, a 'de-dynamization' of relations by means of transnational political structures and strong economic links, such as those which Europe developed in the second half of the twentieth century. Nor, finally, is it excluded that hegemonial and imperial structures overlap – that is, that the same order presents imperial features in many respects and hegemonial features in others.

How does this relate to the question of whether the United States is now an empire or a hegemon? The first point to be made is that the distinction between the two is much more fluid than it is often assumed. If we take interference in the internal affairs of smaller states as the only hallmark of imperiality, and a basic lack of interest in their internal affairs as integral to hegemony, then the United States has been an empire since President Carter launched his human rights offensive, but was a hegemon in the preceding period when it tolerated military dictatorships even within NATO. This, of course, is to turn upside down the value hierarchy between the two concepts. Probably it makes sense to use them both in a completely value-free manner, to indicate different relationships of force among the members of a political order. The hegemon will then appear as *primus inter pares* – where the equality is not limited to rights and duties but includes actual capacities and achievements – while the term empire will apply when the gap between the central power and other members of the political order is so great that it cannot be bridged even with legal fictions concerning equality. The question is simply what kind of power is at issue: economic, cultural, political or military power. And, since it is rare for them all to be heading in the same direction, there will scarcely be unanimity about whether an order should be conceived and developed as imperial or hegemonial.

STEPPE EMPIRES, SEA EMPIRES AND GLOBAL ECONOMIES: A SHORT TYPOLOGY OF IMPERIAL RULE

Of the four sources of power that Michael Mann distinguishes in his world history of power,[1] military and economic superiority were decisive in the early stages of the great empires; they were the basis on which imperial power was built. Political and ideological power, Mann's other two sources, acquired major importance only in the necessary phase of consolidation following a period of more or less dynamic expansion. Certain aspects that had been insignificant in the beginnings of empire then became more noticeable: for example, the costs of administering the area under imperial rule, or the willingness of the population to shoulder the burden of empire.

During the first phase, the question of costs and benefits remained in the background: either expansion brought in more than it required in the way of resources, or people consoled themselves with the thought of future profits. This changed with the passage to the consolidation phase. If the empire was not to collapse through bankruptcy or internal resistance to the burdens, it now had to convert the imaginary balance-sheet into a real one – and that usually meant reducing the costs of rule. The easiest way of achieving this was, in most cases, a strong application of political and ideological power, the latter, in particular, being much cheaper to generate than military power. This is why the influence of ideological power grows as soon as the empire reaches its limits and any further step would lead to 'imperial overstretch'.[2]

Michael Doyle has described an empire's transition from the phase of expansion to the phase of consolidation as the 'Augustan threshold',[3] which alludes to the deep reforms that Emperor Augustus introduced after he had eliminated his last rivals at the battle of Actium (31 BC), and as a result of which the *Respublica Romana* was finally transformed into the *Imperium Romanum*.[4] Many an empire-building project failed at this hurdle. Since the passage from expansion to consolidation is among the most important parts of the history of an empire, it deserves to be given special attention.

Empires come into being either through violent conquest or through economic penetration. We may therefore distinguish imperial orders containing areas under *direct rule* – the classical 'world empires' – from those which rest upon *trade structures* and control of the respective 'world economy'.[5] Only rarely in history have the two types appeared in a pure form. Nearly all world empires have had an economic dimension, especially when they have lasted a long time; and there has scarcely ever been a lasting world economy without elements of power politics.

Crossing the Augustan threshold usually means that existing structures of trade and government are complemented with others, while economic links come about in the areas under imperial rule. On the other hand, the collapse of a world empire usually means the end of the world economy associated with it. Thus, after the fall of the Roman empire in the West, trade among the regions in question came to a standstill, the major towns went into decline, and an overwhelming majority of the population again earned its living from agriculture.[6] In the same way, the break-up of the USSR put an end to the Soviet-dominated economic system, with far-reaching consequences for the living standards of people in both its centre and its periphery. If the gradual decline of the British world empire did not leave deeper traces in the world economy, this is because the United States smoothly took over the functions previously exercised by the British. Of course, the stock market crash of 1929 may be seen as the crisis that attended this transition.

Although the spaces of trade and political rule are never completely separable, it is useful to begin by delineating the two. They too are more clearly distinguishable from each other in the formative stage of empire than at the peak of imperial power. In the formation of the classical empires, the space of rule developed before the space of trade; the reverse was true of most European empires in modern times. But this developmental typology was for a long time complemented with a structural distinction between land and sea empires: the former arose through a consolidation of the spaces under rule, whereas the latter expanded by making their trade relations both more intensive and more extensive. Here too transitional and hybrid forms are visible after a certain time – for example, when areas under imperial rule were used to cultivate economic exchange, or when

trade structures fell apart as a result of political conflict and the political centre intervened to reconstruct them.

In any event, the four sources of power do not play an equal role
in the formation of empire, and sometimes this is true also after it has
reached its maximum extent. However, a deficit in any one of the
four can have thoroughly negative consequences for the empire: it is
expensive to compensate for this by strengthening the other three,
and besides the balance of power within the empire may be perma-
nently disturbed. Thus, neither the Tsarist, the Ottoman nor the
Spanish empire managed to develop its economic power to the same
extent as its military strength – which led either to early infirmity or
to a ruinous expansion of the military apparatus. The Portuguese
and Dutch seaborne empires, on the other hand, were in no position
to develop lasting military and political strength to match their economic power, and so after a time they were forced into the position
of junior partners of another (British) seaborne empire. It would
seem that an empire is most resistant when it can support itself
equally on all four sources of power, or when it has crossed the
Augustan threshold and brought them into equilibrium, as the
Roman and British empires successfully managed to do.

The formation of empires through military and commercial extraction of surplus product

Empire-building by means of extensive political rule or intensive
trade structures serves to underpin two distinct forms of surplus
product extraction on the margins of imperial power: one essentially
military, the other mainly commercial. The steppe empires may be
regarded as examples of military surplus extraction and the maritime empires as examples of the commercial form. What differenti-
ates them is not the degree of exploitation but the level of open
violence, which is clearly greater in the steppe empires. The principal mechanism of exploitation in the maritime empires is not
robbery and plunder but trade and exchange.

The Portuguese and, following it, the Dutch seaborne empire promoted the commercial form of surplus extraction.[7] For a time they
controlled trade in an area stretching from the East African coast to
Southeast Asia, and instead of investing there they built up trading
monopolies from which they derived considerable profits. On the
East African coast and the Indian peninsula, the Portuguese took the
place of Arab traders and either took over or violently severed their

commercial links. On the whole, they were content to build forts or fortified positions at the key trade junctions, mainly on peninsulas or offshore islands, and to defend them with relatively light garrisons; they refrained from making incursions into the interior.[8] From these strong points, they forged links with local rulers and tried to gain their support for Portuguese trading activities. They never showed any interest in the modernization of political rule or social structures.

In the early sixteenth century Francisco de Almeida, the first viceroy of the Indies, developed a conception that took account of Portugal's limited forces and possibilities. This involved the permanent stationing of a naval squadron in the Indian Ocean to act as a floating link among the fortresses and key strategic positions, thereby ensuring that the available forces could be quickly concentrated at any point under threat. As the Portuguese did not want to bear the costs of controlling large areas, they also ruled out the idea of permanent European settlements. Indeed, in the the middle of the sixteenth century, no more than two or three hundred whites were living on the African coast, and the settlement of Europeans in the Indian/Southeast Asian space was intended only to strengthen and maintain the key positions under Portuguese control.[9]

The income to cover the costs of controlling this trading zone came from the Portuguese declaration of the Indian Ocean as a *mare clausum*,[10] a closed space in which they could charge tolls and duties. A monopoly on East Indian trade was combined with a system of permits (*cartazes*) for all non-Portuguese trading vessels, which allowed the Portuguese to fix the price for the spices so highly appreciated in Europe – especially pepper, cloves and cinnamon – without a danger of being undercut.[11] And, when they gave non-Portuguese traders a share in the East India Company, they did so only in return for appropriate licence fees. In addition to its other duties, the naval squadron stationed in the Indian Ocean had the task of enforcing the Portuguese maritime trade monopoly.

All this meant that the Portuguese maritime empire had uniformly positive balances during the century and a half of its existence. 'The budget for 1574 shows', writes Oliveira Marques,

> that the Asian empire (including the fortified positions in East Africa) by no means presented a deficit, but rather a surplus of more than 80,000 cruzados. [. . .] In 1581 this surplus fell to 40,000 cruzados, and in 1588 rose again to 108,000 cruzados. In the 1620s the situation began to change permanently, as constant expenditure was necessary for defence against the Dutch and English. But, even under these circumstances, the surplus still stood at 15,000 cruzados in 1620 and at 40,000 cruzados in 1635.[12]

The Achilles heel of the Portuguese maritime empire was the insecurity of its trading monopoly: the threat came not from those whose products were bought and shipped to Europe, nor from the Arabs shut out from these profitable routes, but from European rivals who fought to capture the monopoly for themselves or to replace it with a system based on market competition. When the Dutch conquered the Portuguese seaborne empire in the East Indies, they also took over its organizing principles – except that they replaced Portuguese state capitalism with private corporations, such as the East India Company, which were able to deploy much greater energy and dynamism than were possible under the state system of licences.[13]

Such 'privatization' distinguishes the commercial from the military form of surplus extraction. Military expansion, which usually takes place on land, is politically driven: its centre is a ruler or a military-political elite that creates the prerequisites for expansion and leads and organizes the military operations. Commercial expansion, by contrast, may be driven by private individuals or, often enough, trading companies, in which case it does not obey an overall strategic plan but grasps the opportunities offered at various points in the imperial periphery. Unlike military expansion, it does not establish a closed space for political rule, but rather a number of trading areas made up of different components, which are linked to one another only through the organization of economic exchange along certain transportation routes. Empires based on the extraction of surplus through trade are therefore mostly maritime empires, which show up on the map not as specially shaded areas but as a tangle of points and connecting lines. Charles Maier has expressed this difference by saying that the one are countries which have expanded into empires, while the other are countries which maintain an empire.[14]

The Portuguese and Dutch seaborne empires were essentially based on the success of the titular power in gaining control over major trade flows. It is characteristic of such imperial trade structures that the centre is systematically preferred over the periphery. They are based on a network of unequal contracts dictated by the interests of the centre. Of course, this does not mean that membership of such a system holds nothing but disadvantages for the periphery, but the centre does benefit from it more strongly than the periphery. From a long-term point of view, the profits have to be high enough to offset the costs of maintaining the system. The imperial centre therefore endeavours to shape the terms of trade in such a way that it does not have to invest more and more in the imperial trading area while others reap the benefits of the resulting order and security.[15]

Is it possible to calculate the profits that an imperial centre gains from control of its 'world economy'? The key point here is probably not the share of the centre in the world economic product – the US share at present, though around a quarter, must have been declining in the medium term as a result of East Asian economic growth[16] – but rather control over flows of capital and knowledge. In the heyday of the British empire, the pound sterling was the world's leading currency and the City was decisive in the formation of interest rates and share prices. British banks maintained and steered the circulation of goods and capital, and it was mainly through their control of the financial system that the British were able to dominate the capitalist world economy in the nineteenth and early twentieth centuries.[17] So long as this remained the case, they also obtained the profits to offset the costs of controlling the trading area, especially the Royal Navy and the military bases along the sea route to India. But the writing was on the wall for the British empire once London lost its dominant position within the international finance system, the costs of governing the imperial space shot up in the face of mounting resistance to its rule, and Britain became entangled in two major wars with hegemonial rivals (Germany and Japan).

The imperial position of the United States should be seen in a similar way, despite the fact that it is economically and militarily more powerful than Britain ever was. Neither the productive capacity of the US economy nor the global system of US bases (reminiscent in many respects of Britain's military control of trade areas) is due to the stability and durability of the American empire; it stems, rather, from a capacity to guide capital flows in the world economy, to influence the value of other currencies in relation to the dollar, and to set economic rhythms by means of constant innovation. The instruments for this are US control over the World Bank and the International Monetary Fund, as well as the research institutes and technology centres that attract a permanent brain drain to the United States. All this ensures that the periphery pays while the USA profits. The costs of the military apparatus do, however, reduce the potential for profit.

A major alternative to this commercial form is the *military* extraction of surplus product, which is most sharply expressed in the fact that the imperial armed forces can be funded only if tribute and booty are regularly drawn from peripheral areas of the empire. This pays first of all for the military apparatus itself, but also for costly building projects in the metropolis that bear witness to the glitter of the empire and its ruler and, now and again, assert a cultural or ideological power that complements military power and takes some of the pressure off it. Such projects can, in other words, replace 'hard' with 'soft' power: the construction of the Acropolis in the Periclean age, or the rebuilding of Rome under Augustus, should probably be seen in this way as a means of converting military into cultural or ideological power. Thucydides, in any event, was convinced that the marvel of the Acropolis made Athenian power appear twice as great as it was in reality.[18] The construction of imperial centres, financed out of plunder from the periphery, may thus help to lower the medium-term costs of rule and give imperial power an element of permanence.

In the pure form of military surplus extraction, this 'culturalization' of power plays only a subordinate role or none at all. An example of this pure form is the Assyrian empire. Basing itself on superior military technology, especially the use of chariots and sickle blades, it managed to achieve supremacy in the Mesopotamian area.[19] But in the long run the Assyrian rulers did not have the means to bear the heavy costs of the military apparatus or to keep control of the periphery and to raise taxes there on a permanent basis, while rulers under an obligation to pay tribute tried to escape it whenever they could. The Assyrian army therefore had the task of waging war all year round to find the necessary resources. A city or a ruler had two alternatives: either it could pay the required tribute to the Assyrians at the approach of their army, play host to them out of its own resources and assure them of its loyalty to Assyria; or else it could watch the tribute taken forcibly in the form of war booty. To be sure that subordinate powers would see regular payments of tribute as the more advantageous option, the Assyrians systematically resorted to a policy of devastation whose notoriety lived on in later centuries. Their extreme cruelty was not an end in itself, however, but a means to maintain the empire, by increasing the risks of a break for areas on its fringes. Such a break took the form of a refusal to pay tribute; the punishment for it was the extraction of booty. More than just an increase in the level of tribute, this involved reducing towns to ashes, laying waste whole areas of land and massacring their inhabitants. The military apparatus was the instrument that carried out this policy, both through threats and through acts of violent enforcement.

Assyria is the paradigm for empire-building in classical times, although the raising of tribute probably never again entailed such harsh methods until the Mongols reintroduced them with their well-known determination. The strategic drawback of this policy was that the relevant empires were in principle incapable of crossing the

Augustan threshold. This was true also of the steppe empires that developed in the wake of the Scythians, in which semi-nomadic horsemen used to alternating between summer and winter pastures greatly extended the area under their rule, though admittedly for rather a short time. The reason why their empires lasted for only a short time is that they usually failed to free themselves from the pressure to expand militarily, and to replace their revenue from tribute and booty with a system of regular taxation. On a strict definition of empire, what we call the steppe empires were too brief to merit more than a footnote. They represent a special type of empire, whose interest here has to do with the fact that they allow military-type expansion and the exclusively military form of surplus extraction to be studied in an almost pure form.

The history of the steppe empires is long, even if it occupies only a marginal place in Western historiography, and even if the nomadic horsemen from the Asian steppes appear in it mostly as disturbers and destroyers of orderly political and economic development. From the Scythians through the Sarmatians, Alans and Huns, the Avars, Hungarians and Khazars, down to the Mongols,[20] all repeatedly threw themselves into the building of empires, most of which began when nomadic horsemen subjected to tribute agricultural areas bordering their winter pastures and thereby acquired the resources for large-scale expansion. The unpredictability of a life in which climate change and animal epidemics played a considerable role forced the nomads to gain some security by imposing a tribute on food-producing areas on the fringes of the steppe. Raids and plunder had always been part of their way of life. But, as soon as these extended to a wider territory and served to accumulate wealth rather than merely to satisfy the needs of survival, the basis was laid for a new round of empire-building.

The formation of the Hun empire under Rua and Attila in the fifth century AD allows us to see certain features of nomadic empires that are more or less pronounced in all the steppe empires.[21] First there is the process of ethnogenesis, whereby a number of tribes come together around a leading ethnic group. Whether this is a success or a failure crucially depends on the charisma (Mongol: *qut*) that the leader consciously tries to develop. Attila, for example, was honoured and feared as a god by his subjects. He himself was convinced of his divine mission, which he saw as the basis of his claim to rule the whole world. He passed on the spoils of booty, ransom and tribute to the (military) elite of his kingdom, thereby assuring himself of their loyalty. He alone decided the series of grades within this elite and expressed it through his choice of gifts and seating arrangements in his tent. In this way, the traditional claims of clans and tribal chieftains were replaced with the favour of the charismatic leader.

The shift within the nomadic social-political order from tradition to charisma – that is, 'devotion to the exceptional sanctity, heroism or exemplary character of an individual person', as Max Weber defined charismatic authority[22] – led to a more dynamic internal organization of the tribes and clans, and this in turn constituted the basis for imperial expansion. Only this can explain the momentum with which a relatively small number of nomadic horsemen overran vast areas and subjugated other empires. But, for the same reason, the steppe empires were often so fragile that they came to an end with the death of the charismatic leader.[23]

The principle of allegiance to a military leader, which took over from hierarchies based on group origin, unified previously hostile nomadic tribes and made them capable of wide-ranging expansion. In particular, this brought an increase in the loyalty and discipline that were notoriously lacking in the nomadic world. For this purpose, the Mongol khan Temüjin (who called himself Genghis Khan, or 'universal ruler') reorganized the existing ethnic units into a new army made up of combat groups of a hundred and a thousand, united only by their loyalty to the leader. In size and composition, they were geared to the requirements of extensive warfare,[24] and rebellious clans and tribes could be split among several army units and rendered compliant. Genghis Khan mercilessly crushed resistance by supporters of the traditional hierarchies, executing every last one of the conservative court shamans who opposed his plans. But the society that the khan dedicated to war also had to wage war in order to survive. It was under remorseless pressure to extract large amounts of booty, because only then could the leader distribute the gifts that ensured the loyalty of his commanders. Genghis Khan therefore had to become involved in a series of risky campaigns, and did not have the possibility of enjoying the fruits of his victories.

Genghis Khan was himself aware of the pressure to conquest he had created: 'The Mongols must subjugate all lands and not make peace with any other people, until it has been destroyed or else submitted to them.'[25] And, indeed, the unity of the Mongol empire, in which individual khans were accountable to a single khagan (or great khan), could be preserved only so long as this expansionist policy continued. With the death in 1259 of Genghis's grandson, Möngke, the Mongol world empire disintegrated into a number of warring kingdoms.

The commercial and military extraction of surplus product represent the two ends of a range of possibilities, where it is not the extremes but various hybrid forms that are the most likely to arise. They may lie closer to the commercial or the military pole, and usually the proportions of the hybrid vary in the course of the history of an empire. At the end of the nineteenth century, for example, the British empire was forced to employ military methods more and more frequently to ensure the commercial extraction of surplus product, and the various Mongol kingdoms that developed in China and eastern Siberia (the so-called Great Khanate) as well as Iran, Iraq and Syria (the so-called Ilkhanate) were able to reduce the significance of military aspects and to place greater emphasis on administrative control of the economy as a means of underpinning imperial power.[26]

It is by no means the case, however, that the founders of empires had a choice between mainly commercial and mainly military extraction of surplus. There were always a number of existing constraints, the most decisive of which were geography, the degree of civilization in the centre, the attitudes and skills of elites, the historical legacy and collective memory, and reactions in the periphery as the expansionist thrust began to make itself felt. A law seems to have operated over many centuries whereby the nomadic peoples of Central Asia periodically founded steppe empires, which then rapidly collapsed and disappeared from history. The traces they left behind do not consist of testimony to their own achievements and grandeur (magnificent cities, temples or churches) but recall the destruction of civilizations that lay in the path of their expansion. The collapse of the Roman empire in the West was not least a result of the advance of the Huns from Central Asia, which set in motion the Germanic peoples settled in southern Russia and put such pressure on the frontiers of the empire that they eventually gave way. Much the same was true of the caliphate of Baghdad, an Islamic-Arab empire whose heyday had already passed before the Mongol assault.[27] Its dissolution in 1258 was especially momentous for the political history of Islam, as there would be no further experience of Arab empire-building. The Arab world was subsequently divided between the Ottoman empire and the Safawid dynasty in Persia. Similarly, Genghis Khan's Mongols broke up the Khwarezmid empire (which encompassed the present-day area of Iran, Afghanistan and parts of the Central Asian republics) and destroyed its economic-cultural foundations.[28] Only the Chinese empire survived Mongol rule relatively unscathed, being formally reconstituted after approximately a century.

Steppe empires had a fundamentally parasitic character: they produced no high culture of their own and no centres of civilization, but merely exploited the wealth and achievements of their periphery. Given their cultural-technological backwardness, they had to concentrate on the only sphere in which they had clear superiority: the military sphere. The speed of their cavalry formations, their vast radius of operations with few logistical requirements, the fighting power of each horseman and the range and accuracy of his reflex bow, the capacity for all-embracing strategic thinking that grew out of their nomadic way of life and was uniformly lacking in their opponents: all this put these numerically small peoples in a position to form great empires such as the world had never seen before. Whereas the civilizations of imperial Rome and China administratively integrated the new territories that they conquered, so that they could expand only slowly and gradually before reaching a point at which the civilizing power of empire was exhausted, the spatial expansion of the steppe empires knew no other limits than the operational reach of their military formations. This made all the weaker the process of imperial integration, which in the periphery often rested on nothing more than a fear that the wild troops of horsemen would return from the steppe.[29]

In principle, an almost limitless expansion of imperial space and a rather weak form of integration are common to the opposite poles of commercial and military surplus extraction. The great Portuguese, Dutch and British maritime empires that came into being with the European voyages of discovery in the fifteenth century – Spain always being less interested in trade than territorial conquest – were only superficially integrated and did not involve a unified administration or legal system.[30]

Both maritime and steppe empires essentially seek to exploit the periphery and make no special effort to spread the achievements of civilization. At least in their formative period, seaborne trading empires limit themselves to the establishment of economic ties between centre and periphery, leaving social-political structures largely untouched in the new areas under their control. Often they cooperate with the existing rulers or play off rivals against each other, but in the end they are interested only in certain commodities. The smaller the investment in the periphery, the higher the profits – such is the calculation in empire-building on the basis of commercial surplus extraction.

Of course, it remains open whether the calculation will be correct in the long term, or whether counter-forces will emerge that eventually reverse the net outcome. A similar problem applies to the economic bleeding dry of the periphery by the armed forces of the steppe empires: commercial contact with foreigners gradually changes a country's social-political order. Empires that rest only upon military or commercial surplus extraction and forgo major investment in infrastructure are scarcely in a position reliably to integrate their fringes into their 'world order', although this is essential for their stability and long-term survival. Empires in which centre and periphery are bound together only through the extraction of surplus product have always disintegrated faster than those which develop regular administration of their provinces, that is, which not only extract resources but also invest in them. None of the seaborne empires and none of the steppe empires attained the durability or stability of the Roman or Chinese empire. The secret of the latter's long life seems to be that, in situations of crisis or defeat, it managed to find in the periphery the means to save or revitalize itself. But the outer areas of the empire were able and willing to contribute to this only if they had a strong sense of belonging to the empire, and only if they were convinced that its collapse would be more harmful than beneficial to themselves.[31]

A decision to refrain from out-and-out plunder of the periphery, and to invest in its infrastructure and the spread of civilization, evidently does not mean that the exchange relations between centre and periphery turn into their opposite or that the periphery becomes a pure winner from empire. But, as the Augustan threshold is crossed, the burdens of empire are more equally distributed and also passed on to those who used only to enjoy its benefits. The costly military apparatus and new administrative structures can no longer be financed only out of tribute and taxation of the subjugated provinces; the population of the imperial centre also has to make a fiscal contribution. Of course, it is not uncommon for this to provoke resistance, and the centre may exhibit a dangerous tendency to putsches and uprisings that promise to lower the costs of empire. Stabilization of the imperial periphery therefore comes at the price of growing discontent in the centre – which is probably the crucial reason why many empires never crossed the Augustan threshold. Instability in the periphery was obviously easier to tolerate than permanent discontent in the centre, and the occasional secession of a province easier to handle than continual unrest in the imperial capital. In historical retrospect, however, it seems more often to have been unreliable provinces than a restive centre which led to the end of empires. In most cases, a decision to spread the bureaucratic-administrative extraction of surplus more evenly within the imperial space increased the long-term stability of the empire.

The two (at least two) sides of empires

Along with the geographical factors that determine the form of expansion from an imperial core, elites have some leeway in deciding on its precise type and structure. These decisions are quite often influenced by historical models or political myths: for example, in the seventeenth century, England was long undecided whether to see itself as a successor of Rome or of Carthage, with the latter's commercial power and the former's territorial empire as particularly important elements in the balance.[32] Behind the eventual rejection of territorial empire lay the idea that it would inevitably come to be ruled by a single individual, as in Rome's passage from republic to principate, whereas Carthage's oligarchic families had held on to power right up to the end. Continental expansion was thus linked to militarism, which, it was assumed, would lead to dictatorship or despotism and cancel England's successful constitutional reforms of 1688–9. The development of a worldwide trading power based on 'informal rule', on the other hand, would be quite compatible with an aristocratic form of government. Since it would only occasionally have to employ mercenary forces, in principle for deployment outside the mother country, there would be no danger of the army's becoming a factor in internal power politics. England's self-limitation to the role of a maritime trading power seemed to offer protection against politically undesirable developments at home.

To be sure, it is also possible to see things quite differently: that is, in the case of Rome, to argue that it was not territorial but maritime expansion which posed the real threat to the Republic, and that the Senate's decision, in the war with Carthage, to abandon the former limits on its policy of supremacy marked the beginning of the end for the Republic. Only the massive turn to maritime expansion allowed power and influence to accumulate in the hands of figures for whom the republican constitution would prove too narrow a framework. Furthermore, the overseas deployment of Roman legions lengthened the average period of military service to the point where soldiers could no longer maintain their small farms back home, and so the veteran problem began to acquire an explosive revolutionary force. The time that an individual held supreme military command also increased, with the result that relations of trust and expectation developed between soldiers and commanders which clashed with the republican principle of rotation.[33] The conquest of new areas brought forth new elites, whose ambition could be satisfied only through further conquests.

This development began in the period between the first and the third Punic War, and then the greatest maritime expansion in the history of the ancient world followed between 67 BC and AD 85.[34] Pompey undertook the initial task of 'cleansing' the Mediterranean of pirates, in order to allow trade to take place smoothly between east and west, north and south. What drove him to do this was no longer a need for security in the face of a direct threat from aggressive rivals, but rather the goal of establishing a universal maritime power in the Mediterranean that would become part of the empire. Until then it had consisted of a number of land territories, but now it acquired a new maritime centre of gravity that fundamentally altered the expansionist dynamic and the prevailing conceptions of an imperial order. From now on, every competing politician or army commander had to measure himself by the yardstick of Pompey's forcible expansion of the Roman empire: Julius Caesar described his British expedition as a move to gain control of the seas, implicitly comparing it to Pompey's achievement, and Augustus formulated his *Res gestae* looking back at both Pompey and Caesar. Augustus' decision to base his posthumous reputation not on external expansion but on inner consolidation of the empire was all the more momentous because it was the main element in what we have called the crossing of the Augustan threshold.

The acceleration of Roman expansion in the hundred years before and after the birth of Christ therefore rested upon an association of aristocratic values with a universal ideology of world rule; travel by ship became a symbol for the victory of human intelligence over the stifling confinement to land that had characterized previous centuries. Thus, in distancing itself from Rome's territorial empire and asserting its ideological affinity with Carthage, the English aristocracy was actually pinning its colours to the wrong mast. Without realizing it, it had for a long time already been following in the footsteps of Rome.[35]

Rome's celebration of its political-military victories as a triumph of civilization reflected an imperial consciousness that could not have grown out of the encounter with the Hellenistic East, which was inferior to it militarily but certainly not culturally. Already in Spain, but above all in Gaul, Germany and Britain, the Romans were convinced that they represented a higher level of civilization than the local 'barbarian' tribes, which had no large towns, scarcely any crafts and only a little trade; inevitably, military pacification of these regions went together with their integration into Roman civilization. In the West, then, Rome had to invest very early in the periphery, whereas in the East it behaved in a more exploitative manner. In fact, it was mainly there that it drew the resources for the expansion of its power, while the sense of itself as a civilizing force grew out of the encounter with the West. The experience of two peripheries, which could scarcely have been more different from each other, was also fraught with political consequences. For Rome disported itself in the East as a hegemon, whereas in the West and North it exercised direct imperial rule.[36] The question of whether to act in a hegemonic or an imperial manner was therefore decided not in the centre but in the periphery.

Differences between East and West long marked Roman politics and repeatedly led to rivalry and misunderstanding between the two parts of the empire – especially when it was a question of whether the legions of the West or the East had the right to proclaim their commander emperor. The Diocletian reforms and then the division of the empire under Constantine were attempts to take these differences into account, but they also consolidated the differences from the bridging of which the Roman empire had drawn its strength and legitimacy. After the West collapsed in the fifth century, the East made no serious attempt – apart from Justinian's occasional efforts – to re-establish its rule over the Western half of the empire. Indeed, it seems to have been not unhappy to rid itself of the West, whose military security had become an endless drain on resources: for example, the Eastern empire raised 65 per cent of the fiscal revenue, which mainly served to maintain an army two-thirds of which was stationed in the West.[37]

In a certain respect, Tsarist Russia may be said to resemble the Roman empire – except that here the East was the part to be civilized, whereas the Russians had a sense of inferiority in relation to the West and endeavoured to reach its level of development. So, the Russians were perceived in the West as semi-barbarian conquerors, and in the East as a civilizing force. In 1864 the tsar's foreign minister, Count Gorchakov, wrote a circular justifying the Russian push to Tashkent, on the grounds that Russia's situation was similar to that of all civilized countries facing wild, semi-nomadic peoples on their fringes which were forced against their will to take the path of expansion.[38] This was intended both to placate the European powers, which suspected Russia of pursuing a course of imperialist confrontation with Britain, and to win the support of Russia's own aristocracy for expansion in Asia. But the Asian conquests had only limited resonance in the population, since the general view was that Russia's history would be decided in Europe. The rulers of Russia, unlike those of Rome, could derive very little political capital from their claim to be a civilizing force.

In the course of the nineteenth century, the two sides of the Russian empire became essentially a problem of the nobility and the intelligentsia, which were torn between an orientation to the West and a longing for the East that kept breaking through. The well-known and often-described disputes between Westernizers and Slavophiles were an expression of this conflict,[39] which mainly concerned a choice of political models and cultural perspectives for the future. Of course, other countries and nations have known similar debates, but the antagonistic form that they took in Russia pointed to a typical intra-imperial controversy in which the two (at least two) sides of an empire fought over the power to shape the future.

From the time of Peter the Great, the Russian nobility – that is, the chief support of empire and 'the one social stratum which embodied its spirit and was responsible for its defence and administration'[40] – assumed an almost schizophrenic dual role as Asian satraps and European gentlemen. Many nobles, and from the nineteenth century most members of the intelligentsia, tried to escape this role by choosing the one or the other side of empire, and inevitably came into conflict with its imperatives. One consequence of this was the basic 'oppositionism' of many members of the leading strata of society, which sapped Russia's strength as an imperial power and eventually contributed to its collapse. For a time the Soviet Union managed to combine the two perspectives, but the toll proved too great in the end;[41] the collapse of the Soviet Union was due also to the excessive demands for integration inherited from Tsarist Russia.

The phenomenon of fringe areas at different levels of political and cultural development points to a fundamental problem of major empires that is not posed in the same way for individual countries, and especially not for nation-states. Whereas the latter develop a relatively uniform political-cultural identity, from which they draw the strength and influence to assert themselves against other states,[42] empires must handle conflicts and oppositions between countries *inside them*, and either make these productive or face collapse in the event of failure.

A good example of such failure is the end of the Austro-Hungarian empire and its disintegration into a number of individual states. Owing to its position between Germany, Italy, Russia and the Ottoman empire, the Danubian monarchy had not just two but four frontier regions and directions of influence, all of which proved to be threatening in their different ways. In line with the Roman model, the imperial government responded to the threats in 1867 by dividing the empire into an Austrian and a Hungarian half, known as Cisleithania and Transleithania respectively (after the name of the

Leitha river). This entailed, however, that the Slav population of Bohemians, Moravians and Serbs did not feel adequately represented and redoubled its efforts to gain independence. A tripartite solution that was temporarily considered, making Bohemia a third component with Prague as its capital, never came to fruition. But the division of the empire into two parts was already enough to release powerful centrifugal forces. The different nations grew apart, the nobility sustaining the cohesion of empire fell into great difficulties as a result of social-economic changes, the economic weakness of the Balkans led to an enduring budget deficit, and a sense that there was no way out or forward began to spread among the population. It was hoped that a great war might dispel the mood of dark despair, but then the dual monarchy collapsed as a result.[43]

Although the Habsburg monarchy was not an empire in the sense of our opening definition, the consequences of its disintegration clearly show that it had the historical significance of an empire that embraces a whole civilization. Over a long period of time it not only politically and culturally integrated the space of Mitteleuropa, but also constituted a bridge between Europe's southeastern frontier regions and the space of Western and Central Europe. After 1918 no other power was able to fulfil this function – with the possible exception of Yugoslavia, and then only for a short time and over a small area. In principle, the European Union now faces the task of finding a lasting solution to the problem.

The division of responsibilities was more successful within the Ottoman empire, where already in the sixteenth century Rumelia was separated from Anatolia as a province in its own right.[44] Each of the two governors or *beglerbeg* not only controlled the administration of his province, but was also responsible for border security and had to raise the necessary funds. Owing to the undisputed position of the sultan and the stronger centralization of the Ottoman empire, however, the two parts did not achieve the degree of independence that marked the two constituents of the Roman empire or the Habsburg monarchy. The fall of the Ottoman empire was the result not of centrifugal tendencies but of other deficits.

The Chinese empire was even more effective in handling various challenges in its periphery without endangering the unity of China that had been won in the Qin dynasty (221–206 BC). From the beginning, it had to reckon with the problem of barbarian incursions from the north, while in the south its relations with a ring of tribute-paying states were quite different from those it had with the semi-nomadic horsemen of the north. The growing apart of the north and south interfered with China's image of itself as the

'Middle Country', which served as a counterweight to the centrifugal tendencies that asserted themselves in periods of decline and
disintegration. A new rise was thus always associated with China's
'reunification'.[45]

The strongly 'middle-oriented' consciousness of the Chinese
probably also lay behind the momentous decision, after the costly
naval expansion under Admiral Zheng He (1405–1433), to withdraw
from seafaring, to burn the fleet and to allow only limited and, if possible, state-regulated coastal trade.[46] Maritime expansion and the
effects of long-distance trade could all too easily have knocked the
country off balance.[47]

The problem of the political, economic and cultural diversity of
peripheral regions was less pronounced for the European maritime
powers (Portugal, Spain, the Netherlands and England) than for the
classical land empires.[48] In India, China and Japan, they encountered
states and kingdoms which were economically capable and politically secure, and so imperial expansion was at first restricted to the
exchange of goods and the opening of markets. Sizeable profits could
be made in the resulting trade area, but the existence of strong local
powers meant that political influence remained slight. Only with the
collapse of the Mogul empire in India (1739) and the decline of the
Qing dynasty in China (second half of the nineteenth century) did
political domination gradually overlay the existing trade relations.

The situation was quite different in the western peripheries of the
maritime empires. In North and South America, a constant stream
of people flowed into newly founded settler colonies. Whatever
their reason for leaving Europe – the lure of quick riches, as the gold
of the Incas and Aztecs seemed to promise, or the quest for a kind of
religious community that was impossible in the Old World – their
economic forms asserted themselves against the existing structures.
Superior weapons gave the newcomers a final trump card, and so
imperial expansion gave rise to areas under the direct political
control of the centre.

The western side of the Spanish and British empires thus sharply
differed from the eastern side, and history took a different course
there. But, since the parts of the empire were separated from the
centre by the high seas, the social-cultural heterogeneity of the
periphery had considerably less impact on the centre than in the case
of the land empires. Sea empires were evidently in a position to
adjust to challenges in far-flung parts, and they also found it easier
to come to terms with the loss of a particular region. One example of
this is the way in which Britain entered a new imperial cycle after the
loss of its American colonies.

Imperial cycles and Augustan thresholds

The interplay of the various sources and forms of power is more apparent in the rise and fall of empires than in the history of states. Whereas interstate structures geared to reciprocity inevitably entail that the four types of power become alike within different countries,[49] the non-uniform peripheries of empires require that now military or political, now economic or ideological power is more strongly emphasized. Military deficits, for example, can there be offset by the fact that peoples fascinated by the imperial glitter may risk everything to become part of it and to place their fighting capacities in its service. They will expect to be paid for it, but the funding requirement will be far lower than if it were necessary to use the empire's own armed forces.

Imperial borders rarely have to be secured against powers of equal strength, and so traders and military advisers, folklorists and influential agents often play a more important role there than the military forces of the empire. This may be observed as much in Rome's defence of its 'barbarian frontiers' with the Germans as in the actions of Britain or America on their 'Indian frontier', as much in the scramble of European colonial powers to occupy supposedly 'ungoverned' areas as in the US overthrow of the Taliban regime in Afghanistan, when the 'buying' of regional warlords for a few million dollars changed the whole power structure in the space of a few days.

Along with money and economic power, the attractions of civilization (hence ideological power) can be decisive in winning the population of frontier regions to the cause of empire. We can already see this in Tacitus' account of the quarrel between Arminius and Flavus, two brothers from the Cherusci tribe, after the former had instigated a momentous uprising against Roman rule while the latter remained in the service of the empire. The quarrel, conducted across the River Weser, began when Arminius asked his brother (who had lost an eye fighting for the Romans) what thanks he had received for his mutilation. 'Flavus spoke of increased pay, a neck chain, a crown, and other military gifts, while Arminius jeered at such a paltry recompense for slavery.'[50] Things grew more envenomed as soon as it was a matter of loyalty to the imperial power or to the ethnic group. Despite Arminius' reference to the fatherland, ancient liberties and native gods, Flavus maintained his loyalty to Rome by invoking the size of the empire and the power of the governor. It was mainly Rome's ideological and political power – not its seriously shaken military power – which gave rise to Flavus' pro-Roman option.

Among the factors determining the rise and durability of an empire are the exchange conditions and conversion forms of the four types of power. A further regulatory function is played by the cycles through which long-lasting empires pass several times. These affect not only the cost problem and the choice of the least expensive type of power, but also its availability at any given time and place. How long an empire can remain in the higher segment of a cycle depends on whether the deficit in one type of power can be offset by a surplus of another type.

The rise of Spain to become a European hegemonial power and a world empire is essentially attributable to its modern and powerful military apparatus, its disciplined infantry and its highly seaworthy fleet. Military power was complemented by political power, which arose from the fact that Spain was a country at peace and had a well-functioning administration. The calm following the end of the *communeros* uprising in 1521 gave it a power advantage vis-à-vis France, which from the 1540s was paralysed by internal strife and a long civil war. What Spain lacked, however, was an independent economic dynamic, 'a banking system with international connections and, above all, a dynamic layer of entrepreneurs and traders who, in collaboration with the state, might have built up the country's economic as well as political and military power.'[51] In the end, only gold and silver from the Americas enabled the Spanish kings to erect and maintain the costly military infrastructure of empire. Yet, despite the permanent flow of precious metals from the New World – estimated at 3,000 billion thalers in the sixteenth century alone[52] – expenditure was regularly 20 per cent higher than income. Spanish power broke into pieces because it had no long-term solution to its financial problems.

A further grave handicap of the Spanish world empire was the narrow demographic base on which it rested. It had a considerably smaller population than its hegemonial rivals, France and the Ottoman empire, and even that declined by some 20 per cent in the course of the sixteenth century.[53] These deficits in the struggle for hegemony in Europe did not initially count for more only because France's internal conflicts put a brake on its external ambitions, and because the forces of the Ottoman empire in the East were tied down. Furthermore, Spain's close connection with the German branch of the Habsburgs gave it the opportunity (which it amply exploited) to recruit fighting men from Germany.

There was also a fortunate turn of events that significantly prolonged Spain's imperial cycle: namely, the takeover of Portugal in

1580, through which the crown acquired an additional colonial empire. It now had the world's largest navy at its disposal, and this allowed it without delay to make up the losses it incurred through the secession of the Netherlands. In the eighty years of war to win back the renegade provinces, however, Spain ate up precious resources without achieving permanent victory. At the beginning of the seventeenth century, the Dutch went onto the offensive and their East Indies and West Indies trading companies managed to capture parts of the Portuguese commercial and colonial empire. The Peace of Westphalia, followed by the Peace of the Pyrenees in 1659, marked the end of Spain's first imperial cycle.[54] The Bourbon reforms granted it one more imperial cycle in the eighteenth century, but this was much more modest and passed quite uneventfully.

We may conclude that the first cycle of the Spanish empire was essentially driven by its military superiority, resulting from organizational reforms and innovations in weapons technology that involved a sharp rise in expenditure.[55] When this could no longer be sustained, and when rivals and adversaries caught up in terms of organization and technology, Spanish power in Europe disintegrated. Another reason why the loss of military superiority had such dramatic consequences is that no other type of power was available in sufficient supply to offset it: Spain's economic power was anyway lesser than that of its European rivals; its political power – especially its capacity to forge alliances and to assert its own will within them – had been reduced as a result of the religious division of Europe and the clash of interests with a newly ascendant England; and it could generate ideological power only through the project of the Counter-Reformation, which earned it at least as much hostility as sympathy and support. With the growth of the 'Black Legend', first in the Netherlands and then throughout Europe, Spain's opponents disposed of a powerful counter-ideology, which made Spanish supremacy in Europe appear worse than unattractive,[56] identified with the cruelty and arbitrary power of the Inquisition, the measureless exactions of Philip II, the moral depravity of the Spanish national character, and the ambition to create a universal monarchy, a world empire in which all other nations would be held subject. We can see in this gruesome vision the first international anti-imperial ideology of modern Europe. Spanish propaganda could find no way to deal with it.[57]

At first, Spain's power deficits made themselves felt only in Europe, not in its lands across the sea; the threat was to its European hegemonic position, not to its extra-European empire. For this reason, the end of Spanish supremacy in Europe should not be equated with the decline of the Spanish world empire, which still had a century and a half to run in Latin America and nearly two and a half in the Pacific and the Caribbean. It is not convincing to portray this long period simply as one of decay and decline.

If we follow the model of rise and fall, the history of nearly all empires is marked by a brief and dynamic period of ascent and a long period of decline; the former is largely identical with military expansion, while all the reforms undertaken after the zenith of imperial expansion are considered with an eye to the more or less gradual decline. Such a model inevitably puts a premium on the *military* side of empires and downplays their *political* capacity for renewal. Reforms of the administration, the economic order, the fiscal and financial system, even the military apparatus then become nothing other than attempts to halt, or at least to postpone, the inevitable decline.

This model has been repeatedly applied to Roman history in particular, until it is scarcely possible any longer to separate historical account and theoretical assumptions. The empire supposedly reached its zenith in the early second century at the latest, in the age of the adoptive emperors, especially as, under Trajan, its spatial extent was greater than at any time before or after. Then it entered a long process of decline.[58] Diocletian's reordering of the empire at the end of the third century, the subsequent division of the empire under Constantine and his successors, the exchange of ideological power through the raising of Christianity to the state religion in 380 under Theodosius[59] – none of this can have any decisive significance for the history of the empire, and so, as in the case of Spain, two and a half centuries are without more ado interpreted as a history of decline. What this leaves out of account – not necessarily in the historical narrative but in the historical consciousness – is the cyclical ups and downs during the long period of ostensible decline. The result is an image of historical inevitability, which makes the politicians of imperial reform into so many tragic figures who, in seeking to arrest the decline, merely accelerated the final demise.

In opposition to the model of rise, zenith and decline, we shall enlist here the cyclical model of political history, which the Greek-Roman historian Polybius developed in antiquity and the Italian political theorist Niccolò Macchiavelli renewed at the beginning of the modern age.[60] According to this, political communities pass through several up-and-down cycles in the course of their history, and both the number of cycles and the duration of the upper segment essentially depend on the skill and far-sightedness of their political leaders.[61]

The cyclical model has several advantages for the reconstruction of imperial histories. *First*, it can represent the ups and downs of empires much more accurately than the rise-and-fall model, with its fixation on merely two tendencies of development. *Second*, the bulk of its attention is directed at the handling of crises, and hence at the crossing of low points and the continuation of periods in the upper segment of a cycle. *Third*, it therefore attaches greater weight to political (and social) players, who, with the resources and types of power available to them, introduce reforms to limit the effect of factors causing decline and to strengthen the forces that give a sustaining impetus.[62]

In recent years, the theory of hegemonial cycles has worked out analytic models that describe the chequered history of empires in a more precise and subtle manner than the traditional rise-and-fall model has been able to achieve.[63] According to George Modelski and William R. Thompson, superiority in the leading sectors of steel, chemicals and electrical engineering allowed the United States to achieve top position in the world economy in the early part of the twentieth century, and on this basis it also advanced to become the leading political power. This hegemonial cycle, in which economic and political development were closely associated with each other, lasted from 1850 until 1973. Thanks to its superiority in the new leading sectors of information technology and microelectronics, the United States then entered a new hegemonial cycle which, after a brief intermediate period of weakness, saw it triumph over the Soviet Union and emerge as the only remaining world power.

One problem with this theory, of course, is the strong determination by economic factors. In terms of the theory of types of power, we may say that it regards economic power alone as decisive and excludes any replacement of one type by another. Consistently, representatives of the theory of hegemonial cycles assume that, before the United States, only Britain managed to pass through two such cycles – one based on its naval and commercial superiority, the other on its primacy in the industrial revolution. The economic determination of hegemonial cycles leaves no scope for political decision. It is therefore insufficiently complex in comparison with the political cycle theories of classical republicanism, in the sense that these understood the ups and downs of history to be determined by social-moral factors and the constitutional order of the polity.

In the analysis of imperial history, then, the concept of different types of power and the two theories of cycles should be combined in such a way as to avoid determinism and to allow decision-making elites greater influence on the course of the cycle (the handling of crises and the length of time in the upper segment of the cycle). This being so, no assumptions should be made about the average duration of a cycle. Empires that pass through one cycle in a relatively short time may also be distinguished from those in which it is possible to identify several cycles, each involving a long period in the upper segment. Examples of the former would be the Mongol empire or Napoleonic France, and of the latter not only imperial China or Rome but also the Ottoman, Spanish and British empires. In these cases the cycle seems to be all the shorter, the fewer the types of power at the empire's disposal or the fewer the types of power in which it has superiority over its direct rivals. Conversely, the length of time in the upper segment of the cycle seems to be all the greater, the larger the available choice between types of power. The ability of decision-making elites to steer the course of the cycle, and to speed it up or slow it down, grows *pari passu* with the variety of types of power.[64] Of course, the leeway for these elites should not be overstated: they are able to influence the course of the cycle; they cannot opt out of it or bring it to a halt.

A key role in lengthening the time spent in the upper segment of the cycle is played by what, following Michael Doyle, we have called the 'Augustan threshold'.[65] The reforms introduced by Octavian/Augustus essentially consisted of three elements: Octavian sought to win the trust of the Roman landed aristocracy, so that with its support he could break the power of the urban oligarchs; he gained influence over the constitutional and administrative order, which could now be changed without provoking a political crisis; and he reorganized the administrative system, transforming the provinces from spaces for oligarchic self-enrichment to efficiently governed parts of the empire. Such was the programme with which Octavian consolidated his power and sought to end the civil wars; it developed into a fundamental reconstruction of Rome's political order, which is generally described as the end of the Republic and the beginning of the imperial Principate. At the same time, however, he created the structures that contributed to the long life of the *Imperium Romanum*. The crossing of the Augustan threshold brought to a close the period of wild, unplanned expansion of the empire and the internal strife and civil wars associated with it. Roman rule was put on a stable long-term footing.

At first, it seemed far from likely that Rome would remain in the upper segment of the cycle for at least two hundred years. After several centuries of devastating civil wars, in which the periphery had been repeatedly used as a base for the conquest of power in the centre, the Roman empire faced the danger of disintegrating into a number of fragments, as the Macedonian empire had done after the death of Alexander. The triumvirate system, for example, which Rome had several times used as a way of ending civil war, assigned the provinces connected with the three rulers as their separate dominions, and this left the way open for them to develop as Macedonian-style rival states. In particular, the division between the West and East of the empire was more than just an intellectual exercise. Yet Octavian managed to bind the population of the provinces to the empire. Troop strengths could be significantly reduced[66] – which lowered the cost of securing the imperial space and made it possible to cut taxes.[67] The power centre in Rome, which since the final victory over Carthage had expanded its rule to the northwest and southeast through the whole Mediterranean in a long succession of wars, now became the *Imperium Romanum* serving to guarantee the *pax Romana*.

The key to the success of the Augustan reforms was the creation of an administrative elite resistant to corruption. In this way, Octavian wagered not only on institutional changes but on a deep reform of the morals of the imperial elite. Recently, many writers on the period have argued that the ethical and religious policies of Octavian (who in 27 BC was given the name Augustus, 'the August' or 'Awe-Inspiring') were an expression of his own deep attachment to conservative values, while others have pointed out that he actually rose to power through methods that he later vigorously combated. The reproach of falsity, which this implies, may be accurate if it is taken in the sense of inconsistency. But then the renewal and consolidation of an empire is essentially a matter of political effect, not moral consistency.[68] Elimination of the widespread corruption among the republican oligarchy was a prerequisite if the imperial extraction of surplus was to proceed through regular and orderly taxation rather than the mechanisms of pillage operated by regional warlords and proconsular officials.[69] For this, it was necessary to ensure that the personnel in charge of taxation were not tempted to increase their own wealth and influence at the expense of the state. Such was the purpose of the Augustan moral and religious reforms, the repeated 'purges' of the Senate (which also, of course, hit at Octavian's more respectable political opponents) and the *lex Julia de ambitu* (whereby contenders for office who had shown themselves open to bribery were excluded from promotion for a period of five years).[70]

Octavian concerned himself not only with the political loyalty and administrative reliability of the imperial elite, but also with its physical reproduction. In the early years after the end of the civil war, he renewed Rome's political class by bringing citizens from the provinces of Italy to the capital, elevating knights to the rank of patricians, and appointing a large number of senators. Although these recruitment methods were an effective way to increase his own following in the top positions, Octavian did not intend them to become the established norm but saw them as a special solution for exceptional times. The main idea in his mind was that the elite would physically reproduce itself, both through its own children and through the widespread Roman practice of adoption. Inheritance rights were restricted in the case of unmarried persons, and the state was given a stronger claim to the property of those who died without children. The emperor introduced financial support for families with more than two children and large penalties for adultery and immoral behaviour. Above all, consuls with many children were given priority over those with few, and they could pick a province to their liking instead of having to be allocated one.[71] Augustus' reliance on this kind of self-reproducing elite naturally limited his own influence over its composition. It may be seen as part of his programme to convert *potestas* into *auctoritas* (power into authority),[72] as well as a measure to ensure the demographic stability of the empire by setting an example for the rest of the population. But it may also be interpreted as a way of increasing the resistance to corruption among the administrative and military elite. People inserted into a family sequence of generations are less prone to bribery than individual careerists, who at most have to worry about their posthumous reputation, not about the fate of their children and grandchildren.

The Augustan threshold therefore denotes a set of far-reaching reforms through which an empire ends its phase of expansion and passes into the phase of settled long-term existence. In terms of cycle theory, the period in the upper segment of the cycle is extended for as long as possible. In the Roman empire's own eyes, this ultimately meant that the Republic's cyclical conception of history, which had been dominant from Polybius to Sallust, was supplanted by the imperial image of *Roma aeterna*, the Eternal City.[73] If the reforms are taken as a whole, we may say that the crossing of the Augustan threshold amounted to a far-reaching change in the types of power: the importance of military power declined, allowing Octavian to make drastic cuts in troop levels, while at the same time the weight of political, economic and, especially, ideological power increased. The last was most visible in the ideology of eternity and the idea of the *pax Romana*, as well as the new legitimacy of empire; peace would prevail as long as the Roman empire lasted, and the greater its security the more secure would be the foundation of peace.

With the crossing of the Augustan threshold, the empire passed from an exploitative to a civilizing relationship between centre and periphery. The construction of an independent bureaucracy, which removed the administration of the empire from the arbitrariness of the Roman civic oligarchy, was followed by the gradual spread of civil rights from the centre to sections of the provincial population. Thus, whereas in 70 BC a census covering the areas under Roman rule recorded a total of 910,000 male citizens, the census ordered by Octavian and Agrippa for the year AD 28 turned up 4,063,000 Roman citizens – an increase which cannot be attributed only to the fact that women and children were now also included. Twenty years later, the figure had risen by another 170,000 to 4,233,000.[74] These are certainly not dramatic changes, but they do mark the beginning of a trend that reached a climax in AD 212–13 with Caracalla's constitution, in which all freemen in the empire were granted Roman citizenship.[75]

This also formally concluded a process in which the differences between centre and periphery had gradually become narrower and less significant. Already Hadrian had ended the political and economic privileges enjoyed by Italy, and treated it as just another province of the empire. At that time the empire's main centre of economic activity was already in the provinces, and its Italian core had entered a period of stagnation whose clearest sign was the depopulation of the South.[76] Now the troops of the empire were also recruited mainly from the provinces in which they were stationed. Military power was no longer an instrument through which the centre ruled the periphery. Rather, the periphery itself produced military power, which in turn increasingly became a guarantee of the empire's continued existence. It was non-Italian emperors, such as the African-born Severus, who placed cultivation of the army at the heart of imperial policy.

The crossing of the Augustan threshold was especially apparent in the fact that political and economic differences between centre and periphery disappeared, and so too, gradually, did the legal privileges that had remained with the conquering people as the fruit of their victories. In Rome, Caracalla's extension of civil rights was followed by Diocletian's great tax reform, which removed the freedom from taxation that all Italians had previously enjoyed.[77] The 'decentring' of the empire finally reached its conclusion with the move from Rome to Constantinople, and the former capital soon lost its position even as administrative centre for the Western half of the empire – in 293 to Milan, then in 402 to Ravenna, which was better protected from enemy incursions.

Have other empires also crossed the Augustan threshold? A comparative historical view suggests that we should distinguish between lingering on the threshold and decisively entering the adjacent corridor. Once more, Spain may serve as our example here. Charles V's abdication in 1556 and the division of the empire into a German and a Spanish line put an end to the peripatetic rule that Charles had exercised, both to be with his troops and to assert his charisma in various parts of the empire. In 1561 Philip II made Madrid the centre of his government and created what, for his time, was a highly modern bureaucracy.[78] Wild conquest of new territory, and the violent, chaotic extraction of surplus in the periphery, were now things of the past. However, since the declining significance of military power could not be offset by a corresponding increase in political, economic and ideological power, Spain did not really accomplish the transition from an exploitative to a civilizing role in world politics.[79] In particular, its decentring of empire was never as strong as in ancient Rome, and so it could not revitalize itself in a comparable movement from the periphery to the centre.

The reason for Spain's lingering at the Augustan threshold should be sought not so much in the relationship between mother country and colonies as in Spain's costly rivalry with the other European hegemonial powers. Its failure was not mainly as an imperial power but as a *hegemonial* power. In other words, its demise as an empire was due to the fact that the struggle for European supremacy stripped it of the resources that might otherwise have stood the imperial periphery in good stead, and its fateful preoccupation with military power may in turn be explained by the constant outbreak of hegemonial wars.

A favourable geographical situation and political circumstances ensured that, after the defeat of Carthage and the empires in the East, Rome no longer had to reckon with any rivals for hegemony; it was able to pocket the peace dividend in full and to invest it for the civilizing of the empire. Spain, on the other hand, was not so favoured. In the confrontation with the Ottoman empire, and *a fortiori* with neighbouring France, it was forced to construct an extensive system of fortifications that recent technological advances had made extremely costly.[80] In the end, as much as 65 per cent of the Spanish budget was being eaten up in debt repayments.[81] Upkeep of the huge army was prohibitively expensive, while the Spanish navy had a hard job protecting trade between parts of the empire from corsairs and pirates operating off the North African coast and the Caribbean/Central America (in the later stages, with covert support from the English).

To keep the losses under control, the Spanish soon introduced a system of convoys between Europe and the Americas, under the protection of the Atlantic armada. This was highly successful militarily, and out of 15,000 sailing trips between 1560 and 1650 no more than sixty-two ships were lost.[82] But, in view of the enormous costs, no independent layer comparable to the English 'merchant adventurers' was able to develop; the transatlantic trade therefore remained under state control. The Spanish world empire always had to rule its trading area directly, with the result that the costs of domination could never be reduced for long.

Another empire that halted at the Augustan threshold was Tsarist Russia. Peter the Great clearly saw that his empire could be sustained in the long run only if the country's population and resources were mobilized behind a Western-style professionalization of the armed forces and the creation of a bureaucratic apparatus.[83] But this was possible only if the feudally organized expansion of the Muscovite empire was directed into state-controlled paths. Peter created a standing army to replace the old feudal warrior contingents that had dispersed every winter, and in 1709 this new force passed its crucial test at the battle of Poltava. Peter's administrative structures, which remained essentially the same down to 1917, separated a bureaucratic apparatus off from the person of the ruler and even more clearly demarcated the temporal from the spiritual domain. He also created a new imperial elite, by fusing the court nobility and the nobles appointed to his service into a single order, whose ranks, first introduced in 1722, placed less value on origin than on personal achievement. In addition, following the advice of Gottfried Wilhelm Leibniz, the tsar tried to establish a scientific elite that would contend with the Orthodox clergy for intellectual leadership. Peter – who took the Latin title *Imperator Russorum* – drove home this fundamental reorganization by moving the capital from Moscow to the new city of St Petersburg, literally raised up out of the swamps and marshes.[84] In place of the Third Rome – a Byzantine-tinged image that had served a central legitimating function since the beginning of imperial expansion under Ivan IV ('the Terrible')[85] – a 'new Amsterdam' thus came into being, which was supposed to underline Russia's claim to be a global maritime power and to bestow cultural glitter on the empire. In the Petrine reforms we can also see a number of characteristics of an empire that has stepped on to the Augustan threshold.

In Peter's Russia, however, empire did not develop as it had in ancient Rome, for reasons that have to do both with the different conditions of geography and civilization and with the different political objectives. When Octavian embarked on his reforms, he was convinced that the empire did not need to expand any further, especially as there were no longer any rivals that could represent a danger to Rome or challenge its claim to leadership. Probably Philip II had a similar sense of satiety after his absorption of the Portuguese maritime empire, but Spain's supremacy within Europe continued to be as precarious as it had been before. Peter I, on the other hand, embraced the Augustan threshold in order to advance Russia's imperial expansion and to take the offensive in the clash with its rivals for European hegemony (especially Sweden, but also the Ottoman empire). His aim was not to reduce the costs of rule, but to mobilize resources and energies for the control and expansion of the imperial space. And at no point in its history could Russia achieve this through increased surplus extraction in its periphery; it also had to place a considerable burden on the population of the imperial centre itself. The Petrine project therefore led to colonization of the centre by the centre, with the aim of expanding the imperial periphery.

Entrance to the Augustan threshold took yet another form in the case of the Ottoman empire, which at the same time had to complete the transition from nomadic conditions to a settled farming mode of production if it was not to vanish with the same rapidity as numerous steppe empires before it.[86] As the nomadic conquerors had not developed any administrative structures of their own, they simply took over the Byzantine system they found in their newly conquered regions and extended it to their whole empire.[87] These two developments – the construction of an imperial administration and the emancipation from pillage and expansionist pressures – were closely associated with each other: an orderly administration was possible only if there was some lasting continuity in the lifestyles of the imperial elite and its apparatus of coercion, and this in turn presupposed that the armed forces were not funded exclusively through warfare. Admittedly the weapons never fell silent on the borders of the empire,[88] but now the supplying of the army rested either on the granting of state lands as benefits (as in the case of the spahis, the heavy cavalry) or on customs and rental income (as with the janissaries).

Despite these measures, military power remained the real foundation of the Ottoman empire: the fighting strength and discipline of the janissaries, always ready for combat in their barracks, was the basis for its superiority vis-à-vis the West. When it began to fade, as innovations in weapons technology and military organization asserted themselves more strongly, the once fear-inspiring Ottoman empire became 'the sick man on the Bosphorus'.

Of course, a certain political power was also present alongside the military. The Ottoman empire was long spared internal conflicts and unrest, and in reality, if not in official eyes, it was an important ally for a few European states in the contest for hegemony on the continent; France, in particular, repeatedly tried to draw on Turkish assistance for the opening of a 'second front' against the Habsburgs. However, the ideological power of the Ottomans was double-edged: while it could temporarily make it easier to win a loyal following in the Islamic world, it aroused intense animosity in the Christian world. After the fall of Constantinople in 1453, a large number of 'Turkish writings' called for a crusade against the new danger from the East, in which all political conflicts within Western Christendom were to be suspended in the interests of a resolute struggle against the common enemy.

From the beginning, however, the real weakness of the Ottoman empire was its lack of economic power, and the shift from nomadism to settled farming changed nothing in this respect. Sea trade, for example, which was quite considerable because of control over the straits, was entirely in the hands of foreign entrepreneurs. The empire profited from it financially only through the tolls it levied.[89] The resources of the empire were limited to what could be siphoned off administratively, and a lot of creative thinking went into this, but it meant that there was no active economic policy, nor any of the usual incentives for the development of an entrepreneurial class.

The uneven distribution of political-military and ideological-economic power led to varying capacities for the handling of crises and recovery from major setbacks. Thus, after the crushing defeat of 1402 near Angora (Ankara) at the hands of Timur Lenk,[90] the Ottoman empire did not collapse but was able to pull itself together and enter a new cycle. This was certainly made easier by the fact that, after Timur's death, his empire fell apart as quickly as it had come into being. In any event, the empire of Sultan Mehmed I was only half as large as that of his predecessor, Bayezid I, who had fallen into Timur's hands and died in captivity. But a new cycle did begin under Mehmed:[91] the empire made considerable advances in the fifteenth century, finally capturing Constantinople and taking over from Byzantium at the border between Europe and Asia.

Economic power was irrelevant in the confrontation with Timur Lenk: all that counted was the clash of military forces. Things were different in the West, where for a long time the fortunes of battle balanced each other out. Economic power here took on decisive significance, so that the strategic weakness of the Ottoman empire became ever more apparent. The frequent idea that the phase of Ottoman ascent immediately gave way to a phase of decline, without a lengthy stay in the upper segment of the cycle,[92] is based on this grave deficit in economic power. However, it does not do justice to the period that the Ottoman empire spent in the upper segment during the sixteenth and seventeenth centuries.

After Rome, China is undoubtedly the most interesting and important example of the crossing of the Augustan threshold. The first point to be made is that China had more space available than any other empire for the consolidation of its power. Under the Qin dynasty (221–206 BC), the geographical core took shape that still largely defines China's borders. In contrast to the spatial changes that the British empire, for example, experienced between its first and second cycles, China always found itself occupying the same geographical area. The Qin period witnessed the administrative unification of previously conquered territories. Emperor Zheng divided the empire into thirty-six provinces, and each of these into several districts, for the administration of which he transferred officials directly under central command.[93] Under the Han dynasty (until AD 220), the civil component of the empire was further strengthened: the court became its cultural centre, and the loyalty of officials was reinforced by the development of the Confucian ethic. In fact, Confucianism[94] grounded imperial administration less on legalistic principles, laws and prescriptions than on a distinctive elite ethos, and whether this could or could not be renewed and maintained was decisive for the course of the imperial cycles. Whereas the fate of the steppe empires hinged mainly on military power, the other forms of power were always more important in China.

Moreover, Chinese empire-building benefited from the fact that, after the period of conquests came to an end, the only remaining military threat was from the north. In the confrontation with the nomadic tribes there, the 'Middle Empire' conducted a mixture of appeasement policies and preventive shows of force, whose purpose was not to expand the imperial space but to frighten its enemies and to break up potentially aggressive tribal alliances. Emperor Zheng had already begun work on wall systems to prevent nomads from advancing into the empire, and Emperor Wudi went on to the offensive by undertaking military expeditions deep into barbarian territory. Most often, however, regular payments of tribute were used to dissuade the nomadic tribes from crossing the frontiers of the empire. As a further guarantee, princes were handed over as hostages and given a Chinese education, in an attempt to 'civilize' them and bind them to the empire. The appeasement policy was therefore characterized by a greater reliance on ideological than military power; the Chinese emperors chose a similar course to the one pursued by Roman emperors in their German policy from the third century AD.[95]

Of course, the limitation of military power typical of the Chinese empire was possible only because, in the 'world' that it ruled, China was not faced with hegemonial rivals and could concentrate on the securing of its 'barbarian frontiers' (Jürgen Osterhammel). This geopolitical framework also favoured the development of the Confucian ethos within the administrative system, for Confucianism was in principle unsuited to an activist or aggressive foreign policy of the kind that would have been necessary in dealing with a hegemonial rival.

For the greatest part of its history, the real threat came not from outside but inside the Chinese empire. At the end of the Han period, for example, the central power lost ground to a hereditary nobility, which fragmented and divided up the administration of the empire.[96] Trade and the circulation of money – the most important means of integrating the imperial space – fell into decline, and China split into a northern and a southern empire. Significantly, the reconstruction of unity under the Sui and early Tang dynasty (618–907) was bound up with revival of the Confucian bureaucratic ethos:[97] the Sui introduced the step-by-step testing of officials and created a bureaucratic elite based on erudition. Then, at the end of the Tang dynasty, the rise of local commanders again strengthened the significance of military power, and once more the empire was divided. In the ensuing period of the 'ten empires', the south in particular was seriously fragmented, but then the Song dynasty (960–1276) managed to restore the unity of the empire,[98] involving more intensive trade and monetary circulation and another revival of the bureaucratic ethos.[99] This cyclical pattern continued until the time of China's encounter with the European powers. The challenge of these new hegemonial rivals, soon joined by a Japan modernizing along Western lines, gave military power much greater weight than it had had in the two previous millennia.

Thus, the kind of power that is decisive for the rise and stability of an empire depends on both internal factors and external circumstances. An asymmetrical relationship develops between the two, and it is this which shapes the characteristic rationality of the empire. The space within which the imperial elites succeed or fail is determined by this specific imperial rationality. It is the concretization of what we have more generally referred to as the logic of world domination.

4

CIVILIZATION AND BARBARIAN FRONTIERS: TASKS AND HALLMARKS OF IMPERIAL ORDER

Large-scale, and *a fortiori* global, empires are under increased pressure to justify themselves. Less extensive political orders, such as those of cities or small to medium-sized states, may have disputed frontiers and even wage wars to define them, but their fundamental structure is not in doubt. Small-scale orders benefit from the assumption that they are natural, in both senses of the word. If the same is not true of large-scale orders, the main reason is probably that they involve a power difference between centre and periphery, which is all the more striking the greater are the areas that they encompass politically or economically. What is most visible in them is the domination aspect of political order. Their subjects question their meaning and purpose in quite a different way from those who live in small-scale political orders, where the power centres balance one another out because of their multiplicity, and the existence of other political entities removes the compulsion for any special justification of one's own entity.[1]

In large-scale orders, the centre's claim to domination or supremacy is repeatedly analysed, if not always disputed, by the periphery. Take, for example, the question that John of Salisbury hurled at the Hohenstaufen Emperor Friedrich I: 'Who has appointed the Germans judges of nations? Who has given these crude and uncultivated people the right to place a lord arbitrarily over the heads of human beings as if they were children?'[2] The implied answer is 'no one': the Germans have taken a liberty to which they have no right, and the sooner they end their presumption, the better things will be. According to Livy, Hannibal said much the same about the Romans when they tried to impose the same restrictions on him in Spain as they had on his predecessor Hasdrubal: 'That outrageously cruel and tyrannical nation claims everything for itself, makes everything dependent on its will and pleasure; they think it right to dictate with whom we are to make war or peace. They confine and enclose us within mountains and rivers as boundaries, but they do not observe the limits which they themselves have fixed.'[3]

Large-scale political orders, when secured and ruled from an imperial centre, are subject to the reproach of arbitrariness and preferential treatment. Irrespective of whether the charge is accurate or not, we have to consider how imperial orders can legitimate themselves in the face of anti-imperial critiques.

Peace as a justification for imperial rule

Peace has again and again been used as a justification for imperial order, the argument being that only large-scale, centrally ruled political orders can avoid the permanent wars to draw or redraw boundaries that are inevitably associated with small-scale orders. Imperial ideology counters the supposed naturalness of small-scale political orders by pointing to their notorious lack of peace. The most famous of these legitimations may be found in the section of Virgil's *Aeneid* that presents the Roman descendants of Aeneas as the future 'masters of the world'. As Jupiter, Virgil's father of the gods, puts it: 'Then shall wars cease and the rough ages soften; hoary Faith and Vesta, Quirinus with his brother Remus, shall give laws. The gates of war, grim with iron and close-fitting bars, shall be closed; within, impious Rage, sitting on savage arms, his hands fast bound behind with a hundred brazen knots, shall roar in the ghastliness of blood-stained lips.'[4]

Dante too, for whom the highest Good was that man should live in peace, was convinced that this was possible only if 'the whole human race' was 'subordinate to one Prince'. 'Therefore when mankind is subject to one Prince it is most like to God and this implies conformity to the divine intention, which is the condition of perfection.'[5] For Dante no lasting peace was conceivable without a universal monarchy (as a Europe-wide empire was known in the Middle Ages and the early modern period), since any order with two rulers would inevitably lead to strife between them. His argument was directed against the champions of the French king Philippe IV (Philip the Fair) and the Italian Guelphs associated with him, who denied the need for a universal monarchy and advocated a system of independent cities and territorial states. In Dante's view, their talk of justice was sheer hypocrisy, as they did not want anyone to assist the actual victory of justice.

In the history of Europe, few political theorists have associated as firmly as Dante did the wish for peace and the creation of an imperial order. Only Tommasso Campanella and (partly) Giovanni Botero laid such consistent emphasis on imperial peace, when they propagated for Europe – and hence for the whole world – the idea of a political order under Spanish rule.[6] The main strand of political thought in Europe has given priority not to the peace of imperial rule but to the *peace of international contract*; not one superior power at the centre of things, but the collective undertakings of theoretically equal players are supposed to be the guarantee of peace. This idea found its most famous and powerful expression in Kant's *Perpetual Peace* (1795).[7] The conception of a contractual peace among states, secured by a league of nations, rejected the idea of peace *at any price* and criticized the imperial 'peace of the cemetery', which always involved lack of political freedom and economic stagnation. Besides, such a peace could have no staying power and after a time would inevitably be destroyed by rebellions and uprisings – not least because of the brutal pillage of the periphery required to compensate the population of the imperial centre materially for their loss of freedom.

One example of the argument that reproached the imperial order for the costs of the periphery was Montesquieu's 'Réflexions sur la monarchie universelle' (*c*.1727). Even the Romans, who devastated the whole world to found the first universal monarchy, did not behave as barbarically as the Spanish, who destroyed everything in order to keep everything for themselves.[8] Montesquieu's critique straightforwardly reverses the civilization–barbarism relationship and characterizes the policy of empires as itself barbaric. But, in his eyes, no power can act barbarically in distant parts without this having repercussions in its own heartland; after a time the same forms of domination and repression will appear there as in the periphery. Empires therefore tend towards self-destruction by their own immanent laws, and in this sense the peace that they undoubtedly defend is not fated to last. Finally, with reference to the disastrous social-economic consequences of Spanish rule in southern Italy, Montesquieu asks whether world empires, which are always based on despotic authority, can still have a place in a commercial world.

In the eighteenth century, Spain became the counter-model to the 'commercial society' of the Enlightenment and the great adversary of all human progress.[9] Since then one increasingly finds in political and economic theory the idea that large areas can be more effectively integrated through trade than through political power, and for a long time commercial integration was conceived as intrinsically non-imperial. The power of Kant's *Perpetual Peace* rests not least on its promise to combine the integration of large areas through economic exchange with the imperatives of peace and freedom. The theory of democratic peace is the counter-model to the conception of imperial peace: it starts from a plural world of states, whose peaceful nature is supposed to stem from the fact that a certain political order (democracy) has become established within them.[10]

Robert Cooper has recently developed this theory into a model of a postmodern international order, but in doing so has qualified its claim to validity.[11] The 'world' of postmodern statehood is, in his view, largely confined to Europe. It stands opposed to the 'worlds' in which the rules of the modern state continue to apply: permanent struggle for survival against other players that follow the same rules. John Mearsheimer, for his part, formulates these rules so as to suggest that only the global supremacy of one of the great powers is really capable of averting the danger of a hegemonial war[12] – a negative formulation which, from the point of view of the 'realist' school of international relations, corresponds to the self-justification of empire that it is the only reliable guarantee of lasting peace.

In his provocative essay 'Power and Weakness' (2002), Robert Kagan takes the postmodern and the modern world of politics, as described by Cooper, and renames them the worlds of Immanuel Kant and Thomas Hobbes. The United States, he then argues, is continuing to operate in the Hobbesian (anarchic) world of mutual distrust and constant readiness for war, while the Europeans are entering a post-historical Kantian paradise. Kagan's point, of course, is that the two worlds do not live in isolation from each other, and that peace in Europe is guaranteed only by the capacity of the United States to wage wars.[13]

The United States has also followed in the footsteps of the great empires by offering a guarantee of extensive peace as the central justification for its claim to supremacy – except that, in the case of a democratic empire, this peace is measured by the assertion and preservation of human rights, which have replaced the claim to a civilizing mission that empires frequently used to declare. At the same time, the promise of future prosperity, which also has a long tradition, continues as before. But, whichever values are central, they can be enforced only if peace prevails, and so the establishment of imperial peace helps to ensure respect for those values. Scarcely any empire has made peace its only justification; nearly all have associated it with a particular mission.

Imperial missions and the sacredness of empire

All empires that have lasted any length of time have chosen as their self-justifying objective a world-historical task or mission that confers cosmological or redemptive meaning on their activity. Hegemonic powers do not need a mission, but empires cannot do without one. In the competition with their rivals, hegemonic powers have to assert their own position; ideological power can certainly come into play here, but the main sphere of operations is foreign policy. The imperial mission, on the other hand, is directed at people within the empire, especially at those in the imperial centre. It is from auto-suggestion more than anything else, however, that the political elites draw the conviction and energy to press on with the imperial project.

It is naturally possible to consider the imperial mission of salvation and its theological accreditation under the keyword 'ideology', and to seek to locate the hard core of the imperialist project in base material interests. If ideology is understood as the (necessary) self-deception of political and social players regarding their own goals and purposes, as Karl Marx proposed in the introduction to his *Eighteenth Brumaire of Louis Bonaparte*,[14] then the critique of ideology can offer a productive and illuminating point of view on imperial missions. But ideology is all too easily identified with deliberate ploys and obfuscation,[15] pursued by a small group of rulers and their intellectual hangers-on to delude the broad masses about the true goals and purposes of imperial policy. Since, in this usage, Marx's discriminating concept of ideology merely reverts to the theory of priestly trickery associated with the French Enlightenment, we shall refrain from employing it in our discussion of imperial missions. Ideology critique, when combined with economic theories of imperialism, all too often reduces the complexity of imperial policy to the mere assertion of the interests of a few players.

In contrast to the usual suppositions of ideology critique, imperial missions actually give rise to self-incurred attachments and duties which cannot be explained in terms of the direct material interests of imperial players, and which, if seen in those terms, nearly always appear as a waste of resources. The mission of an empire binds its protagonists by oath to a project which, if only because of its long-term nature, greatly exceeds the limited horizon of individual interests. For this reason, the mission may also be conceived as a means whereby an empire intended to last for thousands of years imposes its action logic on people who have power and influence within it for only a limited period of time. It requires them to set aside their own interests if they wish to pursue the imperial policy, and is thus directed especially at the imperial elite.

The metaphor of an empire that binds its political and social elites by means of a mission, preventing them from sacrificing its long-term survival to their short-term material interests, may also be described in terms of an interplay among parts of the imperial elite. In this image, the imperial *decision-making elite* relies in the short term on the *interpretative elite* – intellectuals, writers, scholars, journalists, and so on – to give it support in the form of perspectives and visions that justify and reinforce its exercise of power. But these perspectives and visions also bind power-holders and limit their range of decisions, and so intellectuals who would otherwise be power-poor end up exerting considerable influence. In Rome the circle of poets around C. Clinius Maecenas played such a role; in China it fell to Confucius and those who disseminated his ideas, in Spain to the neo-scholastics of the Salamanca school, in Britain to the poets of the Victorian age, and in the Soviet Union to Marxist intellectuals. Neoconservative theorists and political commentators occupy a similar function in the United States today: they have especially taken up the question of American responsibilities in world politics since the end of the East–West conflict and – whether their answers are correct or incorrect – acquired the authority to define the problems and challenges facing the USA.

The imperial mission is more than just self-justification on the part of a world empire, even if it fulfils that function perfectly well. To put it more sharply, we might say that the imperial mission converts self-legitimation into self-sacralization. Its quasi-religious sense of purpose means that empire is no longer in thrall to the random decisions of the politically powerful and the socially influential. Even if these hold power within the empire, it is the empire which ultimately has them in its power. In order to acquire this quality of 'unavailability' for individual purposes, the imperial mission must be given a solemnity that raises it far above humdrum political affairs. This may be clearly seen in the mission of the Roman empire, the imposition and protection of the *pax Romana* in the Mediterranean and its adjoining territories.

It may be argued, of course, that the empire served the interests of Roman-Italian merchants and bankers by putting an end to piracy in the Mediterranean and hegemonial wars in the East, with the result that the risks of trade were greatly reduced and capital investments made more secure. It was equally the case, however, that merchants cooperated with pirates[16] and that bankers profited from wars. The security of sea travel and the stability of peace were thus dependent on group interests and the circumstances of the time. An empire cannot base its central legitimation on such fragile ground; the imperial mission must be given a sacred authority that makes it safe from the fluctuating interests of private players. In the case of Rome, this was achieved through the deification of peace, which already began under Octavian with the construction of the *Ara pacis*; the prince bound himself and his successors to a project that every emperor had to pursue if he wished to keep the recognition of the Senate and people.

The imperial mission may be rooted in a tacit understanding that the empire has of itself, but it may also be publicly evoked and acted out on repeated occasions. The former is more likely to be the case in periods of stability, the latter in periods of crisis. Thus, from the middle of the third century, when the situation became increasingly threatening on some of the Roman frontiers, peace was again more strongly presented as the world-historical mission of empire, and it was made clear what would be lost if the empire were to collapse.[17] What had been a binding attachment on the part of the political elite now had to be impressed on the population as a whole, so that it would be ready to make the necessary sacrifices for the preservation of the empire. Even the Church Father Augustine eventually taught that Christians had a duty to participate in defence of the Roman empire, on the grounds that the peace it upheld created favourable conditions for propagation of the faith and the living of a Christian life, and that, for all its faults and sinister origins, the survival of the empire was in their interests.[18]

But it was not so much political theorists as writers and artists who decisively contributed to the sacralization of the imperial mission. While master builders and sculptors erected the temple to peace, which graphically depicted the civilizing effect of Roman rule, the literary circle grouped around Maecenas (which included Horace and Virgil, the two most important poets of their age) acclaimed Augustus' reform programme as a renewal of the world, which would persist as long as the Roman empire itself. This support was invaluable for Octavian, since his reform programme could not have been implemented through laws and ordinances alone. It also needed the sheen of culture, to provide it with a deeper meaning that bureaucrats were unable to supply.

Virgil, in particular, associated large parts of his work with Octavian's reform programme. His eclogues, which he published together under the title *Bucolica*, attacked the moral decline of urban elites and held up country life as the source for a renewal of the *mos maiorum*, the morals of our forefathers; his hope was that the Iron Age could be overcome and that the Golden Age at the beginning of human history could be brought back to life. Virgil pursued a similar programme in his *Georgica*,[19] and in the *Aeneid*, which remained unfinished because of Virgil's sudden death (and which he himself had wished to be destroyed), the poet completes the tale of Aeneas' travels after the flight from Troy with a series of prophecies looking ahead to Augustus' peaceful rule throughout the world. Here Virgil sketches a vision of universal peace, in which Aeneas appears as a prefigurative model for Augustus and his victories stand for the overcoming of demonic forces on the path to peace. The Roman empire was thus committed not only to peace but to humanity. Virgil endowed with religious solemnity Rome's mission to pacify and humanize the world, putting into Jupiter's mouth a promise of its *imperium sine fine*: 'For these [the Romans as Aeneas' successors] I set neither bounds nor periods of empire; dominion without end have I bestowed. Nay, harsh Juno, who now in her fear troubles sea and earth and sky, shall change to better counsels and with me cherish the Romans, lords of the world, and the nation of the gown. Thus is it decreed.'[20]

Roman rule over the Mediterranean was justified because it ensured world peace, and because integration in the empire opened the gates to the blessings of civilization. Outside the imperial frontiers lay barbarism and the devastation of war. Nor was this all. Through its association with a golden age, the imperial peace was given a sacred quality: it heralded nothing less than a return to paradise by imperial means. Both these ideas – the Golden Age, and paradise as a garden protected from a hostile surrounding world (the 'Garden of Eden') – originated in the East and were initially alien to the Romans' much tougher mode of political thinking. By blending them into his outline of Roman history, Virgil made an important contribution to the cultural integration of the empire. He suggested that, in conquering the East, Rome had not been guided by power politics alone; it was also prepared to absorb its cultural and political-ideological legacy. Aeneas' travels from Troy to Italy became the story of this transfer, and the Trojan conflict itself appeared as a symbol for the self-destruction of the Eastern cultural world in strife and war. Salvation came from the West, in the shape of the Roman empire. One can see why Augustus was so eager that the *Aeneid* should be rescued from Virgil's personal effects and placed in the public domain.

To some extent, Horace too placed his poetry in the service of Rome's imperial mission.[21] Fear of civil war forms the core of his early work, and its hopes are placed in the man who will dispel them: Octavian/Augustus. For Horace, the crisis of the Roman polity was less constitutional than moral; he therefore agreed with Augustus' reform programme. Against sexual licence and adultery, greed and deception, luxury and effeminacy, he celebrated the old Roman values of *moderatio, virtus, pietas* and *iustitia*. Where these were assured, the Golden Age too would persist. Here empire has the function of warding off decline and fall, by ensuring that morals, decency and justice are constantly renewed. It was for such an empire that Horace coined his most famous line: *Dulce et decorum est pro patria mori* ('Sweet and honourable is it to die for the fatherland').[22]

Our glance at the work of Virgil and Horace shows that imperial peace was not only conceived as a special quality of Rome's far-flung rule, but was thought to herald a renewal of time and the reversal of decline. Empires are of world-historical importance, in a cosmological or salvationist sense as well as in terms of power politics. This is another difference in comparison with states and hegemonial powers, which see themselves as acting in time, whereas empires take it upon themselves to shape the course of time. The strongest expression of this is the sacral charge of the imperial mission. The Golden Age of which Virgil and Horace speak is more than a new beginning of the grand cosmic year; the idea underlying it is that the course of the cosmic year itself is subject to imperial influence. The march of time recommences, but by virtue of imperial power it remains at the beginning, and the supposedly inevitable decline through a silver and bronze age to an iron age is held up. In an age when decline and fall were seen as the natural tendency of history, the world-historical role of empire was to arrest the decline and to prevent the end of the world. By contrast, when the idea of progress gained widespread acceptance in the eighteenth century, empires came to be regarded as accelerators of world history: they civilized the world and disseminated progress, and any failure in this regard had momentous consequences. This was the view of both the British and the Americans.

Not every empire has attempted such an extensive cosmological (or salvationist) sacralization of itself. In the case of Rome, as we have seen, this was reinforced by speculative historical narratives originating in the East. Once Christianity became the state religion, it was necessary to give up some of the sacral components of the imperial mission, and in this connection Augustine asserted his famous distinction between the earthly and the divine city (*civitas terrena, civitas Dei*). But the sense of sacrality remained so strong that in the eleventh century the Hohenstaufen chancellery began to speak of the *sacrum imperium* – a term that then passed down into the Holy Roman Empire (of the German Nation).[23] In this formulation too, the holiness of the empire rested on its historical-theological role as *katechon* (restrainer or delayer) of the end of the world, which would inevitably come to pass if the empire collapsed.[24]

For the Spanish world empire, the militant form of the Counter-Reformation could serve as the imperial mission. This was by no means prompted only by the Reformation: it had its roots in the gradual Spanish reconquest of the Moorish-ruled parts of the Iberian peninsula. The spirit of the *Reconquista* drove not only the later *conquista* of the New World but also the expulsion of the Jews and Moors from Spain. Judeophobia, the Inquisition and the persecution of the Reformed Church in the Netherlands became Spain's imperial mission, which towards the end of the sixteenth century turned into a siege mentality. The spectre of a worldwide Protestant conspiracy to overthrow the Spanish empire was significant for this defensive turn, whose strongest expressions are found in the Christian-Catholic coloration of Spain's imperial mission and in the idea that the New World 'savages' must be converted to Christianity. This fuelled Spain's expansionist drive in large parts of Central and Southern America.[25]

It might seem that the Ottoman empire should be regarded as the Islamic counterpart of Spain. But that would be to underestimate the liberal character of its religious policy, which differed sharply from the inquisitorial imposition of Catholicism in areas under Spanish rule. The Ottoman empire was a patchwork quilt of communities (*millet*) with graduated relations of dependence, including Jewish and Christian ones that had their own forms of organization. In the specialist literature, we find heated debates about whether religious plurality was an important part of the Ottoman empire's self-image, or whether, after the conquest of Arab lands in the early sixteenth century, it saw itself as a world empire whose mission it was to defend Islam against unbelievers.[26] In keeping with what has been said so far about the variegated peripheries of major empires, we would rather say that the Turkic peoples which first created the Ottoman empire – and which lacked both organizational competence and a sense of mission – simply tried to combine the two rival

ideas of empire that they encountered: one belonged to the imaginative world of the Arabs, in which the spread of Islam through fire
and sword had been the common practice and was still the central
duty of any empire that saw itself as Islamic;[27] the other stemmed
from the conservative administrative practice of the Byzantine
empire, which the Ottomans largely adopted to bring the newly conquered areas under their lasting control.[28]

On this basis a partial alliance even developed between the
Ottoman empire and the Orthodox Church, mainly directed against
Latin Christendom and the pope's claim to supremacy. In the
European space, in the Balkans, the Ottoman empire for some time
presented itself as the only force capable of defending the independence and self-administration of Christian groups and communities,
and as a result many Christians fought in formation alongside
the Turkish armies. An imperial mission could obviously not be
acquired in this way. Indeed, the price that the Ottomans had to pay
for the two-sidedness of their empire was a fragility of the imperial
mission, which could never become a power factor comparable to
those in other empires. The fact that, once it began to decline, the
Ottoman empire never entered a new imperial cycle was also due to
its weak development of an imperial mission.

The imperial mission of Tsarist Russia had a much stronger religious imprint. Whereas the Ottoman empire came into the organizational inheritance of Byzantium, Russia took over its mission as
defender of the Orthodox Church. This transfer began in 1472 with
the marriage of Ivan III to Sophia Palaiologa, the niece of the last
Byzantine emperor, which soon came to be seen as an act of affilia-
tion to the Roman empire. In the letters of the monk Filofei of Pskov,
the transfer of legitimacy was then worked up into the idea of a
Third Rome.[29] By interpreting the war against the Tatar steppe
nomads as a defence of Christians against their enemies, the tsars
placed their expansionism politically and practically within the
Roman-Byzantine tradition. St Basil's Cathedral in Moscow, built
under Ivan IV, is the architectonic representation of the success of
this mission.[30] That an imperial mission does not have to shape an
empire's history throughout, and that reformers may see it as an
obstacle to modernization, is evident in the policy of Peter I, who
replaced Russia's Eastward mission with an orientation to the level
of development in Russia's Western neighbours.

The opposition between efficient administration and imperial
mission as motivating goals for the elite, already familiar to us from
the Ottoman empire, also appears in Tsarist Russia. In rejecting the
imperial mission of his predecessors and trying to find a bridge to the

West, Peter I created the basis for the tension between Western and Eastern orientations that has been a feature of Russian history down to the present day. For the idea of Russia as defender of the true Christian faith did not simply disappear with the Petrine reforms, but re-emerged again and again in times of crisis. This was the case during the war against Napoleon, and the Russian victory was later attributed to the deep religiosity of the Russian peasantry. The previously Eastward-looking imperial mission was then also turned to the West, in the idea of redeeming it from the fundamental materialism of its way of life.[31] Tsar Alexander I was firmly convinced that he was the bearer of the holy idea that Europe must be reshaped on the basis of Christian morality, and his guiding aim was a synthesis of all Christian denominations in a universal Christendom. The Holy Alliance, proclaimed at the Congress of Vienna in 1815, was supposed to launch a process aimed at the reconciliation of the peoples of Europe.[32] At the latest by 1856, however, after the end of the Crimean War, Tsarist Russia made a strong new turn to catch up the West in development – which was already a necessity if the country was to avoid ending up in the same situation as the Ottoman empire. Indeed, the objective was to take over the Ottoman legacy in Southeast Europe and the straits between the Black Sea and the Mediterranean, in what would have amounted to a completion of the idea of the Third Rome. For that to be possible it was necessary to Westernize. And so, Russia's history has to a large extent been marked by periodic shifts between an imperial mission and an orientation to Western rhythms of development.

Just as the gap with the West was dangerous for Russia, so was the gradual dissolution of its imperial mission fraught with consequences for its internal stability. In the two revolutions of 1917, the old forces could be overthrown and driven out because they were no longer held together by the common idea of a world-historical mission and could not draw a sufficient response from the general population. This situation later repeated itself in the collapse of the Soviet Union, whose imperial mission, as defined in the Constitution of 1977, had been 'to unite all nations and peoples in the common construction of communism' – already no more than a phrase at the time when it was adopted.[33] Among the symptoms of decay was the loss of a sense of mission or the purely cynical invocation of one; it had turned from an internal powerhouse into sheer mystification, leaving the Soviet Union without the driving force on which even Mikhail Gorbachev had still been able to rely for his reform policy.[34]

The two Western empires (the British and American) did without a narrowly religious mission, even if they occasionally presented their purpose in religiously tinged rhetoric. If the British are seen as inheritors of the Spanish empire, then we may say that – in keeping with the history of ideas in Europe from the sixteenth to the nineteenth century – the progress of civilization took the place of the Catholic faith. The British mission was to civilize the world, even if its policy was often limited to one of opening countries to British goods.[35] In Kipling's famous formulation: 'Take up the White Man's burden . . . / To seek another's profit / And work another's gain',[36] the material self-interest entirely disappears behind the civilizing mission – which has naturally aroused the attention of ideology critique. Yet even Karl Marx, an observer of the British empire who can hardly be suspected of ignoring material interests, accorded an *objectively* civilizing function to British expansion.

In his article 'The British Rule in India' (June 1853), Marx first noted: 'England has broken down the entire framework of Indian society, without any symptoms of reconstitution yet appearing.' He attributed these destructive effects to the collision between advanced and backward productive forces: the hand-loom and the spinning-wheel, which for centuries were the connecting link between agriculture and handicrafts in India, became uncompetitive once the Indian market was opened up to British goods. But, 'not so much through the brutal interference of the British tax-gatherer and the British solider as [through] the working of English steam and English free trade', the greatest social revolution that Asia had ever known was called forth. Marx used this as a justification of British intervention in India, and interpreted its subordination to the laws of the world market as a civilizing act:

> [W]e must not forget that these little communities were contaminated by distinctions of caste and by slavery, that they subjugated man to external circumstances instead of elevating man to be the sovereign of circumstances, that they transformed a self-developing social state into never-changing natural destiny, and thus brought about a brutalizing worship of nature, exhibiting its degradation in the fact that man, the sovereign of nature, fell down on his knees in adoration of Hanuman, the monkey, and Sabbala, the cow.[37]

But we should by no means conclude, like Marx, that the civilizing effects of the British world empire were wholly indirect and unintended. Slavery and the slave trade, forcibly extended during the first phase of European empire-building, were abolished or at least curtailed under British influence – and this was not an indirect effect of British maritime supremacy but one of its direct and immediate goals.[38] In the nineteenth century, British naval squadrons patrolled the coast of West Africa to end the still flourishing slave trade, and in Britain itself it was mainly Anglican priests and Quakers who made the abolition of slavery a central plank of the imperial mission. They ensured that, in the British-controlled world economy, human beings came to be seen as illegal commodities, and that the power of empire was deployed against the trade.[39] This also explains why, in the American Civil War, the British did not embrace the cause of the Southern states and seek to weaken and contain the ever more threatening United States – as the logic of great power rivalry would have suggested. Had they done this, they would have been opposing their own imperial mission.

In the end, the imperial mission of the United States may be seen as a further development of the British: market economy, democracy and human rights were its cornerstones, which sustained different priorities according to the various regional challenges and international political constellations. This does not mean that US policy can be reduced to its imperial mission. Security imperatives are as important for it as economic interests, and usually take precedence if they clash with the requirements of the imperial mission.[40] Such factors have given rise to the much-criticized double standards of American policy: that is, the fact that the demands of the imperial mission are often not applied to certain players when US security or economic interests are at stake.

The tension between an imperial mission and imperatives of self-preservation or self-advancement is nothing new in the history of empires: it runs through it like a red thread, at least in empires whose mission was not exhausted in the brutal imposition of their interests. Such an identity between mission and interests is most observable in the steppe empires, but they paid the price for it in their lack of staying power. The binding quality of the imperial mission is especially great in empires democratically organized at the centre, and the sense of duty is stronger there than in autocratically governed or aristocratic empires.[41] Elites that are under no obligation to give an account of themselves can shed their sense of duty more quickly and easily than politicians who must, at regular intervals, canvas for support and face the competition of reserve elites. Besides, increased access to information about imperial policy – and the associated shrinking of the *arcana imperii* at the disposal only of the ruling elite – has often had a serious impact on the character and significance of the imperial mission, which has thus changed in the wake of the *media revolution* as well as the advent of democracy. The electorate in the imperial centre has thus played a role in reducing the tension between imperial mission and imposition of interests, and the population in the periphery may demand that the mission be enforced against the actual policies of the day.

A good example of the scope in a democratic empire for the political handling of tensions between mission and interests is the opposition between US presidents Theodore Roosevelt and Woodrow Wilson. The former, a classical imperialist, attached greater weight to the imposition of interests than to the commitments arising out of the imperial mission. Symptomatic of this was the corollary to the Monroe Doctrine that he drew up in 1904, which threatened to intervene wherever a political movement endangered the repayment of debts to American creditors; the United States, as 'international policeman', would then have a duty to put a halt to 'further misbehaviour'. At the same time, Roosevelt pursued a policy in the Pacific that was far from asserting American claims to supremacy (against Japan, for example),[42] and in 1905 he was awarded the Nobel Peace Prize for his mediation in the Russian–Japanese war geared to the idea of a balance of powers. Roosevelt, then, endeavoured to limit the imperial mission of the USA. Although he spoke of the United States as an 'international police force', he wanted to see this role played only when his country's immediate interests were at stake.

Woodrow Wilson's policy, on the other hand, ascribed a global responsibility to the United States, and in support of this he had to give the imperial mission a normative charge. Without the idea of a mission going far beyond America's immediate economic and political interests, it would have been impossible to win domestic support for its entry into the First World War, with the expected heavy losses in human life. Only the project of a worldwide peace ('a war to end all wars'), including the right to self-determination for all nations and 'a world safe for democracy', gave Wilson the backing to intervene in a region from which a basic consensus in American foreign policy had previously wished to remain aloof.[43] Of course, this support was not large enough to allow a long-term US commitment on the European continent, and the Treaty of Versailles was eventually a political failure for Wilson. The imperial mission that he had envisaged for the United States proved too much for American citizens to swallow.

Theodore Roosevelt and Woodrow Wilson stand for two extremes in the tension between an imperial mission and self-interested politics on a grand scale – a tension that has persisted in the United States down to the present day. It can be seen in the positions taken by presidents and their advisers, as well as in the way decisions are communicated to the American public and commented on by journalists and academics. Here again there are two extremes, with a long line of options in between. On the one side, a mainly self-interested policy is presented as if it were geared to the requirements of an imperial mission; on the other side, the self-interest is itself emphasized when imperial action mainly serves to provide collective goods or even to enforce human rights in geopolitically marginal regions of the world. Nor is this exclusively the domain of anti-imperial ideology critique.[44] Politicians who think they can gain sufficient support for their policies only if they present norm enforcement as a pursuit of national self-interest also make use of such a strategy.

Imperial missions tend to be charged with religious ideas and pathos. The well-known lack of understanding among Europeans for the religious rhetoric of American policy testifies to a lack of understanding for the imperial mission of the United States. The rhetoric in question can be reduced neither to strategic calculation (winning votes in an electorate strongly imbued with Christianity) nor to pure irrationality (as European commentators often suggest). Rather, it goes to the heart of America's political understanding of itself – from Woodrow Wilson's aims in taking the USA into the First World War, through Eisenhower's talk of a 'crusade in Europe' on the eve of the Normandy landings, to Ronald Reagan's characterization of the Soviet Union as an evil empire of 'totalitarian darkness' or George W. Bush's picture of an 'axis of evil' stretching from Iraq to North Korea.[45]

The marked self-sacralization of empire has always provoked strong anti-imperial reactions. The most powerful example of this at the level of political ideas is the Book of Daniel in the Old Testament, where the claim of the Seleucid rulers of the Middle East to have established an eternal empire is disputed in Daniel's interpretation of Nebuchadnezzar's dream, which sees the present empire as one of a succession of four that is already nearing its end.[46] The chiliastic idea of the approaching kingdom of God is here introduced to counter the claim to eternity of the earthly kingdoms. It is no accident that anti-imperial rebels and revolutionaries have returned again and again, in new variants and interpretations, to the story of Daniel and Nebuchadnezzar's dream.

The basic pattern, in which imperial rhetoric relying upon quasi-religious certainties calls forth anti-imperial counter-rhetoric that also supports itself on religious certainties, may be seen in contemporary debate on the status and power of the American empire. The more strongly US policy is communicated in such terms – for example, through the description of its opponents as satanic or demonic – the more strongly do those opponents take up a position in the anti-imperial frontline and counter with religious imagery of their own. Not by chance has this role fallen for some time to political Islam, and even China's growing economic strength will not change this in the near future. Islamism is the most powerful challenge to the American empire because it contests its imperial mission and characterizes the United States itself as 'the Great Satan'.[47]

In principle, imperial demonology is a religiously intensified form of anti-barbarian discourse, in which peoples that do not belong to the sphere of imperial rule are relegated to a lower level and made the potential object of the work of civilization. Anti-imperial demonology pays this back in the same coin, by branding the imperial centre as the hotbed of moral decline and sinfulness.

The idea of the barbarian and the construction of imperial space

The persuasiveness of an imperial mission depends to a large extent on the discursive construction of what it is directed *against*, or which forces it is meant to keep from becoming politically dominant. This will here be considered under the generic term of the barbarian or the barbaric.

The discourse of barbarism is a general feature of empires, or at least of those which set themselves the task of civilizing the areas under their rule.[48] Its central function is to demarcate the frontiers of empire as areas of asymmetrical encounter. Here, unlike at the frontiers between states, those who live on the two sides are not fundamentally alike. Here the higher world of the good gives way to a realm resistant to order and calculation, where one always has to be on one's guard. Imperial frontiers are thus also frontiers between cosmos and chaos. This should make it clear why empires lay such stress on the semi-permeability of their external frontiers.

The asymmetry produced in the discourse of barbarism is especially evident in the fact that it defines some as *subject* and others as *object*, and incorporates them accordingly into the imaginative world of politics. It may be objected, of course, that the division between the roles of subject and object on the periphery of empires conforms to the logic of power politics and does not need to be shaped discursively. But the discourse of barbarism transforms what would otherwise be a mere power difference, or a distinction between a well-organized military apparatus and loosely knit tribal alliances, into a legitimate distinction that can be softened only if the barbarians are exposed to the civilizing efforts of empire and are willing to let themselves be 'debarbarized'. They must become like the inhabitants of the imperial space in order to gain admittance to it. Otherwise they have access to it only as prisoners on public display, testifying to the power of empire and the threat that the barbarian poses to it. This tradition stretches from the triumphal processions of Roman armies and emperors through the ethnological presentations of European colonial empires down to the images of captured Taliban after the recent war in Afghanistan.

The fundamentally asymmetrical discourse of barbarism may assume a number of different forms. It may be conducted ethnographically, so that it is always left open to take the road to civilization by drawing politically and socially closer to the empire. It may be based on religion, in the sense that debarbarization can be achieved by adopting the religion of the empire. Or it may fall back on racist categories, as it often did in colonialism, but then complete debarbarization is ruled out as a possibility. Only rarely, however, does the discourse of barbarism confine itself to one of these forms. Usually they combine or overlap with one another – which may sharpen but also weaken the definition of boundaries. The asymmetrical basic configuration is anyway preserved. On the peripheries, the discourse of barbarism evokes a gap between intra-imperiality and extra-imperiality that only seldom exists as such in reality. For, in the extensive borderlands of empire, the transition between inside and outside is often fluid, and the sense and degree in which a tribe or clan is pro-imperial or anti-imperial is not laid down once and for all. The discourse of barbarism therefore repeatedly assists in the semantic drawing of a boundary that would otherwise be blurred or invisible; it produces an imaginary dividing-line to make up for the actual lack of imperial contours. The asymmetry that is communicated in this way cannot be detected in the border regions themselves, but the empire thereby ensures that it has the frontiers of its rule under control.

In ancient Greece, the concept of the barbarian acquired a political charge only under the impact of the Persian war and the Athenian claim to hegemony. The barbarian became the opposite of the civilization embodied by the Greeks, the figure through which the Athenian policy of conquest acquired a civilizing function.[49] In Herodotus, the barbarian is characterized by a nomadic lifestyle and promiscuous sexual behaviour; he drinks unmixed wine, eats raw meat and does not shrink even from cannibalism. Imperial civilization therefore means – above all, in the mind of the population at its centre – the settling of nomads in frontier regions and the stamping out of human sacrifice, cannibalism[50] and the kidnapping of women (especially common among nomadic horsemen).[51]

As soon as an empire has crossed the Augustan threshold, passing from its expansive to its civilizing phase, the sense of a barbarian threat begins to grow and to take shape especially in relation to female vulnerability. This tendency may be seen from the Romans and Chinese through the European colonial empires to the United States in the period of its westward expansion. In modified form it still appears in the early twenty-first century, in the images and reports of raped and humiliated women in ethnic (barbarian) wars on the fringes of the affluent world.[52] Such reports then come to represent a demand for the so-called civilized world to intervene, if necessary by military means, to enforce a minimum respect for human rights.

While images and reports of barbarian cruelty captured the public imagination and strengthened its willingness to defend the imperial frontiers, the operational policy involved a constant effort to make nomadic peoples in frontier regions adopt a settled way of life. Their conversion from hunters to farmers was meant to establish areas of peace and stability beyond the imperial frontiers and hence to lower the costs of defending them against nomadic predators. Frontier security policy was pushed forward into the realm of the 'debarbarized barbarians'.

An alterative to pacification through settlement was the enlistment of warlike barbarians to defend the frontiers in the service of the empire. Of the classical world empires, the Romans made the greatest use of such methods and the Chinese the least. Cossacks served a similar purpose in Tsarist Russia, as did the military units that European powers raised in their colonies. Washington's use of Afghan warlords to overthrow the Taliban regime may be seen as a modern variant of this risky policy of frontier defence – risky, because cooperation can rapidly turn into confrontation and challenge the empire's claim to be spreading civilization, to the point where the barbarians it has recruited and armed may overrun or gradually take over its positions. The Roman empire, which went furthest down this road, failed politically and militarily through its 'barbarization of the army',[53] at least in the West. In the sixth century, the Western half of the empire broke up into a mosaic of Germanic kingdoms that would prove decisive for the future history of Europe; the one great space of empire fragmented into an order consisting of many small spaces. In China, by contrast, the presence of Mongol conquerors meant for a long time that the barbarians were assimilated to a much greater degree than in the Western Roman empire: the unity of the empire was essentially preserved, with the result that the conquerors could rely on an existing administrative apparatus and had to draw its personnel largely from the militarily subject population.[54]

Mongol assimilation to the superior Chinese civilization began with the decision of the 'Great Khan' Ögödei, one of Genghis Khan's sons, not to convert the Chinese lands into pasture for the Mongol herds, as originally intended, but to turn the conquest to greater advantage by raising taxes from the Chinese living there.[55] However, the Mongols were not capable of implementing this decision, and in order to avoid becoming completely dependent on their military subjects they brought in Muslim tax-farmers, mostly merchants plying the Silk Road between China and the Middle East, who now bought up large territories in the hope of making a fortune. The result was ruinous tax-farming that led to major economic problems in northern China, and the tax-farmers came to be as hated and feared as the Mongol warriors. It was a form of surplus extraction which did not immediately destroy the existing social-economic structures but eroded them over time through constant overexploitation.

After the conquest of the Song dynasty's southern empire, Genghis's grandson Kublai established the Chinese dynastic name Yuan and introduced Chinese rituals into his court. This expansion also made the Mongols heavily dependent on Chinese scribes, without whom they would not have been able to maintain an orderly administration. Finally, in 1315, they reverted to the traditional system of examinations for the state bureaucracy, though they allowed other ethnic groups to participate in them so as not to be completely dependent on the Han Chinese. At the same time, the Mongols tried to avoid complete assimilation to the superior Chinese culture. They prohibited marriages with Chinese women, conducted government business in the Mongolian language and withdrew to Mongolia during the summer months.[56] The Chinese, for their part, kept a Confucian trust in the power of culture eventually to civilize the barbarian conquerors from the North. However, after the collapse of the Yuan dynasty and the withdrawal of the Mongols, Chinese society underwent fundamental change: greater value was attached to force as a means of rule, and to the need for military security against the barbarians in the North.

The discourse of barbarism developed in quite a different way among the Spanish, whose empire was never threatened by barbarian invasions; the 'savages' of the newly discovered world were visible only as objects to be civilized, that is, to be converted to Christianity in accordance with Spain's imperial mission. It was a question not of making nomads lead a settled way of life, but of forcing them to give up human sacrifice. Since most of the indigenous population approved of such practices, the Spanish must have felt, like Francisco Vitoria in his *De jure belli Hispanorum in Barbaros* (1539), that they should intervene to free today's likely victims and to establish a rule that prevented new ones in the future.[57] Far from posing a threat, the 'natives' remained throughout the object of imperial policy.[58]

The Cossacks of Tsarist Russia represent a middle position between the Roman and Spanish experiences of barbarians. Since their nomadism was the prerequisite for them to defend the vast steppe frontiers against attacks and incursions from nomadic peoples outside the empire, the tsars showed scarcely any interest in making them lead a settled way of life. The risk involved in using semi-barbarian peoples to protect the empire stemmed from their strong tendency to rebellion and plunder within the imperial space itself; it was Cossack support which made the peasant revolts of the early eighteenth century so dynamic and dangerous. But, even after the Cossacks were absorbed into the Russian army in the 1750s, they remained a questionable element from the point of view of the imperial mission, and their style of fighting made many Russian observers wonder whether the supposedly civilizing power of the Russian empire was not more barbaric than the population of the conquered territories in the Caucasus and Central Asia.[59]

In the course of the nineteenth century, Arab slave traders acquired in the European imagination the role of barbarians against whom the imperial mission of the colonial powers was directed. The man-hunting and traffic in human beings that the Arab lands had long pushed deep into black Africa became the justification, or at least the pretext, for Europeans to take over power in new territories in West and East Africa.[60] But, even against one another, the European powers staked their claim to leadership by charging hegemonial rivals with barbaric behaviour. In the First World War, for example, the Germans accused the Entente of making the fighting more barbaric through the introduction of colonial troops into the European theatre, while the Entente claimed that the Germans had behaved barbarically towards the civilian population during their offensive through Belgium.[61]

The greater the civilizing element in the imperial mission, the more does the negative image of the barbarian stand out. This can be seen in recent debates about terrorism, and especially the figure of the suicide bomber, but the threat of barbarism appears most sharply in the massacres associated with wars in which inter-ethnic conflict is a major factor.[62] Against both – ethnic mass murderers on the periphery of the prosperous world, and terrorists irrupting into that world – the violence of the new empire is presented in public discourse as a civilizing force. But the barbarian does not only elude the requirements of civilization. When he manages to break into the imperial space, he is also a danger to peace and prosperity.

Prosperity as a justification and programme for imperial rule

Whereas the imperial mission is directed mainly at the elite in its heartlands, and whereas the discourse of barbarism marks off the orderly imperial space from the chaos around it, the promise of greater prosperity is extended to everyone living within the frontiers of the empire. Nor is it a question of long-term responsibilities or imaginary constructions, but rather of tangible advantages in the here and now. The imperial space is a zone of prosperity surrounded by poverty and destitution. It is therefore a blessing for the periphery if the imperial order is extended there. In fact, the promise of prosperity is one of the most convincing arguments that empires use to justify their existence, for their frontier areas are often zones of transition from affluence to poverty. Whether this is actually the case, however, depends on the kind of empire and the way in which it exercises power.

Typically, steppe empires do not accomplish the transition from the exploitative to the intensive or civilizing form of rule, but continue to treat the areas they have conquered as little more than booty. Since the new subjects nearly always have a higher level of civilization, the conquerors can base their rule only on violence and plunder. This being so, even the continuation of their rule is difficult, and it is usually limited to raids of greater or lesser regularity. Any justification of empire by the promise of prosperity would here be scarcely convincing.

As we have seen, however, the mainly exploitative relationship between centre and periphery is by no means seen only in the short-lived domination of territorial expanses characteristic of steppe empires; it also appears in the early phase of maritime empires. Both Portuguese and Dutch commercial domination in the Indian–Southeast Asian area was essentially exploitative rather than intensive in form. But it rested on the preservation, not the destruction, of existing political and social structures, and its characteristic form of appropriation was not violence but exchange. The steppe nomads overran and destroyed the orders in their path, appropriating their treasures and valuable objects for themselves; the commercial adventurers who created the maritime empires in the wake of the great discoverers docked with the existing structures and relations of production, established links among them, brought long-distance trade under control, organized economic exchange across vast spaces and shaped the terms of trade to their advantage.[63]

As the volume of trade gradually increased, the Europeans' commercial dominance undermined the social structures and system of rule they had originally found in place. Imperceptibly yet steadily, the conditions on which the commercial empires had been dependent crumbled away; they provided them with sustenance and at a certain moment were exhausted. Then, if the empire was to survive, it had to invest in the creation of stable political relations and social structures, by funding infrastructural development, by passing on productive technology or building new industries, by stationing garrisons in the large cities and other strategic points, or by sending out the personnel to help develop a modern administrative apparatus. All this inevitably increased the costs of empire, and so a centre that hoped to cash in on an imperial policy nearly always decided to withdraw from direct responsibility for technical commercial matters and to keep a look-out for more favourable ways of deriving a profit from business in general. If we look at the broad sweep of world economic history, we will see that the maritime and commercial empires were replaced in the second half of the twentieth century by global economies which, for a time, were considerably more cost-effective. Whether they can remain so is another question. We shall return to it later.[64]

The crossing of the Augustan threshold[65] may be thought of as an alternative to the gradual exhaustion of the periphery by the centre. At a fairly early date, investments were begun in the periphery with the aim of giving it a stake in the continuation of the imperial order. There were three options that imperial policy could pursue, either separately or – more often – in combination with one another. *The first* was to make available certain collective goods – peace within the imperial space, legal security and opportunities for safe travel and business – that people living in the periphery could enjoy in the same way as citizens in the centre.

The second option was to ensure a great diversity of production across various parts of the empire, so that goods were traded for one another within an imperial area; a conspicuous example of this, in the case of Rome, was the export–import trade involving grain from Sicily, Egypt and North Africa in return for wine and olive oil from Italy.[66] The economic interconnectedness of the imperial space thus rests upon the replacement of regional subsistence economies with surplus-producing economies, which ensure that inter-regional trade remains at a much higher level – although, of course, the actual size of trade and surplus production crucially depends on the security of sea and land routes. The provision of collective goods is therefore closely associated with a greater degree of economic interconnectedness, and vice versa.

But the empire must not attend only to the security of commerce, for the trade area itself is usually opened up only in the wake of imperial expansion. Troops are followed by master builders and engineers, who enlarge the existing harbours and create new ones, and lay new roads and bridges, to make the imperial space an economic space. The great Roman road-building programmes of the second century BC – the via Appia, via Flaminia and via Aemilia – not only involved a well thought-out combination of economic and military functions, but also showed that Rome was ready to develop the capacities and train the people for the work of constructing an empire. The Romans' expertise in bridge construction was essential to the new paved networks of straight all-year roads, which became a symbol of the achievements of imperial civilization as they replaced the old winding trade routes accessible only to pack animals but not goods wagons. Beyond their military and economic functions, they served to advance the Romanization and cultural unification of the imperial space. In the end, under Diocletian, the road network of the empire reached a total of 85,000 kilometres.[67]

The equivalent of the Roman roads for the British empire was the railway (and the telegraph), which meant that bulk goods could be sent not only by sea but by fast and cheap land routes. Other European colonial powers also used the railway, to open up the interior of the lands they claimed and to link even non-coastal areas to the main economic centres of the empire.[68] In this connection, it is worth mentioning that the railway systems which the Europeans left behind at the moment of decolonization were mostly larger and more up-to-date than those which the newly independent countries were able to show a few decades later. The reasons for this may vary, but one factor always played a central role: railway lines were the veins and nerves of the imperial body, and when this broke down the existing infrastructure also began to crumble. Recently, the collapse of the economic area organized and controlled by the Soviet

Union offers an experience comparable to that which occurred in the imperial commercial and economic areas.[69]

For Tsarist Russia, in the late nineteenth to early twentieth century, the opening up of Siberia's vast expanses through new transport technology became the decisive factor allowing it to compete with the Western powers. Finance minister Sergei Witte was deeply convinced that Russia's political independence was increasingly threatened by its economic weakness, and that the empire would soon become a colony to be plundered by Western powers if it did not succeed in making itself an economic centre in its own right.[70] Witte's goal of boosting economic growth involved a major expansion of the railway network, which would open up the country and, most especially, replace the old Central Asian caravan trade with a modern and efficient system. Together with the idea of developing sources of raw materials and product markets in East Asia that would be closed to Russia's economically more advanced competitors, the massive project of the Trans-Siberian Railway took shape as the key link between the European and Asian parts of Russia.

As so often, military and economic factors operated alongside each other. Since the Crimean War in the 1850s, when it took twice as long to deploy reserves from Moscow as it took the Allies to bring in new forces from Britain and France, it had been clear to everyone – including the Prussian General Staff in Berlin – that Russia's future military capability would depend less on the expansion of its armed forces than on their greater mobility.[71] Military considerations therefore argued in favour of a rapid development of the railway system, to make it possible for the first time to transport and supply large numbers of troops across large areas.[72] The economic effects were not slow to appear, however: freight costs fell, and the linking of distant areas to one another gave a boost to economic growth that increased the prosperity of the whole empire. It must have been similar in the case of road-building in the Roman empire, where the direct stimulus was the need rapidly to deploy fighting legions with all their supplies and equipment. But, in the long term, economic integration was an (at least) equally important effect of the new roads radiating through the empire, and in the end the periphery benefited from them more than the centre.

It should be said by way of qualification that the militarily motivated development of transport did not always have economic spin-offs, and certainly not spin-offs in sufficient quantity. Russia is a good example here, in the sense that its projection into East Asia – primarily to bring northern China and Korea under its control – led to a fateful collision with Japan. The disastrous outcome of the war of 1904–5 underlined the weaknesses of the Tsarist empire, this time mainly in the naval sphere. The ensuing revolution of 1905 is generally seen as a harbinger of the final collapse of tsarism.

A comparable evolution may be seen in the case of Spain, where the problem was not the vast external frontiers of the empire but the security of the transatlantic shipping lanes. As the convoy system entailed a certain inflexibility and largely blocked independent economic initiative, Spain in the sixteenth and seventeenth centuries – like Tsarist Russia in the late nineteenth and early twentieth centuries – never achieved a sufficient economic integration of the areas under its rule. In effect, within the European economic system, Spain declined to the status of a transit country for trade with South America.[73]

Reforms corresponding to the principles of neomercantilism were supposed to change this. The new economic policy is already apparent in José de Campillo y Cossío's *Nuevo sistema de gobierno económico para la América*, which was ready in manuscript by 1743.[74] In his stock-taking, Campillo noted that most of Latin America's wealth remained in the Americas and that the links between its economies and the mother country had become weaker and weaker; the economic space therefore had to be more strongly integrated if the empire was to be able to survive. Like Sergei Witte, José de Campillo assumed that the empire could be saved only through the reshaping of its economic structures, and as finance minister he set about introducing the necessary reforms. First of all, he abolished the Andalusian trade monopoly and its obligatory convoy system, the point of trade liberalization being to strengthen Spanish manufactures and to weaken the impact of smuggling. His real aim, however, was to transform Spanish America into a supplier of raw materials and a market for finished goods from the mother country. In this way, the volume of trade between the two parts of the empire would increase, and more value would be created within its Spanish core.

Campillo, then, wagered on product diversification, but intended that its burden should fall entirely on the shoulders of Spanish America. This had the effect of gradually dividing the Creole upper classes from the mother country, which came to be seen not as an engine of reform but as a brake on development. Political independence held out greater economic prospects than Spanish America could have achieved by remaining within the empire, and indeed it took the earliest opportunity to sever the link. Spain's attempt to bring about stronger economic integration, beginning in 1780s, ended with the political collapse of the empire.

Apart from the Roman and British empires, the Chinese empire offers the clearest example of the link between imperial order and economic prosperity. In the period from the third to the sixth century AD, when the empire was divided, the circulation of money declined along with trade; one of the main elements of the imperial economic space thus lost much of its significance.[75] Then the opposite happened after reunification, when the Tang dynasty embarked upon infrastructural development within the imperial space. Through the building of canals and roads, it increased economic links between different parts of the country and ensured China's greater uniformity as a political and economic area.

A new disintegration set in with the decline of the Tang, but a veritable economic take-off under the Song dynasty brought a further growth of internal trade and an expansion of monetary circulation; it was during this period that the imperial government first experimented with the replacement of coins with paper money.[76] Probably nowhere else was the link between imperial order and economic prosperity as directly and plainly observable as it was in China. It would explain the lengthy survival of the empire and its repeated recovery after periods of decline and fall.

The introduction of a single currency throughout the empire may strongly favour the prosperity of the areas under its rule. It is certainly not a prerequisite for foreign trade, but it does make trade considerably easier and increase its extent and density. For this to be true, of course, the single currency must be stable and the imperial centre must itself be solvent. In the case of the Roman and Chinese empires, periodic bouts of inflation had highly negative consequences for trade and therefore economic integration in the empire, and Spain's repeated experiences of state bankruptcy were not only the real weak point of its empire but also a major factor in the deterioration of its economic position within Europe.

The British undoubtedly paid the greatest attention to currency matters, with the result that sterling rose to become the world leader. The Royal Navy and the pound sterling formed the backbone of the British empire, and its slow demise began when Britain changed from a creditor to a debtor nation in the course of the First World War. Then the dollar rose in its place, and New York rather than London became decisive in the economic cycles of the twentieth century.

The third option to guarantee the prosperity of empire was direct investment aimed at raising its peripheral areas to the same economic and cultural level as the centre. Imperialism theories are incapable of explaining such investment and have to fall back on long-term strategic considerations, although these can at best be understood in terms of the imperial mission, not the operational policy of the elites holding the reins of power. In any event, investments with a civilizing purpose have been a recurrent feature of historical empires – not, of course, the steppe empires, or the maritime empires at their height, but every case in which a seaborne empire has established its rule on land (for example, the British) or a land empire (for example, the Chinese) has managed to consolidate itself; the Roman empire should be regarded as a mixture of the two.

When empires manage to fulfil their promise of prosperity, to create imaginative frontiers through the discourse of barbarism, to maintain the persuasive power of the imperial mission and to ensure peace in the area under their rule, then they are rewarded with stability and a lengthy existence. The combination of all these achievements guarantees the empire's survival. But the lack of some or all marks the beginning of its disintegration – and at that point too its enemies get down to business.

5

THE DEFEAT OF EMPIRES BY THE POWER OF THE WEAK

A number of empires have foundered because of strong rivals: either defeated militarily and reduced to the status of a regional power, or so weakened that they have disappeared from the political map in an ensuing revolution or civil war. Napoleonic France and Wilhelmine Germany – more candidates than fully fledged empires – suffered defeat at the hands of other powers, which forced them to remodel themselves as nation-states compatible in power and extent with the functional imperatives of the European equilibrium. In both cases, the military denouement was a repetition, in more dramatic form, of Spain's defeat in the first half of the seventeenth century.[1] By contrast, Tsarist Russia, the Ottoman empire and the Austro-Hungarian empire broke down through a mixture of internal weakness, military defeat at the hands of rival powers and a series of internal revolts and revolutions. Whereas Napoleonic France and Wilhelmine Germany were smashed by the military superiority of their enemies, Russia, Austria-Hungary and the Ottoman empire suffered military defeat only at the end of a long process of disintegration that their rulers had tried to halt and reverse precisely by entering the First World War.

More revealing than the defeat of empires by strong opponents is the case in which they are brought to their knees by weaker ones who were never thought capable of becoming a serious threat. When imperial players are put in their place by forces of equal or superior strength, this shows that they did not sufficiently dispose of an essential feature of empire: that is, world dominion or at least sole dominion in their 'own' world; they were an empire only in a limited sense, since by definition no powers of equal or superior strength confront 'real' empires within their world. What we see here, then, is not the breakdown of an empire but the ups and downs of a great power. Theories of great power politics or hegemonial war may throw some light on the issue,[2] but it has little to do with the problems of imperial order and its eventual breakdown.

Now, as we have seen, the distinctions between hegemonial power and empire are in reality by no means as neat and straightforward as the concepts suggest. Imperial worlds may overlap with one another – as they did in the case of Spain and England in the seventeenth century, or England and France during the Seven Years' War for supremacy in North America, or Britain and Russia in the lines of conflict from the Black Sea to the Hindu Kush. In these zones hegemonial and imperial war mingle with each other, and it is not always clearly discernible whether great powers are fighting for supremacy or an imperial power is trying to break the resistance of anti-imperial players. The so-called surrogate wars during the East–West conflict were examples of this kind of pattern: one of the two imperial powers dressed itself up in anti-imperial garb and supported a resistance movement in the enemy's imperial periphery, thereby keeping within bounds a hegemonial conflict that could not be allowed to escalate into full-scale war because of the presence of nuclear weapons on both sides.

It is therefore not always clear whether empires have to deal only with weak anti-imperial players, or whether behind these stands another imperial centre that has seen a chance to inflict a defeat on its great hegemonial rival, in the latter's own 'world' or in the no man's land between the two imperial worlds. Such a defeat was suffered by the United States in Vietnam and the Soviet Union in Afghanistan, to mention only the two most important examples.

Before nuclear weapons and ballistic missiles entered the picture, small imperial wars on the periphery of the empires, involving a clash between rival interests and spheres of influence, always carried the risk of escalating into full-scale hegemonial wars. This may be seen, for example, in the way in which the European powers stumbled into the First World War. For the chief of the Austrian general staff, Conrad von Hötzendorf, the war against Serbia that he deliberately pursued was a small imperial war, in which a disturber of the peace within the Austro-Hungarian empire was to be put in its place or eliminated. Despite the problems that Austro-Hungarian units had with the Serbian army in the first year of war,[3] there is no doubt that they would eventually have got the better of Serbia militarily; it would then have been just another of the Balkan wars, in which the regional power sought to shape the political configuration in accordance with its own ideas and interests. But when Russia, seeing itself as protector of the Slavs and greatly extending its sphere of influence, took Serbia's side and declared a general mobilization, the small imperial war turned into a great hegemonial war. As a result, Europe's position of supremacy in the world came to an end.

Since imperial wars are structurally limited in space, whereas hegemonial wars have a strong propensity to draw in more and more areas, anti-imperial players naturally tend to make their struggle part of a hegemonial war. If they succeed in doing this, they considerably increase the chances that their political aspirations will eventually win through.

Right from the beginning, the political and military leadership of the German Reich was aware that German intervention would escalate the conflict between Vienna and Belgrade into a great hegemonial war, which would then be impossible to contain as one of the imperial wars common in the Balkans. But, if the war had to expand spatially, there was an attempt to limit it temporally – since it was felt that that was the only way in which it could be won. Thus, the chief of the German general staff, Count Alfred von Schlieffen, planned to win a speedy victory over France and then concentrate all his forces on the confrontation with Russia. A short war was all the more important because of the fear that, for geostrategic reasons, Germany would inevitably fall behind in a more protracted conflict; a fundamentally offensive approach to space was therefore deployed to keep the temporal dimension under control. This was a highly risky game, of course, and when it became clear that things were turning serious a last-minute attempt was made to hold up the course of events.[4] But it was already too late by the final days of July 1914. Berlin had made the mistake of giving Austria-Hungary a free hand for its project of a limited war against Serbia to restore order on the imperial periphery, without taking sufficient care to avoid being drawn into a hegemonial war that would have quite different dimensions and effects.[5] And, once imperial war passed into hegemonial war, Germany's sovereignty over time was gone.

The Serbian example again illustrates the different chances of success that imperial policy has in Europe and on other continents. Whereas the United States was able to conduct its small imperial wars in Central America, the Caribbean and eventually the Pacific without coming up against other great powers – at most it had to deal with one other power, in the Spanish–American war of 1898, not with a coalition of great powers[6] – any imperial war in Europe ran the risk of turning into a great hegemonial war. Tsarist Russia too had been able to fight its imperial wars, in the Caucasus and Central

Asia, without having to fear that they would embroil it in a hegemonial war. Only in East Asia were things different, because of Japan's rapid rise to become a power with imperial ambitions. The war of 1904, which the Russians had planned as an imperial war, soon turned into a major hegemonial war in which it suffered a number of defeats and, as a result, found its position weakened in Europe.[7]

Britain too could pursue its imperial wars without poaching on the preserves of its hegemonial rivals. This was true of its occupation of Egypt and of the subsequent Sudanese war against the Mahdi of Khartoum – an early case of Islamism, one might say. It was also true of the Boer War in South Africa, in which the German Kaiser certainly expressed his sympathy for the Boer cause (in his famous 'Kruger telegram') but offered no actual support.

The greatest danger for the British that their imperial operations might escalate into a hegemonial war came in 1898, when Lord Kitchener's expedition to Fashoda in southern Sudan encountered a small French force under Captain Marchand, and for a number of weeks the imperial rivals were on a war footing with each other.[8] Yet in Africa compromises and retreats were possible which no one dared contemplate in Europe. At the same time, the wars in Africa, the Caucasus, the Caribbean or the Philippines were fought with a degree of brutality against the civilian population that would have prompted cries of outrage in Europe. To put it in another way: whereas in Europe all wars tended towards symmetry, outside Europe forms of asymmetrical warfare were possible in which the technological and organizational superiority of the imperial powers could be fully driven home. Consequently, the problem of 'imperial overstretch' was posed above all in extra-European areas, and quite soon it became associated with the question of whether and under what circumstances anti-imperial players had a chance of imposing their political will against an asymmetrically superior empire. Thus, anti-imperial players had to find an answer to the question of how to convert their weaknesses into strengths.

Forms of imperial overstretch

Analysis of what overstretch means for the stability of an empire goes back to Edward Gibbon's monumental *History of the Decline and Fall of the Roman Empire* (1776–88). Taking Rome as his historical example, but also keeping an eye on contemporary developments in

Britain, Gibbon identified the greatest danger to an empire in its tendency to overexpand in space and to take on unlimited tasks and responsibilities. More recent literature on 'overstretch' and 'overcommitment' suggests that it is in the vital interests of an empire to withdraw from areas of lesser significance to itself, and after a time to shed obligations that it took over under specific conditions. In this respect, the self-preservation imperative of empires and the functional principles of the international community of states point in different directions. Empires achieve the greater stability the less they are tied down in space and bound by agreements. Interstate systems, on the other hand, are more stable and peaceful the more their member-states are territorially fixed and bound by conventions.[9]

The classical meaning of imperial overextension was an excessive expansion of the area to be kept under control, so that avoidance of overextension was nearly always synonymous with withdrawal from frontiers and the handing over of territory. But this concept of overextension or overcommitment essentially referred to land empires and, in the past, had only limited application to maritime empires, where the risks in question appeared only in the event of a push inland from coastal harbours and trading stations. It was the mobility of the navy which reduced the problem of spatial overextension for the maritime empires.[10] In contrast to army units deployed for the defence of frontiers, the navy was a permanent and highly mobile instrument of security and control, for which a greater operational area did not necessarily mean a corresponding increase in costs and requirements. Only this made it possible for a small country such as Portugal to extend its commercial dominance as it did in the Indian and Pacific oceans and to maintain it for more than a century. Similarly, the power of the British world empire was determined not only by the number of its naval squadrons, but also by the quality of the ships, the seamanship of their crews and the skill of the Admiralty in commanding warships over huge areas. A reduction in the number of lay days at harbours was as important for the power of the British empire as the bringing into service of new ships.

Classical land empires could not draw upon such reserves of efficiency for frontier protection and the control of space, and so the problem of imperial overextension was posed quite differently in their case. To put it bluntly, the key problem for maritime empires is not so much spatial extension as the availability of technological innovations. They must ensure that only a part of their resources is committed to the latest shipbuilding and weapons technology, while another part remains capable of force-feeding new innovations and deploying them in sufficient quantity before rival powers can do the same. It is no accident that the first great arms race took place in the navy, between Britain and imperial Germany.[11]

Technological superiority has become even more significant with the opening of air space, and potentially also outer space, as spheres of imperial rule. In fact, the problem of overextended territorial frontiers is no longer of much consequence, and the answer to imperial overstretch can no longer be the drawing of more limited boundaries. Seen in the true light of day, the American empire now has only virtual frontiers, which it defines in accordance with the weapons technology (especially the access to nuclear weapons and delivery systems) of possible counter-players. Otherwise, the US empire's largely unchallenged domination of air space tends to remove all limits to its sway. The territorial model of 'straightening out the front' cannot be used for the redrawing of US-controlled space, for especially in relation to air space and cosmic space that would mean the terminal decline of its imperial power.

The risk of imperial overstretch remains on the ground, however, where technological superiority can be brought to bear only to a limited extent. For this reason, anti-imperial players believe that here they can offset their technological inferiority vis-à-vis imperial forces with a greater readiness for action and sacrifice. Memories of the age of partisan warfare, beginning with Soviet and Yugoslav successes against the German occupiers and their allies and ending with the withdrawal of Soviet forces from Afghanistan,[12] continue to fuel the hopes of anti-imperial players that even the most modern empire can be defeated in the same way. In fact, guerrilla wars in Asia and Africa did considerably hasten the demise of the European colonial empires, and neither the USA nor the Soviet Union was capable, in Vietnam and Afghanistan, of defeating a partisan-style enemy but had to withdraw exhausted after years of war.

Despite their massive superiority, then, empires can be defeated in land wars if they encounter a determined enemy who shuns decisive battles and settles into a long-drawn-out conflict.[13] History provides many examples of this: from the resistance of a German tribal alliance to Roman pressure on the Weser and Elbe, through the Spanish partisan war against Napoleonic forces, to the liberation wars in the course of which the European colonial empires collapsed. In these cases, anti-imperial players exploited the problems of overextension by using the deep spatial penetration of imperial forces to bring out the weaknesses of their position; supply lines became increasingly vulnerable as they extended into more and more territory, offering targets to small enemy groups that were able to mount frequent and costly attacks. With a few exceptions,[14] anti-imperial players have gained victory not on the battlefield but by wearing down the empire, wasting its forces and eventually forcing it to withdraw.

The theorist of war Carl von Clausewitz treated the problem of over-extension (admittedly with reference to conventional warfare) under the title 'The Culminating Point of the Attack'. This culmination is a special problem of what Clausewitz calls the diminishing force of the attack, 'one of the strategist's main concerns':[15] the further an attacker presses into enemy territory, the more his absolute strength declines. This can be handled if, as a result of the advance, the enemy's strength dissipates faster than one's own, so that greater relative strength accompanies the loss in absolute strength. As Clausewitz assumes, however, this is possible only in spatially limited theatres: if the enemy can fall back on great strategic depths, the relationship of forces develops in an opposite direction, since then the resources consumed in the advance are greater than those the enemy needs for defence. Even then the attacker may achieve his objective, but only if the other side is weary of war and, unable to compensate for the loss of territory, rapidly sues for peace. 'The attacker is purchasing advantages that may become valuable at the peace table, but he must pay for them on the spot with his fighting forces.'[16]

Clausewitz's mercantile metaphor illuminates the key problem of overextension: it is not always expedient to avoid it, as it may well lead to the desired success; but the attacker has to pay 'up front', at a moment when it is unclear whether the 'investment' will be worth-while. This depends on the enemy's reactions, which cannot be pre-cisely calculated in advance. And, if the enemy induces the attacker to go beyond the 'culminating point', there may follow a turn-around, a retreat, whose force 'is usually much stronger than that of the original attack'.[17] Independently of its strategic and tactical pecu-liarities, guerrilla warfare may also be thought of as a *political* deci-sion to refuse peace negotiations.[18] The strategic calculation behind it is that the attacking side will always have to pay on the spot, without receiving an offer of peace or surrender; it will then increas-ingly exhaust itself and, after a time, itself have to offer peace talks or initiate a retreat. Henry Kissinger summed up this problem in the famous dictum 'The guerrilla wins if he does not lose. The conven-tional army loses if it does not win.'[19] The danger of imperial over-stretch is that precisely this mechanism comes into play.

Clausewitz's genuinely military-strategic considerations on the culmination of the attack have found their way directly into theories of imperial overstretch, such as Chalmers Johnson's idea that the United States, having passed its climax of expansion and now displaying the first signs of a reverse tendency, is threatened with what he calls 'blowback', especially in the Pacific region.[20] The warning issued by some critics – that Washington should avoid taking the step from hegemony to empire, as it could then end up losing both[21] – is also conceived in accordance with the model of culmination and retreat. But this simplifies Clausewitz's theorem, by suggesting that a reluctance even to approach the culminating point represents a solution to the problem. That is not what Clausewitz thought, of course. His advice was not to avoid risks in principle – indeed, he was convinced that certain challenges can be overcome only if one takes occasionally risky decisions: 'If we remember how many factors contribute to an equation of forces, we will understand how difficult it is in some cases to determine which side has the upper hand. Often it is entirely a matter of the imagination.'[22]

If, however, we abstract from the fact that Clausewitz based his ideas on a territorial model of movement (which already did not apply to maritime empires) and that the opening up of air space and the cosmos has since led to a deterritorialization of military capabilities, then it must be said that his theorem is in principle still applicable to today's circumstances. Especially important is his reference to the many unknown factors in the equation of forces, which is today even more difficult to calculate than it was in his time. Thus, the question of possible overstretch no longer concerns only the relationship between the available military forces and the size of the area to be kept under control, but must above all take into account the economic potential of the imperial power and the 'moral' state of its population. The two together determine whether an imperial power is capable of staying the course: since guerrilla warfare mainly seeks to wear down the enemy, whose political will cannot be broken in any other way, both factors are here of decisive significance.[23]

Imperial overstretch is therefore a danger mainly when the resources of an empire begin to run short, and the danger is all the greater if the anti-imperial forces know which resources are limited and which are more or less inexhaustible. Not by chance have many leaders of anti-imperial wars earlier spent a long time in the imperial centre and familiarized themselves with its strengths and weaknesses. A more likely scenario, however, is that the readiness of the imperial population to stay the course will be exhausted before material resources begin to run out; its 'morale' therefore becomes the main target for anti-imperial players, whether they are employing mainly guerrilla warfare or a strategy of terrorism.

Neither the Roman nor the Chinese empire could be defeated militarily by its enemies, and the same was even true of the Spanish and Ottoman empires. But it was not true of the British empire, nor for that matter of Tsarist Russia. Neither Napoleon nor Hitler was capable of directly attacking Britain, and indirect strategies in North Africa did not bring the desired results. The decline of the British empire was economic – a slow process that gradually unfolded between 1914 and 1956.[24] The costs and losses resulting from two hegemonial wars in Europe, and from the war with Japan over its East Asian possessions, weakened Britain so much that it could no longer steel itself for an energetic long-term defence of its colonies against the various independence movements; it therefore took the decision to withdraw, largely without a struggle.[25] Once again this demonstrated the imperial astuteness and far-sightedness of the British establishment, which, unlike the French, realized that the frontiers of empire were overstretched and had to be rolled back. It is true that in the late 1940s, when the decision was made to grant Indian independence, no one could have thought that the frontiers would end up virtually identical to those of the mother country. It is also true that, for a time, the British spared themselves this conclusion by dreaming up the survival of empire as a Commonwealth.[26]

Except in a few cases, such as Kenya and Burma, the British refrained from seeking to preserve their rule by military means. The French, who tried to do precisely this, were defeated militarily in Indochina and economically and psychologically in North Africa. When they surrendered their swampland fortress at Dien Bien Phu in 1954, at the key junction between Laos and Vietnam, they lost the Indochinese war on the battlefield – not least because the USA had refused to give the logistical support that would have made it easier for them to fight on.[27] In Algeria, the situation was quite different: there were more than one million French settlers, who had become native to the country; Paris could rely on sizeable support from local military units; and the French had considerable backing among the Algerian middle layers, whose original aim was not at all complete independence but full political rights. By 1962, however, following eight years of war that had led to a deep split within French society, France was in such bad shape that it agreed to Algerian independence and signed the Evian accords.[28] The Algerian War, which the French had fought with political resolution and military competence, showed that colonial powers could be defeated politically even if they could not be overcome militarily. The methods of guerrilla warfare had succeeded in wearing France down both economically and psychologically.[29]

The Algerian War became the model for all anti-imperial and anti-colonial wars from the 1960s to the 1980s – from Vietnam through Mozambique, Namibia and Angola to Afghanistan. In each case, the guerrilla forces sought to convert the military presence of a great power or colonial ruler outside its mother country into a form of imperial overstretch; the use of force no longer served, as in classical wars between states, to render the enemy powerless as a prelude to the imposition of one's own political will, but rather became a lever with which to weaken the enemy economically and, in this way, to sap and eventually destroy his political will. After some time, it was thought, the imperial centre would realize that its presence in the periphery cost considerably more than it brought in, and this would strengthen political forces who were no longer willing to bear the costs of empire in far-flung areas of the world. This is indeed what happened in the United States, where the middle layers increasingly turned against the Vietnam War, then in Portugal, where a group of senior officers staged a putsch and brought the colonial empire to an end, and finally in the Soviet Union, where reformers around Gorbachev pushed for a rapid end to the Afghanistan adventure on the grounds that it was impeding the capacity for reform inside the country.

Imperial overstretch is thus not an objectively measurable quantity corresponding to the specifications of geopolitical or geostrategic theory. The rediscovery of guerrilla strategy during the Second World War, the subsequent longing for peace in European society and, not least, the focus on rebuilding a shattered continent made a significant contribution to the way in which the lines of imperial overstretch were redrawn. Then, with the political mobilization of peoples in the periphery, regions that for decades or even centuries had been fixed parts of an imperial space suddenly became areas of imperial overstretch. This is precisely what Harold Macmillan meant during his trip to Africa in 1960, when he spoke of a 'wind of change' blowing across the empire. People sat up and noticed overstretch where no one had seen it before, in part because of the strengthening of the periphery along with the weakening of the imperial centre.

The weakening of the centre was discernible in the statistical data, the strengthening of the periphery in nothing. The beginning of decolonization was not preceded by any economic take-off in the colonies, protectorates and mandated territories; their strength was due almost entirely to their striving for independence and a willingness to make sacrifices to achieve it. The times were gone when the British had been able to control huge territories with a few hundred officials and a few thousand soldiers. The independence struggle dramatically raised the costs of imperial rule, and completely shifted the lines of imperial overstretch.

Those who, following the collapse of the Soviet Union, spoke of the end of all empires[30] were mainly using the tendencies we have just outlined as their basis. What they did not see was that imperial overstretch is a dynamic quantity, which changes not only with the resources available to the parties in conflict and the readiness to deploy them, but also with the form of imperial rule against which the resources for domination and resistance have to be weighed. In so far as the US empire shifted from the control of territory to the control of flows (capital and information, goods and services), and in so far as it refrained from the assertion of direct control on the ground because it could operate much more cost-effectively from the air or space, the classical forms of guerrilla warfare lost much of their capacity to raise the costs of imperial domination. They are now mainly a way for warlords to raise funds,[31] not a threat to the global instruments of control at the disposal of American power. Guerrillas cannot attack stealth bombers or cruise missiles, and popular support in the areas of conflict is of little use if their military objectives lie outside those regions.

From time immemorial, imperial players have used their asymmetrical superiority to push out the lines of overstretch and to open up areas that would otherwise have been closed to them. This was already the case for the classical empires of Rome and China: their armies were more efficiently organized, better equipped and generally better led than those of their adversaries, but the key point was that the empire was able to make its superiority last by institutionalizing it. Of course, the asymmetries in question were quite weakly developed[32] and could often be counterbalanced by an appropriate effort on the enemy's part – for example, the copying of imperial military organization or the kidnapping of craftsmen and engineers to make use of their knowledge and skills.[33]

The asymmetrical superiority was much more pronounced in the case of maritime empires, whose warships and cannons represented a technology, and required nautical skills, unavailable to potential enemies in the periphery.[34] The industrial revolution subsequently spread these major asymmetries to land warfare. A lasting symbol of this was the battle of Omdurman (1898), when a British expeditionary corps under Lord Kitchener used its artillery, and especially the new Maxim machine-gun, to defeat the numerically far superior troops of the Mahdi of Khartoum. The real symbol, however, was not the victory but the asymmetry of losses: 48 men on the British side, 13,000 on the Sudanese.[35]

So long as anti-imperial players opposed superior enemies with symmetrical means, they had no way of avoiding defeat. Only when they began to develop asymmetrical methods of combat, attacking supply lines or small units and avoiding pitched battles or frontal assaults, were they able to compensate in part for their technological and organizational inferiority. Through technological developments as well as strategic and tactical creativity, through changes in the forms of imperial control as well as a greater capacity for political mobilization on the part of anti-imperial players, the lines of imperial overstretch were constantly redrawn. The notion that this process has dramatically slowed down in today's world, or even that it has become fixed by state frontiers, has little plausibility. However, the new lines of imperial overstretch are to be found no longer on geographical maps, but rather in capital flows, competitive access to information and differences in relation to technological revolutions and strategic innovation. The contest between technological innovation and strategic-tactical creativity is still under way.

Political mobilization and military asymmetry: the strategies of anti-imperial players

For reasons of self-preservation, empires take great pains to prevent their rivals, especially potential anti-imperial players, from gaining access to militarily important innovations.[36] The more they derive their superiority from a technological lead, the more intent they are on secrecy and non-proliferation. This exclusion never functioned in the European system of states, however, where all path-breaking scientific or technological developments spread to Western and Central European rivals in the shortest space of time.[37] Perhaps this is why no lasting empire developed within Europe; or perhaps it was rather because there was no empire that other countries were never excluded from technological developments. The mutual *arcana imperii* of rival states – size of the war chest, undisclosed treaties, dispositions in the event of a war or international crisis, and so on[38] – become, in relation to empires ruling 'their' world, the secrets of a technological superiority to be protected at all costs.

Security guarantees are one of the means to this end. By undertaking to protect its friends and allies from attack, an empire keeps them from making greater efforts to close the technological gap. The more these powers are capable of doing this, the more prepared the empire will be to offer them appropriate security guarantees. One example was the nuclear umbrella that the United States extended over Western Europe and Japan during the Cold War; the empire thereby maintained its lead by allowing others to participate in its positive effects,[39] while the others – with the exception of France – were happy to be 'bought off' because it allowed them to invest in other areas, or to consume in the form of social benefits, the money they would otherwise have had to spend in developing nuclear weapons of their own. This kind of imperial policy, which, as we have seen, first manifested itself in the alliances forged by Athens, has been called 'empire by invitation'.[40]

The situation is much more difficult when smaller rivals, or even anti-imperial players, seek to end military asymmetry by acquiring weapons, especially nuclear missiles, that allow them to confront the empire as a potentially symmetrical adversary. If North Korea, for example, did not have a nuclear capability, it would be a negligible power in world politics, having at most regional significance, one of the poor countries to which no one pays much attention because it has no mineral resources of interest to the world economy. Nuclear weapons, we might say, are a functional equivalent that can make up for the lack of strategic resources. Above all, however, they can give a small and rather weak country considerable power to deter an empire from attacking it. A number of countries therefore have a strong incentive to develop a nuclear arsenal of their own, instead of placing themselves under the shield of an empire or a regional hegemon.

Unable to accept such things without losing power and prestige, any empire will take active steps to prevent them. Thus, after the end of the East–West conflict, the United States moved at first gradually and tentatively, then ever more resolutely and purposefully, from a policy of blocking proliferation by agreement to one of active 'counter-proliferation' (including military strikes against a nuclear capability before its actual deployment). Any state that does not agree to forgo nuclear weapons, that secretly or openly breaks agreements, or that otherwise gives the impression of wanting to join the nuclear club comes under enormous pressure from the United States. In no other area is it so clear that the international community does not consist of equals – and that the inequality refers not only to their present size and strength, but to also to the future possibility of becoming equal. Non-proliferation and *a fortiori* counter-proliferation policies are ways of actively preventing equality, and the argument that nuclear weapons might fall into the hands of terrorists is often simply a pretext for the denial of such weapons to certain states.

The shift from nuclear deterrence to active counter-proliferation has shown itself first of all in the array of weaponry: mini-nukes with an explosive power of less than one kilotonne and 'robust nuclear earth penetrators' (so-called bunker-busters) are typical of what might be termed disarmament warfare. The Bush Doctrine[41] announced in September 2002 summed up a number of long-existing trends as the basis for new directives governing US policy.[42]

A prerequisite for this move away from prevention is the asymmetrical superiority of US forces in conventional as well as nuclear weaponry, the backbone of which is American dominance of space for the purpose of warfare or contact with the enemy. This is supposed to preclude the use of guerrilla warfare against US forces, giving an adversary no chance to attack supply units, protective positions or small combat units. The deployment of high-tech weapons and special forces should reduce to a minimum the enemy's opportunity to counter asymmetrical superiority with his own strategies of asymmetrization;[43] US losses will be kept low and the fighting will be over as quickly as possible. Otherwise the public at home might rapidly turn against the war, and political support for the military might evaporate. This is the Achilles heel of empires that wage wars to pacify, rather than to plunder, their periphery. It is a weak point all the easier to attack, the greater is the democratic control of governments and the more pronounced the development of post-heroic attitudes.

The attempt of subordinate states to achieve something like military equality by developing or acquiring nuclear weapons of their own may be understood as a policy of resymmetrization, whose logical conclusion – the possession of nuclear weapons by every country on earth – would restore symmetrical-reciprocal structures in international politics. The symmetry would then be much more radical than ever before, since the possession of nuclear weapons would render meaningless differences between countries in respect of land surface and population size, economic strength, conventional military forces, and so on. The only thing that would count in terms of power politics would be the capacity to inflict nuclear annihilation on another country. Just as Thomas Hobbes argued that all men in the state of nature were equal because anyone could kill anyone and even the weakest could, with cunning and deception, take the life of the strongest,[44] so could radical equality prevail in international relations if each and every state acquired nuclear weapons. But then Hobbes's state of nature would also prevail, in which everyone is in 'continual fear and danger of violent death', and 'the life of man [is] solitary, poor, nasty, brutish, and short'.[45]

If every country must go nuclear for there to be a global symmetry of power politics, it is scarcely an attractive option – especially when we consider that even nuclear states can collapse and their weapons fall into the hands of infra-state or even private players.[46] A policy of nuclear non-proliferation that maintains imperial asymmetries, but also a policy of active counter-proliferation, wins support even in places where there is otherwise little sympathy for the imperial dominance of the United States. For, through a non-proliferation policy geared to its own power interests, the empire creates and maintains a collective good – relative security from nuclear war – of which we could not be assured without the dominance of the imperial power.

Since the road to symmetry is blocked, anti-imperial players – that is, those who seek not only to mobilize world opinion against the imperial centre through rallies and demonstrations, but actually to combat it by means of violence – have to fall back on the pursuit of systematic asymmetry.[47] And, since neither the weapons at their disposal nor their degree of military organization enable them to overcome the imperial power, they must try to wear it down in a protracted small war. In the second half of the twentieth century, guerrilla warfare was the main asymmetrical strategy. But now it looks as if its place has been taken by terrorism.[48] We shall look more closely below at the differences between the two, but first we should examine what they have in common.

Both guerrilla warfare and terrorism avoid direct confrontation with the professional armed forces of the power they seek to attack; they operate at the enemy's rear, so to speak, and try to exhaust his military apparatus by constantly harrying its supply lines and maintaining the nervous tension. Strategies based on asymmetry aim to make the adversary deploy greater resources where it is most vulnerable. This increased deployment of resources may be provoked not only by direct guerrilla attacks and physical casualties, but also by actions designed to provoke an overreaction and to draw the enemy into imperial overstretch.

Generally speaking, guerrilla warfare and terrorism – qua asymmetrical forms of anti-imperial warfare – seek to demonstrate that the empire's promise of peace and its associated security guarantees are an illusion. The imperial order has to be stripped of its attractiveness, not only at the core but in the periphery and beyond, so that people's acceptance of it melts away in the medium to long term. If the empire can no longer deliver what it promised, or can do so only at hugely increased cost and with major restrictions of civil liberties, then consent to the imperial order will disappear and support for it even in the centre will eventually crumble. In other words, the *object* of asymmetrical strategies based on force is to stimulate the quest for alternatives to the imperial order; their strategic *aim* is to wear down the population of the imperial area both economically and psychologically; and their *means* is a diffuse violence directed at the political, social and economic order of the empire.[49]

The power of the weak, which is brought to bear in strategies based on asymmetry, also has two main components: to make the empire appear not at all as strong as it claims to be; and to place it under such pressure that it further increases certain strengths and finds itself in a process of overstretch and overcommitment. The first element is essentially symbolic, the second mainly instrumental. What both come down to, however, is that 'soft power' is replaced with 'hard power' (to use Joseph Nye's terms) and that the costs of rule constantly increase. Finally, the asymmetrical strategy aims to force the empire back over the Augustan threshold, which it crossed in order to keep the costs of rule to a minimum.[50] If the opponents of empire manage to do this, they hasten the decline of the world empire from the zenith of its power and ensure that the process further accelerates under its own steam. Their prospects of success, however, depend not only on their own skill but also on how the empire reacts. Asymmetrical conflicts, like symmetrical conflicts, unfold in accordance with the model of action and counter-action, in which each side has a chance to cut across the plans and intentions of the other side – except that asymmetrical conflicts are not fought on a single battlefield or with a single set of rules.

The asymmetry of the parties to the conflict can be seen not least in each side's legitimation of the use of force by presenting the other as the embodiment of evil. As we have seen,[51] imperial demonology is matched by a similarly structured anti-imperial demonology, which paints one side as holy and the other as the devil's work. The lack of symmetry and reciprocity here crystallizes in an intensification of enmity.

In the eyes of anti-imperial players, empires are fundamentally methods and forms of repression and exploitation; the collective goods such as peace and security that they claim to provide serve only to maximize the advantages of the imperial centre and to set the periphery at a systematic disadvantage. This line of argument can already be found in the classical anti-imperial ideology of nationalism, which condemned imperial orders as the 'prison house of nations';[52] many an empire would be broken by this perception in the course of the twentieth century. Nationalism too was incapable of creating a stable world order with its favoured model of the nation-state, and its failure was nowhere more evident than in the areas from which it drove out old empires (the Balkans, the Near and Middle East, sub-Saharan Africa). Earlier, however, it released powerful forces and energies against the suppression of the right to national self-determination, claiming not only Tsarist Russia but the Ottoman empire, the Austro-Hungarian empire and the European colonial empires as its victims.

The nationalist critique of empire was generally flanked by a socialist critique, which focused less on the enslavement of nations than on the pillage of regions and an ethnic hierarchy of exploitation. And where empire played the role of modernizer, undermining ancient ways of life in the periphery, the guerrillas fighting for independence could gain considerable support by presenting themselves as defenders of tradition.[53] Together, all these critiques sapped the legitimacy of the imperial order, inducing the peoples in the periphery to turn first away from empire and then actively against it. The resulting wars and uprisings could legitimize themselves as liberation struggles and, in view of the high value set on the concept of freedom in the modern world, thereby gained considerable sympathy and support.

From the point of view of empire, these were wars and disturbances against an order that acted in the interests of all people of good will living within it; there was therefore a duty to take the harshest and most decisive measures against its enemies. The pacification wars of empire appeared in this light as just – indeed, the very idea of *just war* took shape right alongside the imperial order. In Rome, for instance, it developed after the defeat of Carthage, the last rival for hegemony in the western Mediterranean, at the battle of Zama, when the task of the hour was to pacify or overcome any disturbers of the imperial peace.

The idea of just war may be traced back to the influence of the Hellenistic Stoics Panaitios and Polybius, whose suggestions were taken up and further theorized by Cicero.[54] From the point of view of practical politics, it was evidently a reaction to the imperial position that Rome had carved out for itself in the Mediterranean. It meant that imperial wars were not fought on the basis of symmetrical rights, on the model of the duel, but constituted a particular kind of action against lawbreakers. The idea of just war thus rested upon asymmetrical legal grounds. This theory runs like a red thread through the history of imperial warfare: we find it in the Salamanca school in Spain but especially in Tommaso Campanella,[55] then among the loyal intellectual supporters of the British empire, in the ideology of the Soviet Union, and finally among neoconservatives in the contemporary United States.[56]

The asymmetrical configurations of imperial or anti-imperial wars are matched by asymmetrical patterns of legitimation. First, they display a strong tendency to criminalize the adversary, who is not regarded as an equal and legitimate party to the war, nor usually as a combatant against whom the rules of international law must be observed. The reason for this is that imperial or anti-imperial wars are fought with unequal forces, for disparate goals and in accordance with disparate principles. Guerrillas and *a fortiori* terrorists derive their strength precisely from the fact that they elude the reciprocal system of rules that ostensibly applies to war between states; they would not stand a chance against their enemies if they played by those rules. But imperial armies too do not feel bound by the rules of international law in their conflicts with anti-imperial players; they indeed develop a strong tendency to overreact to the constant pinpricks they receive at the hands of an elusive enemy. The history of imperial and anti-imperial warfare reads like one long sequence of massacres which, when they have a military function and are not mere expressions of panic, are designed to instil terror and thereby dissuade the civilian population from lending further support to the other side.

The asymmetry of imperial and anti-imperial warfare is evident not least in the differential involvement of civilians. Whereas the centre initially sees only minor disturbances in the periphery, expecting its military apparatus to put them down in short order and not wishing its own population to have its peace troubled by them, anti-imperial players seek precisely to shake up the population in the region of their operations. They must mobilize people for their ends, and if they cannot achieve this through agitation they rely on enemy repression to confirm their claim that the whole imperial order is intolerable. Unless this happens, the anti-imperial struggle falls at the first hurdle. But, if the idea of an anti-imperial war finds fertile soil among sections of the population in the periphery, a conflict develops there which soon becomes a festering wound for the empire.

Both guerrilla warfare and terrorism target resources that are available to the empire in only limited quantity. The nature of these resources has changed repeatedly in the history of anti-imperial wars, but it is possible to make some general points about them. Political thoughtfulness combined with astuteness and far-sightedness is in principle one such scarce resource, since the capacity to process and evaluate information soon comes up against limits in the imperial centre. This is especially true if, in several parts of the periphery, the empire faces challenges from various anti-imperial players.

A good example of such cognitive overload is the way in which the Kennedy administration stumbled into the Vietnam War without being clear about who was the real enemy or what kind of war it was entering.[57] For President Kennedy and President Johnson, as well as for Defense Secretary Robert McNamara, it was part of the global East–West conflict. But it became that in reality only in so far as the USA got involved in Vietnam with military advisers, then with air force units and finally with ground troops. At that point the Soviet Union and China thought that, by supporting North Vietnam, they could draw the United States into an enervating conflict in which they themselves would be only indirectly involved. For the majority of Vietnamese, on the other hand, the East–West conflict was not the heart of the matter; they were fighting a national liberation war and saw the USA as the successor to the former colonial power, France. Therefore they were prepared to bear the huge costs and casualties of the war, and to keep up with each escalation without making political concessions. Washington, for its part, thought that it could push up the costs for the North Vietnamese until they were forced to stop assisting the Vietcong; the enemy in the South would then be starved of supplies and easily defeated. As it turned out, however, this plan was based on an illusion.

For the US administration, and especially for McNamara, Vietnam was an *instrumental war* for a definite political end: namely, to maintain the status quo, in which North Vietnam belonged to the Eastern bloc and South Vietnam to the West. For the Vietnamese, however, it was a *war of survival* in which their national existence was at stake.[58] This is what the US administration, in its obsession with the East–West conflict, failed to grasp. Cognitive overload of the imperial elite means, in particular, that the empire's various conflicts on its far-flung borders and periphery are perceived and handled in accordance with a single model. In the late 1970s, the Soviet leadership made a similar error in Afghanistan. But, whereas Vietnam was only a severe setback for the resource-rich United States, Afghanistan became the beginning of the end of empire for the Soviet Union.[59] In both cases, the power of the weak owed a lot to the faulty judgements and decisions of the strong.

In theory, both the United States and the Soviet Union repeated the learning process that the European colonial powers had undergone between the late 1940s and the early 1960s. The lesson, in short, was that modern empires are not able to keep large territories under their control in the event of a large-scale popular mobilization against the local government. That kind of resistance has nearly always meant the beginning of the end for imperial rule in the area.[60]

The conditions of success for anti-imperial players in the twentieth century were thus markedly different from those in earlier times, when imperial powers could crush resistance movements with an iron fist and then instal a regime capable of nipping any rebellion in the bud. At the beginning of the twentieth century, it was still possible for the British to crush the Boer rebellion in South Africa and to re-establish their own rule on a stable footing; nor, in order to deprive the Boer partisans of support, did they shrink from herding civilians (mostly women, children and old people) into concentration camps, where wretched hygiene was the rule and many died in misery.[61] One may doubt whether the British would have been able to maintain such a policy for long after the emergence of the global audio-visual media in the 1960s and 1970s. Pictures of suffering and death would have triggered massive protests in the imperial centre, and the empire would have been under such pressure from international public opinion that it would soon have had to open the camps. It is even unlikely that the British could have won the Boer War if it had taken place in the second half of the twentieth century.

This example is also revealing because the Boers skilfully used all the forms of warfare which, half a century later, had largely become a guarantee of success. Evidently, victory and defeat in anti-imperial wars depend on more than just the creative development of new military strategies and tactics. But, before we attribute the greater chances of success in such a war purely and simply to twentieth-century changes in the media, we should remember that the American settlers had already wrested their independence from Britain through what was essentially a guerrilla form of warfare.

Now, it might be objected that the Americans could not have been certain of victory in the War of Independence if they had not had the support of the French, who for a brief but crucial moment possessed naval supremacy on the East Coast and were able to force the surrender of British forces at Yorktown.[62] The Boers' lack of comparable support from any other power (the German Reich, for example) certainly limited their capacity to hold on politically and militarily. But it was probably much more significant that the Boer fighters, numbering little more than 30,000, did not manage to widen their political support in the course of the war; they would have had to appeal to the black population of the territories, in whose eyes they were far worse oppressors than the British. In the end, the Boers lost the war because, though employing guerrilla warfare in a technical sense, they were unable to make use of the well-known mechanism of political escalation – the mechanism which, as the anti-guerrilla campaign develops, makes the imperial power appear increasingly as a repressive rather than a pacifying force, thereby allowing partisan groups to count on ever growing support in their area of operations.

Surprisingly, the literature on guerrilla warfare has seldom discussed this mechanism whereby empires refute their own claim to be a force for peace and prosperity and come to be seen by the local population as an occupying force.[63] This is what happened to France during the Algerian War.

The characteristic feature of guerrilla warfare, as it developed in late eighteenth- to nineteenth-century America and Spain from 'small war'[64] into a distinctively anti-imperial form of warfare, is the combination of military and political aspects in a way that works to the advantage of insurgents and the disadvantage of the imperial power. From the moment at which the empire, reeling from armed attacks on its installations and personnel, starts to employ military methods to stamp out unrest, it loses legitimacy and hands it over in equal measure to the guerrillas. We may call this the original asymmetry between imperial and anti-imperial legitimacy, which in the history of ideas arose with the spread of conceptions of liberty in the eighteenth century and has grown deeper in the course of time. Guerrilla war brings out this latent asymmetry, and this is the main reason why in the twentieth century it became a guarantee of the success of anti-imperial insurgency.

The empire's recourse to military methods becomes a confirmation of what the anti-imperial propagandists always claimed: that the empire first established control over the territory to oppress its population and to exploit its resources; that all the supposed advantages of remaining in the empire are pure ideology, or benefit only a small layer of exploiters associated with it; and that the mass of the people will therefore have a better life once they conquer independence. As soon as the guerrilla war spreads to large areas of the country, any measures to combat it tend to confirm these statements. At first indifferent, the majority of the population moves through withdrawal of support for empire to active support for anti-imperial forces, with the result that the guerrillas grow stronger and stronger precisely because of the military campaign against them.

The classical land empires escalated anti-guerrilla violence to a level far beyond what the British practised in South Africa, sometimes even exterminating the inhabitants of whole areas or resettling them in order to break their ethnic unity.[65] 'The scattering of nations' is the biblical term for this policy, as seen from the viewpoint of those subjected to it. One example is the widespread 'ethnic cleansing' of the notoriously rebellious Jews by the Assyrians and Neo-babylonians.[66] The Mongols pursued the same kind of policy. The conquerors of the New World decimated the indigenous peoples, and Russian policy towards the peoples of the Caucasus was extremely harsh and brutal in the nineteenth and twentieth centuries. Similarly, the Ottoman empire repeatedly used ethnic resettlement and expulsions against rebellious populations, and when it applied this to the Armenians during the First World War it turned into a genocide which was reported in the world's press and had disastrous consequences for the political position of Turkey and its allies.[67] The Roman commanders Vespasian and Titus, who put down the Jewish insurrection of AD 66–72, were subject to no such mechanisms of scrutiny, and the uprising ended with the dissolution of the Jewish polity in Palestine.[68] This action on the part of the Roman empire was finally annulled only with the founding of the state of Israel in 1948.

Modern empires are barred from escalating small wars on their periphery to the point where they use all weapons at their disposal, because that would contradict the principle of proportionate response. Thus, American politicians and generals who wanted to use nuclear weapons to win wars on the periphery of their sphere of influence did not find the necessary support among the electorate: for example, the temporarily popular General Douglas MacArthur, who was keen to force the issue in the Korean War by bombing China, or the Republican presidential candidate in 1964, Barry Goldwater, and the presidential candidate of the American Independent Party in 1968, who both thought the Vietnam War should be won through a nuclear attack on North Vietnam.[69] It was not fear of escalation into a nuclear war between the superpowers that stood in the way of such attacks, but rather a strong sense that they would discredit every political ideal to which Americans felt attached. This self-limitation of democratic empires in relation to uprisings and wars on their periphery may be said to have considerably increased the chances of success for anti-imperial players. We may therefore also assume that the liberalization and democratization of China will expand the room for manoeuvre of the Tibetans.[70]

Of course, empires with a democratic constitution – which have usually been maritime or trading empires – have ways of reshuffling their rule and control that the classical land empires never had. The empire may withdraw from administration of the area in dispute and grant the local population political autonomy, then return after a while as the force controlling flows of goods and services, information and capital. This gives rise to forms of soft dependence that cannot be overthrown by insurrections or guerrilla wars. In such circumstances, the classical weapons of anti-imperial warfare prove blunt: because empire no longer exists as the repressive power that guerrilla forces targeted, and because the forms of imperial repression and exploitation have become more elastic and sophisticated than they claimed. In the struggle on the periphery of imperial zones of influence, the key question is whether the empire has really changed from a repressive and exploitative structure to a regime that ensures peace and promotes prosperity, or whether imperial repression and exploitation have not fundamentally changed but simply become invisible.

Cultural identity struggles and terrorism as a strategy for wars of devastation

What may be said of war in general since the transition from agrarian to industrial society is also true of guerrilla warfare: its costs are greater than its benefits, regardless of whether one emerges as winner or loser; and it takes years, if not centuries, for a society devastated by such a war to regain the economic level it had before its outbreak. Since, however, anti-imperial guerrilla wars have been fought exclusively in regions with an agrarian economic and social order, their medium to long-term costs for anti-imperial players have not been immediately visible. Industrial systems based on expensive technology were not present, and large-scale mining of roads and fields was not often a feature of decolonization wars but became common only in the civil wars of the 1980s and 1990s and in the arsenal of warlords.

The negative impact of lengthy guerrilla wars was thus at first social rather than economic: it involved the dissolution of existing social orders, the erosion of traditional authority and the growth of at least one generation deeply marked by war. In contrast to the expectations of Frantz Fanon, a theorist of the anti-colonial struggle, the climate of war and violence fostered the development not of free, self-confident people who had overcome the humiliation of colonial oppression, but rather of traumatized characters who hindered the building of a new society more than they advanced it.[71] Often they expected to be rewarded for the trials and tribulations they had suffered, and it was not easy to convince them that the real work of construction lay ahead and would decide whether the goals of the war had actually been achieved. Veterans of the guerrilla campaigns were (and are) one of the great burdens in the development of a new society and the stabilization of a new state. As a rule, they lay claim to lifelong benefits and expect to be better off materially than the rest of the population. The predictable consequences are corruption and mismanagement of the economy.

By the end of the twentieth century, hardly any of the countries that won independence through a guerrilla war was anywhere near achieving the goals set for the first few years after independence. There are thus good reasons to believe that the economic situation of the imperial periphery cannot be improved through a long war. To be sure, if one's own population is prepared for limitless suffering and sacrifice, it is possible with the help of guerrilla war to compensate for technological and organizational inferiority, to increase the costs of imperial rule, and eventually to force the colonial power to withdraw. But this usually goes together with such a degree of social devastation that political stability and economic prosperity become impossible for decades in the newly freed territories.

This balance-sheet can, of course, only be drawn retrospectively; it could not have been apparent to the contemporary players. Indeed, basing themselves on the revolutionary theories of the time, they were convinced that the political mobilization accompanying the popular uprising or guerrilla war would be directly carried over into a process of social modernization and economic development. This belief was illusory in every respect.[72]

So, anti-imperial players in the late twentieth century would have had good reason to avoid guerrilla warfare, at least if they saw the main objective of liberation as an improvement of the economic situation for people living in the territories at issue. Anyone concerned about living standards and social prosperity did well to avoid such methods. In any event, as soon as leaders decided that they wanted to participate in global economic development, they had to come to some new arrangement with the former imperial powers and to allow them considerable influence over their own social and economic order, especially if they wanted to have loans from the International Monetary Fund and the World Bank.[73]

Guerrilla warfare therefore turned out to be a double-edged form of anti-imperial struggle. The decline of Marxism, formerly the leading ideology of the liberation wars, is closely bound up with recognition of this fact. For, once social-economic considerations weighed more in favour of cooperation with the imperial centre than of struggle against imperialist exploitation, the Marxist approach to social-economic issues was no longer appropriate. In fact, long before the collapse of the Soviet Union, ethnic-nationalist and especially religious-cultural ideologies had largely taken the place of Marxism: they had the advantage, one might say, that they no longer made the success of the anti-imperial struggle dependent upon social-economic indicators, but laid the main emphasis on the assertion of ethnic, cultural or religious identity. Cost–benefit analysis is powerless to overcome this kind of identity anti-imperialism, whose rise, accompanying the decline of Marxism, led war and violence to lose their instrumental character and to acquire an existential dimension. They are no longer just a means to certain ends, but techniques of self-affirmation and self-confirmation. Those who have not mastered them go under, or at least forfeit their cultural identity. More important than the outcome of the struggle, then, is struggle for its own sake. What this means can be seen most sharply in the new forms of international terrorism, and particularly in the figure of the suicide bomber.

The relative value of cultural identity, in comparison with the opportunities and dangers of social-economic change in the periphery of the zones of prosperity, is therefore a key issue for future wars in the world and the nature of terrorist threats to the imperial centres. To put this more trenchantly, if the elites in the peripheral countries embrace economic growth in an effort to participate in material prosperity, certain compromises or ways of balancing interests are possible. But, if their main concern is to defend identities under threat from lifestyles in the imperial centres, there can be no compromise or balancing of interests. For, in a world of global economic, informational and media systems, the Western way of life cannot be restricted to particular regions; its spread is not under anyone's direct political control, but is driven by a variety of players in the economy and civil society, by the opening of new markets for Western goods, and by programmes to introduce mass education and equal rights for women. Besides, on the periphery of the imperial order, there are always influential groups who feel strongly attracted to, and wish to adopt for themselves, the values and lifestyles of the imperial centre. The struggle of anti-imperial players therefore begins as a civil war in peripheral societies over the values by which they are to be shaped.

If, in traditional civil wars, the struggle for political power was indissolubly bound up with a conflict over social values, we can now see two different types of civil war taking shape outside the imperial centre. On the one hand, warlord groupings fight one another for nothing more than military control of a certain territory, which is of interest to them because valuable mineral resources or raw materials are to be found there.[74] The values and religious-cultural orientations of people living there are of no concern to the warlords, who want to tyrannize the local population, not to educate or change them. On the other hand, there are civil wars in which control of mineral resources and political power play only a secondary role in comparison with cultural identity, because the people involved in them live by the customs of their ancestors, consider religious values as unconditional obligations, resist the hedonistic temptations of the West, and so on.

The imperial centre can remain politically and militarily detached from the first kind of civil war: the victorious party will enter the imperial economic cycle by itself, at the latest when it wishes to capitalize on the mineral resources over which the fighting took place; the raw materials in which the zones of prosperity are interested, and on which they have to rely, will therefore flow out to them, regardless of precisely who runs things in a particular area. If the imperial centre intervenes in these wars, it usually does so not in pursuit of political or economic interests, but because the crimes and atrocities of a warlord go beyond the hitherto accepted threshold and because a coalition of NGOs and media are demanding humanitarian action to stop the violence. Any intervention will at best be hesitant, however, especially if a quick end to the fighting is not in sight.

In the second type of civil war, where norms and values are the issue, the imperial centre shows just as little readiness to intervene. But, as the belligerents see things, it is already implicated, simply because the enemies of the regime currently in power attribute its persistence to imperial support and therefore become anti-imperial players. What they mainly reject and fight against is the soft power radiating from the imperial centres to the periphery, and so Joseph Nye's advice that the United States should rely more on soft power than hard power does not lead anywhere in such cases.[75] In fact, soft power exerts considerably greater influence than hard power on the lifestyles of societies: it changes people's identity, whereas hard power only affects power relations. Fundamentalism, in its various forms, is principally a kind of resistance to the soft power of an imperial centre. The resistance does not have to be violent. But, faced with the dynamic of the soft power that empire deploys, it is continually tempted to have recourse to violent methods.

Fundamentalist groupings, which engage in a fight over the internal values and orientations of their society,[76] become anti-imperial players if they hold the direct or indirect influence of the imperial centre responsible for the erosion of the values they cherish, and if they see in armed struggle the only way of halting a collapse of morals. An early variant of this religious-cultural anti-imperialism was the Maccabee revolt against Seleucid rule in Palestine, in the second century BC.[77] A group oriented to the morals and beliefs of their ancestors saw the gradual spread of Hellenistic culture, first to the Diaspora Jews and then to the upper layers in Jerusalem and Judaea, as a threat to their identity – especially their monotheism – and rose up in revolt against it.[78] The Seleucid king Antiochus IV Epiphanes tightened the repression in response, and this in turn helped to spread the rebellion, which was soon being fought along the lines of a guerrilla campaign. Only small units of the Seleucid army could operate in the mountain wildernesses in which the guerrilla groups were firmly entrenched. It was also to their advantage that Antiochus was under severe pressure from the Parthians in the East and faced the expanding power of Rome in the West, while in the centre rivalries and power struggles ensured that decisions could no longer be made with long-term effect. The Jewish rebels were therefore able to hold their ground politically and militarily, and in the end to win the struggle for political and religious autonomy.

Whatever the mix of political, religious and identity-centred motives among the Maccabees, the fact remains that at the beginning, when it seemed highly unlikely that little Judaea could assert itself against the mighty military apparatus of the Seleucids, religious factors played the main role in carrying the revolt along. However, the group of rebels was split into two: the moderates, who were content to recover the autonomy of Jerusalem's Jewish community, under a high priest not appointed by the Seleucids; and the radicals, for whom the real issues were far-reaching changes in the world and preparations for the coming of God's kingdom. What eventually emerged was the Jewish kingdom of the Hasmoneans, a largely independent state in Palestine, which was possible because the Seleucid empire had been weakened by decades of battles for the throne and gradual Roman penetration of the Middle East (although, of course, the Romans were not yet in a position to bring the whole region under their direct political control). In this post-imperial space, the kingdom of the Hasmoneans survived for more than a hundred years.

The political framework to which the Hasmonean kingdom owed its existence does not explain, however, the combativeness and spirit of self-sacrifice with which it was constructed. This inner dynamic was much more strongly marked by religion and identity issues than by politics. And the actual outcome of some fifty years of fighting scarcely corresponded to the defence of religious identity that had been the main concern of the rebels. The struggle began as a defence of tradition, soon became more radical, and finally assumed the dimensions of a fundamentalist movement. If the minimal prospects of success did not rapidly lead the rebels to give up, this certainly had something to do with the emergence of apocalyptic ideas; the myth of the four empires in the Book of Daniel, whose final end was supposed to have come, first appeared in the age of the Maccabee revolt.[79] In particular, the two Books of the Maccabees – the first of which gives a detailed historical account of the revolt, and the second a synthetic view of its course and motives – are imbued with the spirit of a religious-cultural 'anti-imperialism' that rejected on principle the unification of laws and customs within the *Oikumene*. The Hellenistic cosmopolis was perceived and fought against as a cosmodespotism.

The account in the Books of the Maccabees downplays the political dimension of the conflict and places the issue of religious identity at the heart of things. Jewish outrage at the cultural influence of the Seleucids was on the increase, and the building of a *Gymnasium* (a place for sports taken over from Greek culture) came as the last straw. Not only did pious Jews regard as a provocation the organization of physical exercises in the nude right next to the Temple; the cult of Heracles commonly observed in Hellenistic gymnasia would have brought the worship of pagan idols into the Holy City itself. While the first Book of the Maccabees emphasizes this introduction of pagan worship, the second lays greater stress on the secularization of everyday life under the influence of Hellenism. This makes it clear that the revolt was by no means only about the rejection of presumptuous Seleucid demands, and that from the beginning elements of intra-Jewish conflict were also present.[80] The collaboration of Jewish upper layers with the Seleucid authorities meant that civil war and anti-imperial struggle were often associated with each other.

Along with wars over economic resources, uprisings to defend religious-cultural identities have repeatedly caused empires to intervene militarily in their periphery. Political or religious motives have combined with issues of cultural identity, and the diffuseness of goals and intentions has not signified their weakness (as one would suspect within a Marxist tradition) but rather contributed to the fact that the groups in question have not fallen out with one another in debates over the correct political line. This is not the least of the reasons why the Jewish uprising against Seleucid rule, as depicted in the Books of the Maccabees, is an appropriate historical mirror for us today, since power politics once again runs together with issues of religious-cultural identity, and accounts of the Maccabee revolt always involve a decision about which of the two components carried greater weight.

Most important of all, the Maccabee revolt allows us to see how hard power and soft power worked together in the Seleucid empire. The military power of the Seleucids, which underpinned their occupation of Jerusalem and Judaea, was certainly an important reason for the uprising, but the attractiveness of Hellenistic culture was even more decisive (at least from the point of view of the Second Book of the Maccabees). This soft power threatened the religious identity of the Jewish community in Palestine, and it was this which ultimately led to violent action against the bearers and propagandists of Greek culture. Moreover, since religious traditions command unconditional recognition and their bonding power is weakened by secularization or enlightenment tendencies, traditionalists become fundamentalists in the event of a conflict between the two. This kind of conversion, often described as a radicalization but actually something more, takes place in the course of an uprising. Those who take up arms are no longer traditionalists but already fundamentalists: they wager on a restoration of community, and the renewal of its values takes the form of armed struggle. This becomes for them a moral purification, in which the community rids itself of traitors and apostates. But such a purification, which is a classical component of all civil wars, can fulfil its purpose only if it takes place in struggle against the seat of depravity, the imperial centre.

Here the parallels between the Maccabee rising and the terrorism of the last decade originating in the Islamic world reach their limits. The end of the Seleucid occupation of Jerusalem, together with the expulsion from Judaea of all devotees of Hellenistic culture and the establishment of the kingdom of the Hasmoneans, led to a stabilization that exempted Jeruslaem and Judaea from the Hellenization process in the Middle East. Today such solutions are no longer possible: the more intensive interchange of people and information means that cultures can no longer be kept isolated from one another. Cultural globalization increases the soft power of the imperial centre, whose attractiveness ensures a constant brain drain and a further increase in the soft power. The results are visible in a range of phenomena, from academic performance to the power to shape popular culture. The idea that this is all a deliberate manoeuvre to level cultural identities is certainly false, yet anti-imperial players seem to gain additional strength and support from precisely such convictions. If this is so, it is clear that anti-imperial struggle is no longer a means to liberate territories on the margins of empire – as it was until far into the twentieth century – but is being carried deep into the imperial centre itself. The form in which this happens is terrorism.

The difference between terrorism and guerrilla warfare is not only that the former is geared mainly to the *physical* consequences of violence and the latter to its *psychological* consequences, but also that guerrillas are in their innermost being *defensive*,[81] whereas terrorists may at any time act offensively. Furthermore, guerrillas rely for both support and cover on the population of the areas in which they operate. This is no longer the case with transnational terrorism, which is funded out of supporters' contributions and uses the infrastructure of countries in which it carries out attacks; some of the most important elements here are the high media density in the modern world, mass transportation systems, easy flight connections, access to the Internet and, not least, the anonymity of big cities. As the attacks in New York and Madrid showed, this infrastructure provides everything necessary: from the introduction of the operational unit through its ongoing supply to the conversion of aircraft into weapons and mobile phones into detonators.

But what is the strategic objective of the new forms of terrorism? Classical terrorism, as it arose in Russia towards the end of the nineteenth century, was directed against leading figures in the Tsarist regime and sections of its repressive apparatus. The aim was to intimidate the decision-making elite and, at the same time, to win over the people to the cause; the terrorist attacks were supposed to be the initial spark for a mass insurrection to bring down the existing regime. This worked better in national-revolutionary than in social-revolutionary movements. For transnational terrorism, however, the basic strategy is quite different. Attacks against civilian targets, in which anyone might be a victim, cannot win any sympathy; what we are really talking of is a modern variant of 'blowdown', a war to cause devastation in enemy territory. In essence, today's terrorists are following the same strategy as the nomadic horsemen did when they carried out a quick raid in a peaceful area of an empire, burning and pillaging their way through and disappearing before the imperial troops could catch them.

What speed of attack meant in this classical model is matched by the anonymity of terrorist players in the big city, their disappearance in a mass of strangers, and the high mobility they must achieve, not even by their own efforts but thanks to a convenient public transport system. The aim is not physically to destroy villages and towns, or to lay waste whole areas of land, but to cause serious damage by playing on the psychological volatility in post-heroic societies, by producing a state of terror and hysteria that interrupts normal life and economic and financial processes. It is not so much the strength of the attackers as the dramatic vulnerability of those they attack which ensures the effectiveness of the strategy. One effect may be that the imperial power finds it necessary to attack the terrorists' supposed places of origin and then becomes entangled in a classical guerrilla war, in which the asymmetrical superiority of the empire counts for little but the ability of anti-imperial players to create asymmetry can be fully brought to bear. Here weakness can change into strength, just as previously the terrorist attack, by virtue of its form, had turned the strength of empire into weakness.

In the twentieth century, when the periphery gained considerable power from the fact that an empire could no longer use everything it had to crush an uprising, the idea that the age of empire had come to an end had a certain plausibility. But it soon turned out to be a rash judgement. Instead of an end of all empires, there was yet another change in the form of imperial order. First the imperial power gave up trying to control territory on the ground, which made it vulnerable to attack, and switched to control from the air or outer space. This made it possible to strike partially and selectively. What the empire lost in political options, it made up for with various technological developments. Anti-imperial players responded to this by changing the main form of resistance from classical guerrilla warfare to new kinds of transnational terrorism. The arms races that had occurred under conditions of classical symmetry gave way to a race between technological innovation and strategic creativity. Therefore, it is now a fiscal rather than a territorial burden that poses the greatest threat to empires.

THE SURPRISING RETURN OF EMPIRE IN THE POST-IMPERIAL AGE

The mood changed in the space of a decade. Whereas, in the early 1980s, many Americans thought that their country was steadily declining, and that Japan or Europe (admittedly not the Soviet Union) might gain the upper hand, a new 'triumphalism' developed in the 1990s which celebrated the United States as by far the mightiest country on earth, with no end in sight to the 'American century'. Of course, the perception of such mood swings may have something to do with a changed focus on the part of the observer: he thinks he can detect a far-reaching change in attitudes when he has just slightly turned his head and caught sight of different debates and personalities; what appears to him as a change of object is simply a change of his field of vision.

In the late stages of the Cold War, when West Europeans mistakenly thought the United States was on the path of decline, they were mainly taking note of increased expressions of concern in America itself about the future of the country: about its falling industrial output, high crime rates, growing gap between rich and poor, problems in health and education, mounting national debt, low rate of savings, and notoriously high trade deficit. However, following the Soviet collapse and the American demonstration of power in the Gulf War (1991), it became a firmly established view in Europe that the USA had achieved a position of global dominance without parallel in history. What people then mainly noted were the voices depicting America in the role of a global policeman, which no longer merely stopped the worst villains from doing their evil deeds, but also ensured that the process of neoliberal globalization, from which the USA profited economically, could continue undisturbed.

A change in external perceptions of the United States may have exaggerated the mood swing, for many of the warnings and analyses that were being voiced in the 1980s are still audible today, especially as the problems of that earlier decade have by no means disappeared. But the impression that Americans now see themselves differently and have a new self-confidence is more than just the result of a changed perspective in Europe. The promotion of the USA to 'the only remaining superpower', the economic upturn of the 1990s, the accompanying realization that, in the economic competition with Western Europe and Japan (which precisely then were showing signs of exhaustion), America could not only hold its own but regain the lead, and finally the overcoming of the long trauma of Vietnam through the Gulf War: all this helped to dispel the idea that the zenith of American power already lay in the past. Americans felt confident of being equal to the challenges of the twenty-first century, and what had previously seemed a sign of decline was now a complicated problem for which a solution could be found. For, if the USA can't get on top of it, who can? The new self-confidence found expression in Madeleine Albright's striking image of the United States as 'the indispensable nation'.

For a long time, the central importance of the 1991 Gulf War for this change in mood was probably not fully appreciated. Not the least reason for this is that, despite the success of the war, George Bush Sr. was not re-elected to the presidency but had to hand over to the little-known Bill Clinton. In any event, the significance of the war for America's new mood of self-confidence can scarcely be overestimated. The Vietnam trauma had not only involved the bitter experience of military defeat at the hands of the Vietcong and North Vietnamese or humiliating memories of the hasty flight from the US embassy in Saigon on 29 April 1975. There was also the related fear that, after a century in which it had gone from one victory to another in foreign wars, America's history of military successes had come to an end. The collapse of the shah's regime in Iran in 1979, the holding hostage of USA embassy staff in Tehran for nearly fifteen months and the fiasco of the attempt to free them in April 1980 seemed to confirm such fears. But then the rapid military victory in the Gulf desert put the Vietnam experience into a new perspective, allowing it to be seen as a brief interlude in the history of American successes that could now finally be handed over to Hollywood for social-moral reprocessing. Perhaps the clearest sign of the mood change was that films critical of the Vietnam War gave way to the kind of 'epic' through which Americans usually anchor their wars in the collective memory of the political community.[1]

Victory in the Gulf War did not only have a therapeutic function in relation to the Vietnam trauma; it also showed that the USA had clear superiority over the still-existing Soviet Union (which had supplied the Iraqi army with weapons and the basis for its military strategy), and that the economic performance of Japan and Germany was not to be feared so long as it could be roped into service for America's own ends. It is well known, in fact, that Japan and Germany paid the bulk of US war costs in 1991. But the most important point is that the USA suffered a minimal number of casualties: it had built up such an asymmetrical superiority in weaponry that it could again wage war successfully at any point on the globe.[2] In the aftermath of the Gulf War, the military became a convenient instrument of US foreign policy. What this meant became clear in the course of the 1990s, and even more so after 11 September 2001, when the US government increasingly used the military as a political problem-solver.

The Gulf War experience must have been a major reason why the US administration, unlike its counterparts in Europe, did not take the end of the East–West conflict as an opportunity to cut its arms expenditure and pocket the peace dividend, but made further investments in building up its military capability. This would have been a wrong decision on Washington's part if it had seen Europe's and Japan's success in catching up economically as the real threat to the US position. But the nightmare scenario actually looked quite different. In continuing to build up the military apparatus, even in the absence of a challenge from a direct competitor, Washington was wagering on the option of an imperial policy for the country. This was all the more remarkable in view of the general consensus at the time that empires were a thing of the past. As the historian Alexander Demandt put it: 'The self-dissolution of the Soviet Union on 31 December 1991 brought the age of empire to an end. For three thousand years world politics was shaped by world empires. Now that is over.'[3]

Analyses of the end of empire and the problem of post-imperial areas

The twentieth century – especially if we follow Eric Hobsbawm's view of it as a short century, beginning in 1914 and ending in 1989[4] – was characterized by a succession of waves that brought about the collapse of empires. Already before the First World War, the

Ottoman, Austro-Hungarian and Tsarist empires were thought of as unstable, unreformable and doomed to fall. At a certain point, the leading politicians in Vienna, St Petersburg and Istanbul began to think that war might help them stave off the threat. None of them was successful, however: the Tsarist empire did not even survive until the end of the war, and the peace negotiations at Saint-Germain and Sèvres were already conducted with the successor states to the Habsburg monarchy and the Ottoman empire. Of the major empires covering Central, Eastern or Southeastern Europe and the Middle East/Arabia, Germany was the only survivor – albeit with a considerable loss of territory, and only because its internal structure was more that of a nation-state than an empire.

It can scarcely be said, however, that a stable order of nation-states emerged in place of the imperial order; the population in the new states was too heterogeneous for that, and so too were the interests and motives of the Western victors that could have kick-started it. It is true that US President Woodrow Wilson proclaimed the right of nations to self-determination, but the negative attitude of Congress made it impossible for him to provide American support for the process of reconstruction and stabilization in Europe. Besides, he was unable to assert himself against the divergent interests at Versailles and returned to Washington a failed politician.[5]

Eric Hobsbawm has described the attempt to apply the right to national self-determination as a disaster that left an enduring mark on twentieth-century European politics. It soon became the cause for a flurry of wars and civil wars, because nation-state frontiers could not structure the areas formerly under imperial rule without creating new minorities, injustices and repression.[6] The problems of Central and Southern Europe, starting with the ethnic expulsions from Turkey or Greece and ending with the eradication of Czechoslovakia in the spring of 1939, before the whole area was repeatedly shaken up by the Second World War,[7] may be seen as paradigmatic for post-imperial configurations. Many of the interwar developments there – from attempts at infiltration and destabilization by the former imperial powers through military putsches to ethnic conflicts and civil wars in the successor states – would recur in a different form in the post-colonial and post-Soviet era.

In 1918–19 the United States was not willing, and indeed not capable, of guaranteeing the political order in Central and Southeastern Europe. So, the post-imperial area was largely left to its own devices: the USA pulled back, defeated Germany was too weak and had its hands tied by the Versailles Treaty, and the newly emerging Soviet Union initially failed in its attempt to establish ideological or even political dominance in the region. After 1945, however, Central and to some extent Southeastern Europe became Moscow's so-called external empire, and when the USSR finally fell apart the United States and its West European allies assumed the functions from which they had recoiled in the interwar years, ranging from economic aid through political stabilization to military intervention. In Bosnia and Kosovo a military operation was presented as a humanitarian action; no doubt it was that too, but in essence it was an external intervention that was supposed to prevent a repetition of what had happened between the wars. That the USA, the 'power alien to the area' [*raumfremde Macht*],[8] took on the main responsibility was due initially to the fact that it alone had the necessary military capacities. It also had the advantage of being able to fulfil the imperial *task* of keeping the peace, without having to fear – as European countries would – that it was falling into an imperial *role*.

A focus on Central and Southeastern Europe, where the dawning post-imperial age had to face its first test, reveals a peculiar dialectic which appeared many times in the twentieth century with the collapse of an empire. Post-imperial areas have to rely on stabilization from outside in order to have a stable order within; they need time to develop their own political structures, and can sustain them only if they find a power which – temporarily – fulfils some of the functions of imperial order without assuming the position of the old empire. It was not least this challenge which favoured the rise of the United States to the position of global power. The post-imperial age, so often proudly proclaimed in the twentieth century, therefore rests upon a paradox: it has to rely on a player which, according to its own suppositions, should no longer exist. Niall Ferguson, referring to the United States, has called this the 'imperialism of anti-imperialism'.[9]

After 1918–19 Woodrow Wilson put his trust in the ability of the League of Nations, newly founded in Geneva, to stabilize the post-imperial areas. Certainly, only such an international body could have been expected to carry out these tasks without slipping into an imperial role. But the fact that a construct is theoretically convincing does not at all mean that it can work in practice. The history of the League of Nations is a history of failure in the face of this challenge. Precisely out of fear that it would overfulfil its duties and end up in an imperial position, the League of Nations underfulfilled them.[10] It proved incapable of stabilizing the post-imperial formations in Central and Southeastern Europe, and this became one of the causes of the Second World War. It cannot be doubted that Nazi Germany actually started the war, but its very possibility had to do with the failure of the League of Nations.[11]

The interwar power vacuum in Central and Southeastern Europe therefore made the construction of new empires more or less inevitable. The foreign policies of Hitler and Stalin may be regarded as attempts to destroy the nation-state system and to return to an imperial order, in Central as well as in Northern and Southeastern Europe. For the Germans this meant a revision of the Versailles Treaty, for the Russians a revision of the Treaty of Brest-Litovsk (which they had only partly achieved at the end of the Civil War).[12] The coalition between Hitler and Stalin came as a surprise only to those who had focused on ideological contradictions and overlooked geostrategic interests.[13]

Hitler's empire-building foundered on a worldwide coalition of the great powers, while Stalin's finally collapsed – forty years after his death – because resources had become overstretched. At the end of the Second World War, Stalin used the power vacuum created by Germany's withdrawal from Eastern and Central Europe to shift the western frontiers of his empire to the Elbe and the Vltava. In this way, however, he provoked the formation of an anti-Soviet coalition between the United States and Western Europe, whose potential was greatly superior to that of the Soviets. Thus, in order to maintain a structural military balance, the Soviet Union had to spend five to six times more of its GDP than the USA and Western Europe.

In the hope of gradually undermining the West's superiority, Moscow began systematically to support liberation movements in the Third World. But it was an illusory hope, and all that remained of it in 1991, when the Soviet Union fell apart, was accumulated Third World debts totalling 130 billion dollars.[14] Even by Western standards such a level of irrecoverable debt was enormous; for the Soviet Union it was a disaster. The pressures of imperial power had led it to push its external lines too far and to overstretch its internal resources, and no withdrawal from empire could now be enough to restore a balance.

The last imperial power, which had ruled western Eurasia for centuries, thus departed from the political stage. Already, in other parts of the globe, all the signs had been pointing to the end of the imperial age: by 1945 not only Nazi Germany but also imperial Japan had failed in their attempt at empire-building, and the European colonial powers, which had lost a lot of territory during the war, would lose the rest over the next two decades (Portugal being the one exception). The East–West conflict did not work in favour of a restoration of the old colonial empires, and the supreme Western power, the

United States, had a considerably reduced interest in helping the Europeans to recover them. Commenting on the attempt by Britain and France (acting together with Israel) to regain control of the Suez Canal after its nationalization under Nasser, President Eisenhower once asked the telling question: 'How can we possibly support Britain and France if in doing so we were to lose the whole Arab world [to the Soviet Union]?'[15] One of the few cases in which Washington took a different line was Indochina, and even then it did so only because the Vietminh, the national liberation movement, had close links with the Soviet Union and China.[16]

With a few exceptions, the age of the European colonial empires ended without bloodshed, and the Europeans handed over power to indigenous elites whom they had poorly prepared for the job.[17] The problems we have just outlined in relation to the post-imperial areas of Central and Southeastern Europe made themselves felt here at a very early date, and there was no power 'alien to the area' which could have fulfilled the long-term tasks of imperial order without claiming for itself an imperial position. At the time of the East–West conflict, it is true, both blocs exerted a temporarily stabilizing influence, but both sought a reward for their imperial tasks by claiming an imperial role for themselves. The Soviet Union, like the United States, acquired considerable influence over the internal affairs of Third World countries that it helped to keep stable with military and economic aid. It therefore long escaped notice how internally weak and endangered were most of the post-colonial states, and the fact that each of them gained a seat in the United Nations was considered sufficient proof of their viability as states. When the Soviet Union broke up at the beginning of the 1990s, and the remaining American superpower lost interest in the Third World, it suddenly became clear that many of the new states created in the 1950s and 1960s were no more than façades which would collapse at the first major upheaval.[18] The replacement of an imperial order with a pluriverse of states had again turned out to be beset with risks and difficulties. However, none of the problems regarding the stabilization of post-imperial areas changed the view that the age of empires had come to an end.

There were (and still are) three basic arguments for this view. *First*, there is the relative decline in the power of any potential imperial player. Paul Kennedy put it like this in 1989: 'The United States today has roughly the same massive array of military obligations across the globe as it had a quarter-century ago, when its shares of world GNP, manufacturing production, military spending, and armed forces personnel were so much larger than they are now.'[19]

For Kennedy, then, everything suggests that the USA should cut back on its commitments to avoid hastening its decline through imperial overstretch.[20]

Second, some writers emphasize that the greater self-confidence of today's subject peoples and their much-increased capacity to resist a single world empire have hugely increased the costs. Along with political rationality, measured chiefly in cost–benefit terms, the extension of public scrutiny by omnipresent media is supposed to have made a neo-imperial policy unattractive, if not downright impossible. Not even the resurgent idea of just war, which has always had a strong affinity with imperial policies, can make up for this handicap.

Third, doubts are raised about whether an empire can ever be profitable under modern conditions: if, as some economic historians suggest,[21] nineteenth-century and early twentieth-century imperialism already cost more than it brought in, it should be assumed that the disproportion has meanwhile become even more pronounced.[22] Imperial ambitions are therefore antiquated projects, which will soon founder in the changed conditions. They are bothersome irruptions of the past into a present that is moving in a different direction.

The idea that the age of empire was at an end could therefore point to a number of persuasive arguments, which rested not upon the normative desirability of certain circumstances but upon economic considerations and power politics. All the more surprising, then, was the way in which the United States suddenly began to redefine its perspectives in terms of a new empire.

The United States: the new empire

The numerous analyses of the end of empire that ran through political journalism at the turn of the twenty-first century often looked ahead to a new world order, but certainly not to a return of empire. However, Europeans in particular continued to have great hopes that the United Nations would finally assume the responsibilities that had been planned for it when it was founded at the end of the Second World War. Until the collapse of the Soviet Union, blockage in the Security Council had meant that this mission could be only partly fulfilled, if at all. But now, with the end of the East–West conflict, such problems had been overcome.

Another reason for the greater weight of the UN was the declining sovereignty of states, which could no longer play the two roles that had once made them great: the creation of external security and the underwriting of a stable currency.[23] The state's decreased powers of control, together with the growing necessity of handing over sovereignty to transnational institutions, led to an expectation that the era of global organization was beginning in earnest. This feeling was especially widespread in Western Europe, not least because of its good experiences with the Organization for Security and Cooperation in Europe (OSCE) and the European Union (EU). It was thought that Europe's evolution after the Second World War should serve as a model for the new world order.[24]

Along with the model of a community of states, there was a growing sense that the state was withdrawing from the spaces of the economy, that these were becoming globally interconnected and structurally independent of territorial boundaries.[25] The kind of national state that took shape in the sixteenth and seventeenth centuries has gradually disappeared; it was not a system of spaces and structures but one of movements and flows, whether it was a question of capital, services, information or labour. The state lost some of its power along with its functionality, and this part of its power dissolved into the self-regulation of market regimes and the political activity of non-governmental organizations (NGOs).[26]

Both perspectives of a new world order – the UN-centred international community and the network of global metropolises – underestimated the importance of the periphery and its repercussions on the centre. It was these, above all, which led to the unexpected revival of the model of imperial order and created a certain sympathy for it even among liberal intellectuals. (One thinks of Richard Rorty's statement that, in the current situation, *Pax Americana* is the best the world can hope for.)[27]

In the state system in which the UN was the central locus of negotiation and the supreme decision-making authority, it was simply assumed that stable states existed throughout the world which had only to be made part of a legally binding regime based on negotiation. The ill-conceived and ultimately false character of this assumption became apparent in the 1990s, when the term 'failing states' came to be widely used in relation to the incipient breakdown of states. For only in Western and Central Europe, North America and East Asia does one find the form of state required for a functioning world order in the sense defined above. In Central and South America, Africa and the Middle East, the Caucasus, Central Asia and parts of Southeast Asia, such a state system first has to be created (or re-created), and the question is whether globalization will eliminate it more quickly than it can be built up. At the same time, successful nation-building is fraught with consequences not only for the importer of stability but also for the exporter of stability. Protectorates and mandated territories come into being, and those who prevent the open use of force there, build up new infrastructure and superintend the whole conversion process end up assuming a quasi-imperial role, even if it is defined in advance as temporally limited and is designed to make itself eventually superfluous.[28] Time and again it has been the United States which, in assuming the responsibilities, has also played the role of the pacifying empire. Bosnia, Kosovo and Afghanistan are examples of this.

With regard to the network of metropolises that a fluid system is supposed to produce, it has been evident at least since 11 September 2001 how delicate its structures really are. The wealthy and dynamic centres are not interested in areas outside the network, and unlike in the nation-building model they do not invest in the creation of order there. But those areas can serve as a base for attacks on the highly vulnerable lines of communication among the metropolitan centres, and so it becomes indispensable to make them secure.[29] In short, in the face of new forms of war and warfare, the blueprints for a new world order have proved inadequate or illusory. In the case of the UN order, the international community has been unable to control the resource wars among warlords, liberation movements and religious warriors. As to the idea of metropolitan networks, transnational terrorism has inserted itself into the global flows of goods and capital, people and services, using them for its logistical purposes and for the staging of surprise attacks.[30]

As discussion resumed on the political-economic model of empire, it soon became clear that it promised precisely what the UN-centred international community and the network of metropolises were incapable of delivering: namely, a decisive push into areas without a state, in order at least to prevent genocide and massacres, and to protect the fragile lines of communication among the world's great economic centres. The first of these tasks now traded under the name of humanitarian military intervention, the second under that of the war on terror; it was scarcely surprising that the two rapidly merged in the deployment of imperial power. Accordingly, the debate on empire started up again as a critique of empire.

The first question to be thrown up was whether the return of empire was a process of political will, and therefore one which could be undone, or whether structural exigencies were shaping the behaviour of leading players in the United States, irrespective of who held office in the White House. More specifically, the question was whether the United States would have taken the road of political unilaterialism if George W. Bush had not been elected president and the neocons had not gained any influence over policy. In fact, not a few critics hold the view that American politics has acquired an imperial character mainly as a result of personal decisions by the president, under the influence of his advisers and their ideological orientation.[31] If that were the case, the question of the logic of empire would be settled, and we would have to turn our attention to the psychopathology of George W. Bush and his entourage; that is indeed what the film-maker Michael Moore has done in his highly journalistic manner. The more complex variant of this question asks instead whether the rise of empires is due mainly to imperialistically minded politicians in the centre or to structural problems on the margins. What has been said above would suggest that an imperial mission creates a sense of duty among political elites, shapes the way in which they see problems, and provides a not insignificant legitimation resource for the corresponding decisions.

Probably this question cannot be answered once and for all. The Mongol world empire, for example, would never have come into being without the person of Genghis Khan: it was he who created a military organization which, by virtue of its internal structures, not only proved capable of extensive conquests but was *compelled* to engage in a whole series of them. On the other hand, the history of the steppe empires shows the regular formation of allegiance groups capable of expansion – a phenomenon observable from the Huns through the Avars to the Mongols, which suggests that the geographical conditions in Central Asia did not merely favour but actually prompted the emergence of charismatic imperialists. As we have seen, this may have continued down to the Tsarist empire, or even the Soviet Union, the last imperialist power in the area. There are power vacuums and differences in economic development which, alongside the decisions of charismatic conquerors, are decisive for empire-building.

It may be objected that a foresighted policy has to resist this undertow, at the end of which usually lies some form of imperial overstretch. Whether this is possible or not depends on the degree to which the decision-makers rely on the greed of their coercive apparatus and the moods of their population. In empires with a strong military aristocracy or a dynamic bourgeoisie, the undertow may be so strong that the political leadership is unable to escape it. And, in democratic empires, the electorate may place demands which, combined with the pressure of pictures and reports of massacres, famines and endless civil wars, force politicians to intervene and thereby increase the suction coming from the periphery. The concept of liberal or democratic imperialism[32] – or what Michael Ignatieff calls 'Empire lite'[33] – has been introduced to describe this.

For a long time it was not at all acceptable in the United States to speak of an American empire. Paul Kennedy, in his much-noted book, referred instead to Great Powers,[34] and talk of empires was reserved for the past,[35] except perhaps as a critical label for the Soviet Union. Its affirmative use breaks a taboo, as those who indulge in it must have considered beforehand.

When critics of the Vietnam War charged the USA with imperialism, it was a polemical usage designed to shake a nation proud of its anti-imperialist self-image. If there was ever positive talk of an American empire, it could scarcely have been intended in the sense of a continuation of earlier empires; the point would have been to underline how different it was from them, and especially from the policy of imperialism – and for that reason terms such as 'informal empire', 'empire by invitation' or 'consensual empire' were introduced.[36]

What, then, is really new about the American empire? Michael Ignatieff speaks of a 'new form of imperial rule for a postmodern age', characterized by a commitment to human rights and democracy as well as the creation and safeguarding of free markets. For Andrew Bacevich, the novelty has to do with America's lack of satellite states in the classical sense and its exercise of global influence through intermediate institutions, such as NATO, the UN, the International Monetary Fund and the World Bank. Charles Maier sees it in a mixture of economic interchange and security guarantees, while for Dan Diner the key point is nothing other than America's safeguarding of the world market through power politics, whose constant expansion leaves the rest of the world less and less power to shape things.[37]

Many critics of American empire see nothing substantively new in its form of rule, which they place within the tradition of classical imperialism.[38] A key indicator of this is said to be Washington's division of the globe into five regional commands, which ensure that US interests are not endangered. The regional commanders for Latin America, Europe, the Middle East, the Pacific and North America, who are sometimes compared to Roman proconsuls, can currently draw on 250,000 troops spread around more than 700 bases in more than 150 countries, from where they can be rapidly deployed without a long march. But, even if no troops are actually used, the bases themselves exert a constant influence in each region. With their help it is possible to stabilize or intimidate governments.[39]

For the critics, they are the backbone of the new empire and permit Washington to continue an imperial policy tradition going back to the nineteenth century. 'Our imperial history', writes Johnson, 'is littered with bases on foreign soil.'[40]

Other critics argue that, already by the nineteenth century, imperialism no longer limited itself to administrative-military governance or the control of trading stations, and that the *modern* form of imperialism has sought above all to open up markets for cheap goods industrially produced in the imperial centre.[41] This was what the British did in the Opium War of 1840–42, which brutally ended China's separate trade policy. And Commodore Matthew C. Perry's demonstration of gunboat power in Yokohama harbour, which in 1853 forced open Japan for European and American trade, was significant not militarily but economically. It was a question not of geopolitics but geo-economics – also a kind of imperial policy, even if it did not employ the usual forms of colonial rule. Market imperialism was already complementing the classical forms of colonial imperialism in the nineteenth century, and since then the globalization process has gone so far that 'gunboat economics' is scarcely required any longer. The IMF and World Bank have taken its place as instruments of global economic and financial policy, which in large measure corresponds to American interests.[42]

In this view, empire-building through the control of globalization processes is not the novelty that Dan Diner and others assume it to be, when they identify open-door policies to break down protectionism as an American *nomos* distinct from the path taken in continental Europe.[43] Britain's free trade imperialism in the Victorian age also pursued that objective, and it went together with a liberal internationalism which believed that the victory of free trade principles over state protectionism would help to generate peace in the world. Yet, within a few decades, the opening of markets to European goods and European capital undermined the political stability of the areas exposed to them, and Europeans had to try to restore it by sending out troops and building up administrative structures of their own.

Critics of a US empire based on economic globalization argue that the cycle of American empire-building will also follow this model: globalization produces 'failed states', because economic development there erodes the state monopoly of force; warlords then take control of territory in which mineral rents can be extracted for a long time; and, as a result, the globalization process has to be safeguarded on the margins of empire through military intervention and nation-building. Gradually, then, global markets give rise to an imperialist interventionism and a succession of peace-making wars,[44] which may yield a precarious kind of global supremacy but not a new world order. Increasingly the United States will be forced to bank on its military strength rather than economic integration and cultural attractions – that is, to convert soft power into hard power. The American cycle, like the British before it, will end in peripheral wars and increased deployment of its armed forces. But today war and military force are much less capable of solving problems than they were in the late nineteenth century. The American empire will therefore fail in a relatively short time because of a mismatch between the problems requiring solution and its limited capacity to solve them. What will be decisive, these critics argue, is that America has too little of the kinds of power that matter in the twenty-first century, and too much of those which are today of only limited relevance. 'The American empire', writes Michael Mann, 'will turn out to be a military giant, a back-seat economic driver, a political schizophrenic and an ideological phantom.'[45]

Of course, peace-keeping wars in the periphery may also be seen as a consequence of imperial overstretch, so that they become less important the more supremacy is concentrated in the *inner* rings and ellipses of the zones of prosperity, safeguarding them against threats pressing in from the periphery. This is precisely what characterized the policy of the Romans and Chinese after their imperial areas had been consolidated. *Imperial* policy, we may say, differs from *imperialist* policy by virtue of this focus on the centre: it pays only the attention that is strictly necessary to areas outside the empire, whereas imperialist policy is veritably obsessed with the periphery and is convinced that the greatest challenges lie there. Accordingly, imperialist policy sets greater store by the military side of things, whereas imperial policy attaches relatively little importance to it in comparison with economic, political and cultural power.[46]

On this analysis, what the critics of US empire see as the cause of its inevitable decline is due more to a misguided entanglement in the problems of the periphery; a clever game of divide and rule would seek instead to get its adversaries to weaken themselves. Thus, for Chalmers Johnson, Clinton was a more astute politician of empire than George W. Bush, who has given in to the temptations of an imperialist policy.[47]

An imperial, in contrast to imperialist, policy would mean that the United States saw itself mainly as guarantor of the denser economic links among Europe, America and East Asia, playing the role of 'ideal total capitalist' to ensure that their level of commercial and scientific exchange did not suddenly sink as it did at the end of the 1920s (to regain its former level only in the 1990s).[48] If the survival of empires – including maritime and land empires, though perhaps not steppe empires – is conditional on the development of denser and more intense economic exchange within the imperial space, then the most important tasks of imperial policy are to establish legal rules for this economic area, to prevent competition from taking a military form, to ensure a stable currency (or stable exchange-rates among the several currencies), to promote technological innovations that make the imperial space superior to its surrounding areas, and to safeguard it against external attack: in short, to fulfil the role that it assumed in crossing the Augustan threshold. For an empire to last, it has to stop military spending from getting out of hand in the economics of imperial power.

The possibility of such an optimal weighing of tasks naturally depends not only on the shrewdness of government politicians, but also on whether the strategic resources for the economy are available within the imperial space itself or have to be imported. The latter case may set up constant pressure to exercise direct rule over parts of the periphery, and in this sense the need to control oil supplies and the price of oil is the Achilles heel of the American empire.

A perspective of ensuring supplies by peaceful means, rather than by military expansion, leads to a moral paradox with far-reaching implications. Any kind of humanitarian intervention in the periphery or beyond – what we described above as a core element of the imperial mission – then becomes a moral luxury that the empire is unable to afford for economic reasons and in which it should not engage. Within the logic of an empire geared to its own economic prosperity, it may be rational to intervene militarily to safeguard and control oil supplies, but not to end civil wars or to 'build nations' outside the central zone of empire. Such a conclusion would mean saying goodbye to the imposition and safeguarding of human rights – a project so favoured by liberal intellectuals,[49] but the kind of ideological trap into which empires fall when, overestimating their capabilities, they allow themselves to be enlisted for goals that contradict their own survival imperatives.

This would not be the first time in history that a conflict has developed between imperial rationality and imperial mission, which could then be resolved only through compromise. It occurred to the Spanish world empire, for reasons of self-preservation and resource protection, to pull back from its militant project of the Counter-Reformation. But it was unable to do this because of its imperial mission, which gave the empire its legitimacy and the ruling elite its motivation for action. When the mission became less important in the seventeenth century, this was a sign that the imperial momentum had been exhausted – and was interpreted as such by other political players.

The United States today finds itself facing just such a dilemma. The peaceful safeguarding of resources would imply not taking on too many global commitments. In order to hold its subglobal world, an astute imperial policy should keep out of the problems of the global world and protect itself from them by drawing 'imperial boundaries with the barbarians';[50] what happened outside would then concern the empire only if it posed a threat to its own security. To a large extent, the policy of long-lasting empires – the Chinese and the Roman, in particular – was geared to such a perspective. But it is scarcely an option in the age of democracy and media saturation: it would continually contradict the imperial mission of the United States, and without such a projection of moral purpose the US empire would lose much of its strength. To put it plainly, it may be that the American empire will founder not on external enemies but on the moral overload associated with its mission, because this makes it impossible to maintain the required indifference to the external world.

A democratic empire?

Many have doubted whether a democratic order can be lastingly combined with the deployment of imperial power. As a rule, empire goes together with authoritarian or even autocratic leadership in the centre, so that democratization would be synonymous with collapse of the empire. The end of the Soviet empire would seem to confirm this thesis. In fact, it bears the strong imprint of Roman history, in which Rome's military expansion in the Mediterranean destroyed the republican order and triggered a century of inner turmoil and civil wars. Under Octavian/Augustus the republican institutions became a mere façade, concealing a system in which neither the people nor the patriciate had decisive political influence.

The establishment of the empire and the demise of the republic went hand in hand: this idea impressed itself on generations not only of Europeans but also of Americans, whose political system is more strongly geared than that of any European country to the Roman model.[51] It is true that the Roman example played a role in the French Revolution, but it was relevant mainly to the extension of

French power in Southern and Central Europe, during the rise of Bonaparte to first consul, and finally to emperor. Players and observers alike saw the reflection more of imperial than republican imperial Rome, whereas in America it was precisely the institutions of the Roman Republic that were supposed to offer a way of avoiding the emergence of factions, the rise of party leaders and the eventual destruction of the republic itself.[52]

This is the anti-imperial foundation on which the United States came to understand itself. It crucially shaped that detachment from the challenges of world politics which again and again marked American politics in the nineteenth and twentieth centuries. It is therefore scarcely surprising if radical critics repeatedly draw parallels with late republican Rome, to demonstrate the incompatibility of a republican order with imperial politics, and to argue that democracy is being eliminated in the contemporary United States.[53] The evidence for this claim that is usually mentioned first is a growing uniformity of the media, which are seen as propaganda instruments for government policy.

But those who are more positive, or at least open-minded, about America's imperial position see a tension between its democratic system at home and the requirements of its policy abroad. Michael Ignatieff expresses this in the formula that the burdens of empire are long-lasting, but democracies have little time and are always in a hurry.[54] The frequent checks on high office in a democracy, together with the limitation of the US presidency to two four-year terms and the people's expectation that problems will be solved in a reasonably short period, do not fit well with the exigencies of imperial policy, where success can usually be promised only in a matter of decades. Here, action taken under time pressure generally leads to negative results. Whereas, in internal politics, bad outcomes can be corrected in the medium term or reversed by a change of government, mistakes in foreign policy, especially those of a global 'number one', nearly always have long-term consequences and may be very difficult to correct.

Probably, Washington's growing tendency in recent years to use the military for problem-solving also has something to do with the time pressure built into democratic mechanisms. Military solutions offer themselves with a suggestion of speed and finality, so that an 'empire in a hurry' may grasp at them more often than would be sensible or advisable. If this is true, it points to the surprising conclusion that democratic empires resort more readily than authoritarian empires to military methods. This would explain the number of wars in which the USA has been involved since 1945.[55]

On the other hand, democratic societies are less belligerent: they do not regard wars as a way of gaining fame and honour, but subject them to a cost–benefit analysis that often shows them to be ineffective and overly expensive. On closer observation, it may be hard to win popular support for a presidential decision to go to war, and so many wars may be concealed from view or begun under false pretences. American military interventions have drawn on a wide range of lies and deceit: from the so-called Tonking incident in 1964, which was used as a pretext for the first air strikes against North Vietnam; through the supposed killing of Kuwaiti babies in incubators, which ostensibly motivated an American attack on Iraq in 1990–91; down to the claim that Saddam Hussein's weapons of mass destruction were a threat to the free world.[56] Such trickery has regularly been cited as proof of the thorough duplicity of the foreign policy of the United States, which conjures up threats and dangers to impose its own interests and to extend its sphere of influence. What this usually overlooks, however, is the structural pressure to conjure up threats as the only way of motivating a democratic public to take on imperial obligations. The politics of deception and stage-management serves to close the gap between democracy and empire.

The danger to democracy that this represents in the long run is not open to doubt. Not many commentators point out, however, that it is also a perilous makeshift from the point of view of the requirements of empire, since democracy, in our conception of ourselves, has a higher value than empire (if the latter is held to have any value at all as a political system). The most dangerous threat to democracy yet uncovered has to be Operation Northwoods, a plan devised in the early 1960s by US Chief of Staff Lyman Lemnitzer, in which terrorist attacks were to be staged in the streets of American cities, and civilians gunned down without warning, in order to win the support of the American people for an invasion of Cuba.[57] It is true that Lemnitzer had to withdraw this plan after it leaked out, but the suspicion has remained that the US government not only invents threats but actually stages attacks against its own people. Since 9/11 this has given rise to a number of veritable conspiracy theories.[58]

Of course, in the first half of the twentieth century, the United States had a number of experiences of war which differed markedly from those of continental Europe, and which help to explain why American voters have repeatedly been prepared to assume at least some of the military burdens of the imperial project. In the two world wars, in particular, the United States emerged as the only victor – in the sense that it had fewer casualties than the other main belligerents, but also gained the most economically.[59]

The United States entered the First World War as a debtor nation and came out of it as the largest creditor. At the same time, owing to the burdens that the war had left for its European rivals, it gained access to markets in which it had previously had almost no presence. After the Second World War, when Germany and Japan were for a long time out of the picture and the British empire was on its last legs, the United States was able to come forward as by far the strongest political and economic power. Thus, although US capital profited the most from war, ordinary Americans knew from their own experience that it could be closely associated with good times economically.

The long period during which people were willing to bear the burden of the Vietnam War is explicable in terms of this memory of the world wars. But then confidence in the expediency of war was so badly shaken that it resulted in a period of economic as well as psychological depression; only with the Gulf War in 1991 could Americans again 'plug into' the experiences of the second half of the century. Nevertheless, although it is generally true that modern wars cost more than they bring in, this can be applied without reservation only to individual countries. Empires, under certain circumstances, can certainly show a net profit on wars, both politically and economically – that is, when rival powers weaken one another in them and bear the brunt of the costs. A war can also be useful for an empire if the external threat associated with it helps to strengthen the internal cohesion of the imperial space. Such wars stem centrifugal tendencies and make empire appear a more rational proposition. The Gulf War had this effect, whereas the Iraq War had the opposite effect. It remains to be seen what will be the medium- to long-term consequences of the 'war on terror'.

According to Andrew Bacevich, even if the American people broadly supported the imperial project – which he doubts – one would still have to say that the US political system was not the best suited for it. As soon as demands are made on it for long periods of time, the public support turns out to be unreliable, since people 'expect the benefits of empire to outweigh the burdens and responsibilities, and to do so decisively'.[60] In contrast to authoritarian empires, those with a democratic form of rule or a highly responsive population are scarcely able to endure long periods in which imperial policies cost more than they bring in. We might even say that the pressure to come up with booty is greater in the case of democratic than authoritarian empires.[61]

Of course, in so far as post-heroic societies do not attach a central importance to war, this concept of booty pressure has only the force of metaphor in relation to democratic empires.[62] Whereas, in the period of ascent of earlier empires, war booty was not just a motive but a *resource* for expansion, it has not been possible to say this anywhere since the German and Japanese attempts at empire-building collapsed in 1945. In principle, however, the industrial revolution already changed the motivational structure of empire-building and the imperatives of imperial policy; expansion no longer involved mainly the appropriation of foreign resources and possessions or the exploitation of militarily subjugated labour-power, but had as its main purpose the opening of markets for goods produced in the economically advanced countries. What was taken as booty was not the wealth of subject peoples but their consumption needs or – given that industry in the imperial heartlands could produce goods more cheaply than peripheral handicrafts – their technological backwardness.

The chief prerequisite for this kind of imperial policy is therefore economic (rather than military) superiority. The only resources that play a role are mineral resources, whose exploitation becomes economically attractive precisely when the industrial revolution converts them from fossil substances or ore deposits into a valuable natural *resource*. The British empire pursued this course most assiduously; the continental Europeans and North Americans followed its model, while the Tsarist empire remained caught up in old ways for which it paid a heavy price in the defeats of the early twentieth century.[63]

The problem with empire-building on the basis of economic rather than military superiority is that it cannot avoid military deployment to safeguard newly opened economic areas. No serious difficulties arise if small contingents are sufficient for this purpose – especially if, as in the case of sepoy units in the British army, they are funded and controlled by trading companies. But the picture changes if uprisings and disorders make it necessary to deploy large units for a lengthy period of time: both because this entails considerable costs, and because troop losses can rapidly erode popular support at home. Once again the British were the first to attempt the obvious solution (as well as the ones who applied it most extensively): that is, to recruit troops on the periphery of the empire, where they cost significantly less and serious losses do not attract such great attention as in the case of units originating in the imperial centre.[64]

Elements of the same practice may be found in the American military, which since the 1970s has consisted of fixed-contract and professional soldiers, not conscripts. One of the most important lessons of Vietnam was that such a war could not be fought with middle-class

kids, because they combined a protest potential with political articu-
lacy. Today, moreover, 44 per cent of the manpower in US army units
comes from ethnic minority groups.[65] They stood no chance in the
ordinary labour market, but in the army they experience a degree of
social integration and recognition that ties them more strongly to the
service. Of course, the military subculture that has developed in
American bases and ships around the world is increasingly remote
from everyday life in the United States, and only time will tell
whether this is compatible with democracy. In any event, it has been
one important means for Washington to build combat-ready armed
forces with global reach, despite the fact that they are the armed forces
of a post-heroic society.

The real functional equivalent of the colonial troops that
Europeans used in the nineteenth and twentieth centuries to control
their empires would seem to be the new crop of mercenaries and
'private military companies' (PMCs), which mean that the need for
self-sacrifice in the imperial centre can be replaced with monetary
payments.[66] It has been estimated that a fifth of US forces deployed
in Iraq are in fact 'Greencard soldiers', who hope to acquire US citizenship through several years of military service, and that PMCs
supply an additional 20,000 soldiers. In return for money or future
citizenship, these men (and women) are prepared to shoulder the
military burden of imperial policies, thereby raising their level of
acceptability in the American electorate.

That leaves the cost problem, which ultimately determines
whether the advantages of empire outweigh its disadvantages. The
central imperial power does not always have such cost-effective
solutions at its disposal as it did in the 1991 Gulf War, when its allies
covered 80 per cent of the total cost of $61 billion. It is therefore ques-
tionable whether the US electorate will in the long run be willing to
tolerate the considerable burden of the imperial arms budget. It is
true that today's defence is 3.5 per cent of GDP, down by a half since
the days of the Cold War, but this is due less to a cut in absolute
figures than to favourable economic trends in the 1990s.

The burden of defence spending should thus be seen in relation to
the economic strength of the United States, and it is doubtful
whether this can sustain over a long period an annual trade deficit
of roughly 5 per cent of GDP. With its 27 per cent share of world economic output, the United States can count on a more solid economic
base than the British empire used to have,[67] but it is still less than the
40 per cent share it had in the interwar period or in the years after
the Second World War – and the figure is set to decline further in
the years ahead. If the USA wishes to keep its position of military

superiority, it will therefore have to make public spending cuts that affect the lives of its citizens. We can hardly suppose that this will fail to erode popular support for the imperial project.

A comparison of two figures is enough to give an idea of the weight pressing down from the military apparatus. The US share of world economic output is as large as that of the next three countries together (Japan, Germany and France), but the US military budget, in absolute terms, is as large as the combined military budgets of the next twelve countries.[68] This explains why Andrew Bacevich came to the conclusion that the greatest vulnerability of the American empire lies not in external threats but in 'the questionable willingness of the American people to foot the imperial bill'.[69] The costs issue – that is, the medium-term relationship between the costs and benefits of imperial policy – is in all likelihood the chief problem of a democratic empire. Not by chance do both its internal opponents and its external enemies seize on precisely this weakness.

When the US administration decided, at the end of the East–West conflict, to cash in only part of the possible peace dividend and to increase still further its lead in military technology, its reasoning was that a greater threat came from the margins of the imperial area than from rivals within it. The growing number of terrorist attacks on US installations, reaching a climax on 9/11, appeared to confirm the correctness of the decision. Confidentially, it was also implied that the Europeans were incapable of catching up economically and technologically to the point where they could seriously challenge American supremacy.

In fact, the creation of a single European currency area represents a much greater challenge to American dominance than Islamist terrorism ever can,[70] and an integrated European research landscape, with corresponding inputs into the economy, could have similar effects to the introduction of the euro. It cannot be ruled out that the stronger US orientation in recent years to military instruments of domination also has to do with Europe's closing of the gap in the world economy. By shifting the rivalry to the realm of military capabilities, the USA could, at least temporarily, keep Europe at a distance and, by means of political disputes between them, diminish the power and influence that Europe gained from its single economic area.

In connection with what was said above about the four sources and forms of power,[71] this would mean that the United States compensated for the narrowing of its lead in economic power by widening its lead in military power, where the Europeans do not appear to be making a major effort to draw level. Of course, the costs of dominating the imperial economic areas thereby increase for the United States, and it has only a limited ability to pass these on to the Europeans. There are two possible ways in which it can react to this: one is to divide Europe through a classical policy of divide and rule; the other is to involve it more closely in safeguarding the imperial area. In the end, it also depends on the Europeans which of these options is taken up.

Europe's imperial challenge

The changed situation following the end of the East–West conflict and the collapse of the Soviet Union has posed a considerably greater challenge to Europe than one could have imagined, or wished to imagine, at the beginning of the 1990s. At first, it was taken as an opportunity to overcome the division of the continent into two opposing political camps, by gradually extending to Central and Eastern Europe the process of economic and political integration begun among the nation-states of Western Europe. In retrospect, we can see that fears of Russian resistance to this were exaggerated, while the economic and social problems associated with it were underestimated. Some observers foresaw that a 'reunified' Europe would play a more important role in world politics, and more often than not the expectations on this score tended to be inflated. But the fundamental change that would occur in NATO as a result of its extension to Central and Eastern Europe was only imperfectly perceived and, in most cases, wrongly evaluated. A common prediction, for example, was that NATO would be weighted more heavily towards Europe, whereas in reality the influence of Europe declined and that of the United States grew into an unlimited claim to leadership.[72]

The real challenge for the European Union was (and is) that, on the one side, it faced an area in which all the conflicts and instabilities typical of a post-imperial area were developing at great speed, while on the other side the Western 'number one', which until then had acted as a benevolent hegemon, was turning into an imperial player that paid scant regard to the wishes and ideas of its allies. Most European politicians were particularly surprised by these developments because they had not built the action logic of an empire into their calculations; they had thought of national states as the units of political calculation, and were now faced with post-imperial areas on the one side and an imperial player on the other.

Signs of irritation first appeared over how to respond to the wars surrounding the break-up of Yugoslavia, then grew into political ructions in the run-up to the Iraq War. Has Europe, as some claim, now won increased weight and influence? Or has it, as others object, been losing both?

Europe's imperial challenge is made up of two distinct, and dissimilar, parts. On the one hand, Europeans must keep up a two-way relationship with the more powerful United States; they must take care that they do not simply provide resources for its operations and step in afterwards to handle the consequences, without having any say in the fundamental political-military decisions. Their task in this respect is to resist political marginalization. Europe must assert itself as a subcentre of the imperial area and ensure that a centre–periphery structure does not take shape between the United States and itself. On the other hand, however, Europeans have to concern themselves with their unstable periphery in the East and Southeast, to prevent collapse and war there without being drawn into a spiral of expansion that would overtax Europe as it is presently constituted. Here the paradoxical danger is that they could suffer imperial overstretch without actually being an empire.

Up to now Europeans have found no answer to this twofold challenge – indeed, they have not even seen it for what it is. A glance at the specialist literature reveals two reactions to the problem we have just outlined. The first, to be found in what we might call the *literature of reassurance*, lays the main stress on Europe's relationship to the United States: the challenge of the US empire, it is argued,[73] is not as great or as dangerous as it first appears, since the USA is already in the process of decline or is so overstretched by its worldwide commitment that it will soon lose its leadership over the Europeans. These authors emphasize Europe's economic strength and note a tendency to equilibrium between Europe and the United States. But, in doing so, they overlook or downplay two points: the erosion or collapse of US world leadership would pose greater problems for Europe than it would solve; and the prospect of economic equilibrium with Europe could induce the United States to turn even more to the range of military solutions, with the idea that this could again make dwarfs of the Europeans and giants of the Americans. In short, the literature of reassurance underestimates the globally stabilizing function of the US empire and overestimates the significance of economic factors for short-term power relations. The effect of economic factors makes itself felt in the long rather than the short term.

The second reaction, to be found in a complementary *literature of identity*, looks at the progress of European integration within a purely internal perspective. Abstracting from the EU's significance in Eastern Europe, the Middle East and North Africa, it focuses on the constitutional-political order and European cultural identity.[74] This assumes that Europeans will still have long time-frames in which to reach decisions and to bring together different political cultures. During the period of the East–West conflict, the slowing down of political processes and the lowering of the political temperature led, as it were, to a change in the general situation that favoured European integration. Since the end of the East–West conflict, however, the factors of deceleration have disappeared and political processes have returned to their normal tempo – which, because of the need to catch up, is actually faster than in other parts of the world. In the slowing-down period, Europeans could afford the luxury of a search for common identity, but the acceleration tendencies since the early 1990s have removed that possibility. The literature of identity evidently ignores the problems of the periphery and trusts to luck that they will not escalate until identity issues have been sorted out in the centre. This is clear from the public debate on Turkey's application to join the EU.

As regards the relationship with the United States, the ancient Athenian thalassocracy that we described earlier may serve as a warning. So long as it was locked in acute conflict with the Persian empire, Athens treated its allies as weaker but accepted that they had equal rights. Once the Persian threat faded, however, the allies cashed in the peace dividend, and Athens agreed that they should fulfil their obligations in the form of monetary payments. From allies with equal rights, they thereby turned into dependent subjects who had to comply with the wishes and demands of Athens – a development that also made it easier for them to be played off against one another. If Europe is to escape a similar fate, it must constitute itself as a single political unit in which outsiders, including its closest ally, have no say in the major decisions.

The pressure on Europeans to act together comes from outside, and developments within Europe must adapt to it. Whether this is possible or not will depend less on the new members from Central Europe than on the United Kingdom, which must make up its mind whether it wants to be a junior partner of the USA or a leading power in Europe. The European integration process will have to be organized in response to this British decision. If the result is not a Paris–London–Berlin triangle (which is inherently desirable), another continental power will be found to convert the Paris–Berlin axis into a triangle. London will then, of course, be repositioned on the periphery of a United Europe. But, in any event, the generation of a European capacity for joint external action will lead to more hierarchical decision-making structures, unlike in the case of the Common Agricultural Policy, where it has been impossible, but also unnecessary, to develop such structures. Conversely, there will be no European capacity for joint external action without a stronger hierarchy among European states. This is the reason why many small and medium-sized countries balk at the idea of stronger community-wide action in foreign and security policy. What they must realize, however, is that they are not increasing their own room for manoeuvre, but rather strengthening America's influence over European politics. Washington is happy to play on the difference of small and medium-sized New Europe, but its need for EU support in an increasingly difficult world situation creates an opportunity to stop it from continuing along that path.

The need for a common European external and security policy derives not only from the challenge of the US empire but also from the fact that it is essential to intervene in the European periphery to help stabilize the situation there. The suction effect of an unstable periphery, which the Europeans first encountered during the post-Yugoslav wars of the 1990s, is likely to increase in the future; it will no longer be confined to relatively manageable regions such as the Balkans, but will stretch in a long arc from Belarus and Ukraine through the Caucasus to the Middle East, and from there to the African shores of the Mediterranean and Morocco. Since state failure, social strife and economic collapse in this arc have much greater implications for Europe than for the United States, Europeans will have to work to ensure that Western policy there is not shaped by the USA alone. It would be best, of course, if they took overall charge in their own 'backyard', with the United States in second place, but that is scarcely a possibility in relation to the Middle East. On the other hand, the constellation of interests and moods can rapidly change in the United States – and then Europeans must be in a position to take over the American role in proposing solutions and developing the capacity to implement them.

Europe is a continent with imprecise boundaries; only in Norway and the west are these defined in advance by the geography. To the south and east, it remains unclear how far the political and economic community can and should extend itself. It is true that the Mediterranean forms a natural limit in the south, but its effect in the past has been more to join than to divide. For the Roman empire it was the centre, not the frontier, and this first changed only with the Arab advances of the eighth and ninth centuries.[75] But then the Italian maritime republics, Venice and Genoa, again made the Mediterranean the centre of their trade relations, and the Ottoman empire at its height was essentially an Eastern Mediterranean power. There are many reasons why Europeans continue to regard the Mediterranean as the outer limit of their political integration, but this does not remove the pressure on them to ensure that its opposite shores are politically and economically stable. Europe has a vital interest in the stability of North Africa.

What has just been said about Europe's southern frontier applies all the more to its eastern frontier. Paul Valéry once spoke of Europe as a promontory of Asia,[76] and often in its history Europeans have looked nervously east to the Asian steppes from which invasions have come at irregular intervals, from the time of the great migrations to the Russian empire-building efforts that made Europe's eastern frontier unsettled. At a certain point, Europeans began to counter with attempts to expand their own sphere of influence and culture eastwards. Russian empire-building thus acquired crucial significance, so that the question of Europe's eastern frontier came to depend on whether Russia was perceived as a mainly European or a mainly Asian power; the Janus face of Tsarist Russia was an expression of its repeated oscillation between these alternatives. If the ancient geographers placed Europe's eastern frontier on the Don, the geographers of the eighteenth century moved it to the Urals in response to the reforms of Peter the Great. Russia thus became a European power.[77] The progress of European integration has converted this largely cultural issue into a genuinely political problem. Should the EU and Russia have a common frontier with each other, or should Belarus and Ukraine remain as a buffer zone?

The trickiest frontier lies in the Southeast, of course, where the continents of Europe, Asia and Africa meet up. Broadly defined, the region takes in the lower Balkans, Asia Minor and the Near East, which in the last few decades have witnessed varying degrees of crisis that sharply differentiate them from postwar Europe. The EU will not be able to avoid considerable investments in the stabilization of this area. A glance back reveals it as a breeding ground since antiquity for large-scale imperial ventures, but also for wars that early on involved an ideological clash between East and West, despotism and liberty. The Byzantine and Ottoman empires, at the height of their power, saw themselves as bitter rivals of Europe. And, when the Ottoman empire entered its long death agony in the nineteenth century, shifting coalitions of European states sought to stabilize it in order to ward off dangerous developments within its imperial space. Since time immemorial, the Southeast has played a special role in European history.

Neither geographically nor politically, then, does Europe have clear-cut boundaries, and especially in the East and Southeast it has borderlands typical of a large-scale imperial order. Yet European history is also marked by the formation of territorial states, which later developed into nation-states. This form of polity rests on the principle of combined or consolidated boundaries: the frontiers of the nation-state are not only political and economic, but also linguistic and cultural; and the resulting homogeneity has ensured that players exceptionally capable of action have appeared there on the political stage. In the confrontation between nation-states and the empires of Central and Eastern Europe, the latter nearly always came off worse.

The boundary consolidation model led to a situation, however, in which the energy stored up internally was time and again released in border conflicts, since the nation-states could not agree on precisely where the demarcation lines should be drawn. Moreover, the nation-state model that had taken centuries to develop in the West could not be directly transferred to the East, where the strategy of boundary consolidation resulted in policies of discrimination or even expulsion against ethnic and national minorities. It is true that the postwar policy of European integration was still based on a model of multiple nation-states, but it complemented this with a systematic disentanglement of political, economic and cultural boundaries. The dissolution of highly cultivated political-cultural identities was put forward as the royal road to peace in Europe. Already in the 1980s, as plans were drafted to complete the European integration process, the model of boundary diversification began to give way to the idea of a redefinition and reconsolidation of frontiers – the European identity debate is the result of this tendency. Clear-cut breaks at the external frontiers of Europe thus became exclusion points, causing more and more countries to seek to join the EU in an endless series of negotiations. Paradoxically, it was above all the policy of boundary consolidation which set in train the permanent process of EU enlargement.

An alternative to this is the model of an imperial order involving diversification of the various boundary lines. In fact, imperial orders usually have 'soft' boundaries, where the centre's regulatory claims gradually lose their force and where borderlands take the place of borders. If Europe is not to overstretch itself and eventually end in failure, it will have to take over this imperial model of boundary demarcation. In principle, such an order is already inscribed within it, but the EU's external borders are not the same as those of the Schengen area or those of the Eurozone. This model must be developed further, to make Europe's external frontiers at once stable and elastic. This will include exercising influence in the periphery of the EU, in ways that have a greater affinity with the requirements of empire than with those of an interstate system. For Europe's future will not be able to do without borrowing from the imperial model.

The Maritime Empire of the Athenians *c*. 450 BC
After the Persian Wars, the Athenians built up a sea empire, which was at first
held together by the continuing Persian threat. As this threat waned,
hegemony turned increasingly into imperial domination. This was expressed

Black Sea

Thrace

Byzantion

Sea of Marmara

Samothrace

Imbros

PHRYGIA

Lemnos

Makestos

Lesbos

Aegean
Sea

Mytilene

Pergamon

LYDIA

Hermos

Khios

Sardes

Persian Empire

Kolophon

Maeander

Andros

Ephesos

Tenos

Samos

Ikaros

Priene

Miletas

KARIA

Siros

Mykonos

Delos

Patmos

Halikarnassos

Kyklades

Leros

Naxos

Siphnos

Amorgos

Kos

Sikinos

Anaphe

Telos

Rhodes

Lindos

Sea of Crete

Karpathos

Crete

Gortyn

M e d i t e r r a n e a n   S e a

| 0 | 50 | 100 | 150 | 200 | 250 km |

in the transfer of the treasury from Delos to Athens. The Aegean Sea was the
centre of the Athenian thalassocracy.

The Roman Empire in the Age of Augustus (63 BC – AD 14)
Roman expansion effectively ended with Augustus. A few smaller conquests
or acquisitions followed: Dacia in the north, Armenia and Arabia in the east,

Mauretania in the south. The empire had fortified borders only in the north, where it was constantly under pressure from the barbarians.

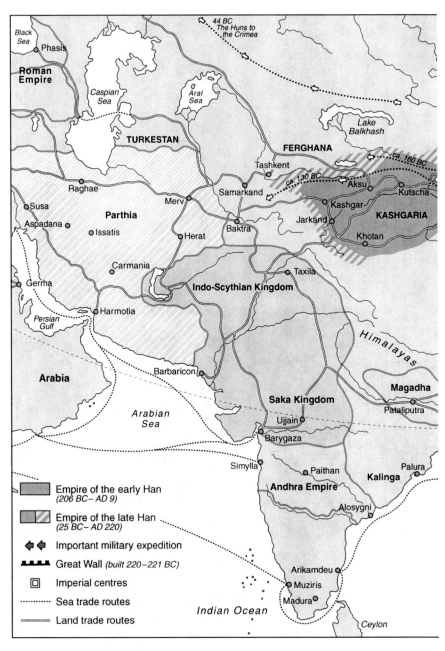

Black
Sea

Phasis

Roman
Empire

Caspian
Sea

Aral
Sea

TURKESTAN

Lake
Balkhash

FERGHANA

ca. 160 BC

Tashkent

ca. 130 BC

Aksu

Kutscha

Raghae

Susa

Merv

Samarkand

Kashgar

Aspadana

Parthia

Issatis

Baktra

Jarkand

KASHGARIA

Herat

Khotan

Carmania

Taxila

Gerrha

Harmotia

Indo-Scythian Kingdom

Himalayas

Persian
Gulf

Arabia

Barbaricon

Magadha

Saka Kingdom

Pataliputra

Arabian
Sea

Ujjain

Barygaza

Simylla

Paithan

Palura

Andhra Empire

Kalinga

Alosygni

44 BC
The Huns to
the Crimea

Empire of the early Han
(206 BC – AD 9)

Empire of the late Han
(25 BC – AD 220)

Important military expedition

Great Wall (built 220–221 BC)

Imperial centres

Sea trade routes

Land trade routes

Arikamdeu

Muziris

Indian Ocean

Madura

Ceylon

The Han Empire, 202 BC – AD 220

Under the Han the Chinese empire took the form it would maintain in essence
for the next two millennia. As in the Roman empire, there were also fortified
borders in the north, where invasions from nomadic peoples could be

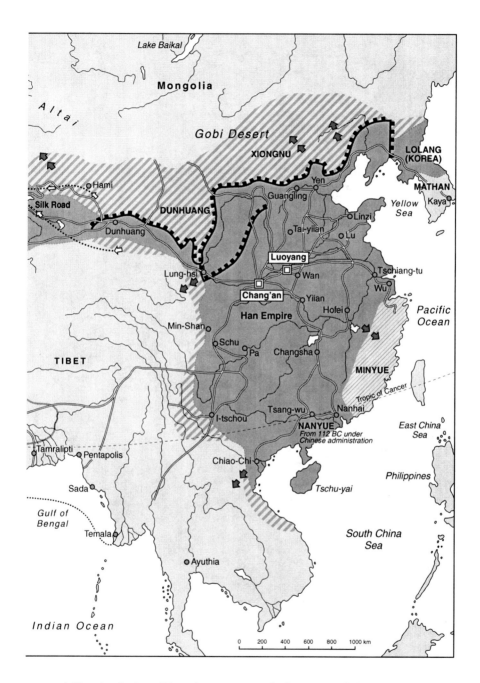

expected. Despite the later Han advances towards the west, it did not come
into direct contact with other empires.

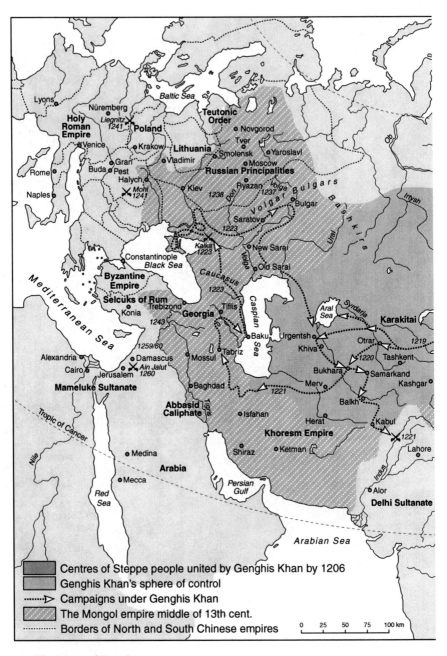

Legend:
- Centres of Steppe people united by Genghis Khan by 1206
- Genghis Khan's sphere of control
- ·······▷ Campaigns under Genghis Khan
- The Mongol empire middle of 13th cent.
- ·········· Borders of North and South Chinese empires

0 25 50 75 100 km

The Mongol Empire
The starting point of Mongolian empire-building was a unification of nomadic
peoples in the Asian steppe by Genghis Khan. By the middle of the thirteenth

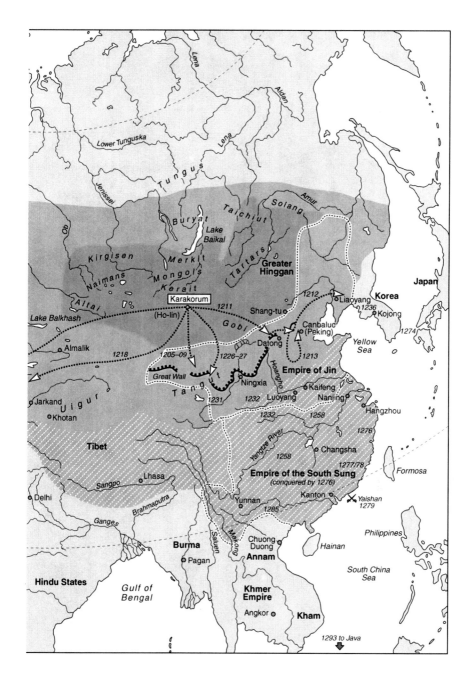

century Mongolian armies had advanced to the Oder and the Danube,
forming the largest continental empire that had ever existed.

The Russian Empire, 1551–1914
The Russian empire belongs among the great territorial empires: the sea
represented a border rather than an internal imperial space. The speed and
extent of expansion from the centre in Moscow towards the west, the south

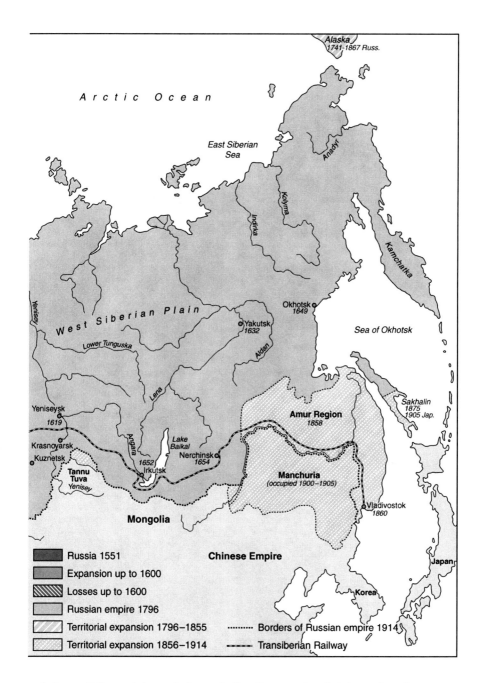

and above all the east depended on whether it encountered states or loosely integrated tribal groups.

The Ottoman Empire by 1683

Situated at the junction of three continents, the Ottoman empire in the period of its ascent had opportunities for expansion towards Europe, Asia and Africa, all of which it utilized. But after it passed its imperial zenith, this

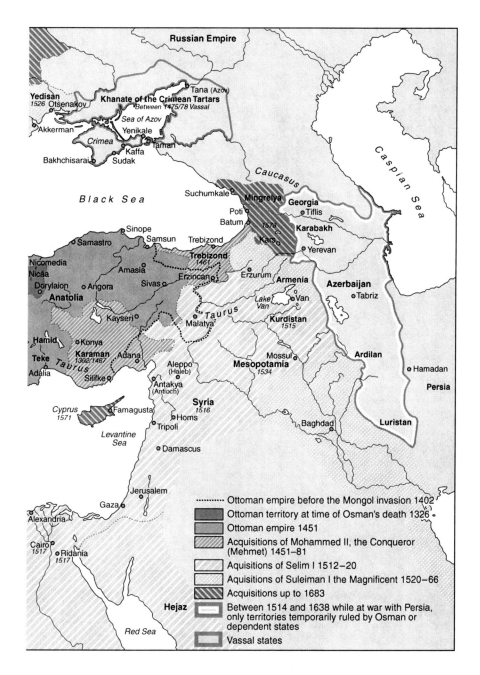

central geopolitical position inevitably led to imperial overextension, as a result of which the powers of the empire were exhausted and it became 'the sick man of the Bosphorus'.

Labels on map:

Greenland

Britain
London

Paris
France

Portugal Spain
Lisbon Madrid
Algier
Ceuta Oran
Masagan Melilla

Flemish Islands (Azores)
1431 Port.

Santa Fé
1609 Span.

1512 Span.
Florida

Atlantic Ocean

Fortunate Isles
(Canary Islands)
1341 Port.
1496 Span.

Viceroyalty
of New Spain

Cuba
1511 Span.

S. Juan Bautista
1509 Span.
1670 Engl.

1441/56 Port.

Mexico Vera Cruz

Acapulco

1662 Engl.

Espaniola
1492 Span.

Mosquito
Coast

Puerto Belo

1482 Port.
1637 Dutch
Elmina

São Tomé
1483 Port.
1599/1600,
1641–1643 Dutch

Belém
São Luis

Recife

Lima
Bahia

Terra do Brazil

Pacific Ocean

Potosí

Viceroyalty
of Peru

Rio de Janeiro

Valparaíso

Buenos Aires

Legend:

- Portugal and overseas possessions
- Spain and overseas possessions
- - - - - Boundaries of spheres of interest between Spain and Portugal after the Treaty of Tordesillas 1494

Spain and Portugal *c.* 1600
The Portuguese maritime empire was at first confined to the acquisition and construction of bases from which it could open up the South Atlantic and especially the Indian Ocean to commerce. By contrast, Spain embarked on

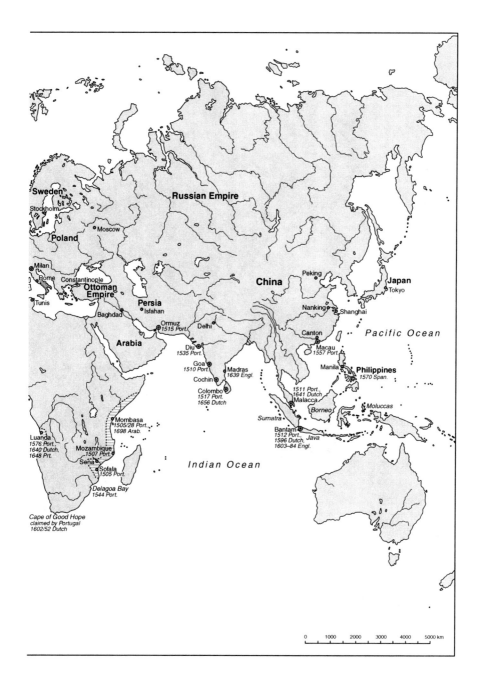

Sweden
Stockholm

Russian Empire

Moscow

Poland

Milan
Rome
Tunis
Constantinople
Ottoman
Empire
Persia
Isfahan
Baghdad

Arabia

Ormuz
1515 Port.
Delhi

Diu
1535 Port.

Goa
1510 Port.
Cochin
Madras
1639 Engl.

Colombo
1517 Port.
1656 Dutch

Mombasa
1505/28 Port.
1698 Arab.

Luanda
1576 Port.
1640 Dutch,
1648 Prt.
Mozambique
1507 Port.
Sena
Sofala
1505 Port.

Delagoa Bay
1544 Port.

Cape of Good Hope
claimed by Portugal
1602/52 Dutch

China
Peking

Nanking
Shanghai

Canton

Macau
1557 Port.

Manila

Japan
Tokyo

Pacific Ocean

Philippines
1570 Span.

1511 Port.
1641 Dutch
Malacca

Sumatra

Bantam
1512 Port.,
1596 Dutch,
1603-84 Engl.

Borneo
Java

Moluccas

Indian Ocean

0   1000   2000   3000   4000   5000 km

territorial expansion from the beginning, which led to a constant stream of
soldiers and adventurers to the 'New World'.

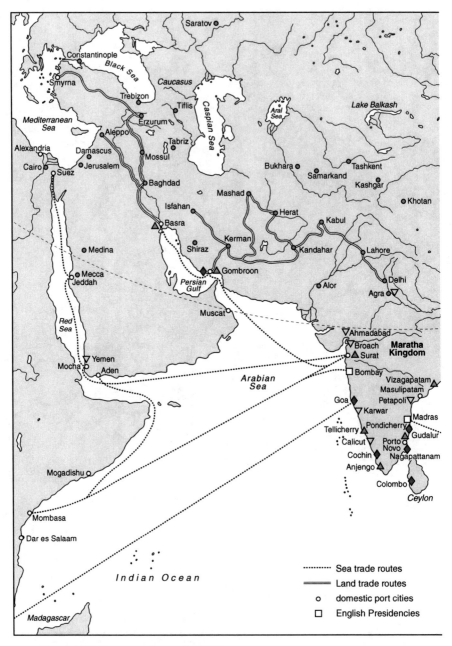

East India Company bases by 1760
In the eighteenth century England joined the tradition of the seaborne empires, Portugal and the Netherlands. The British imperial order also confined itself at first to a network of port cities, trading posts and trade routes, woven together

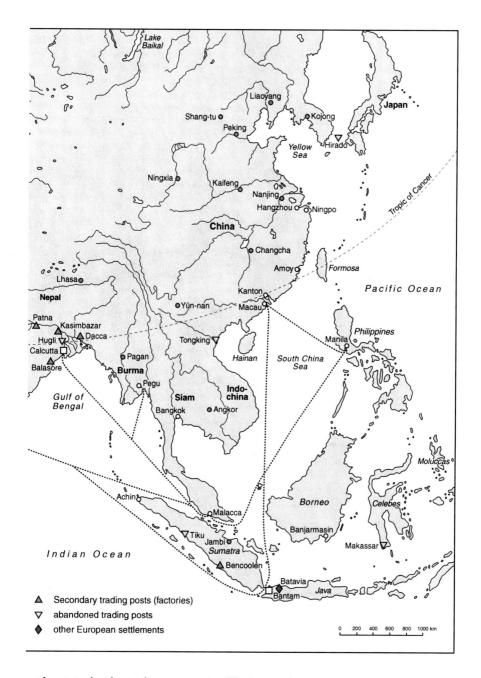

not by states but by trading companies. The imperial power grew essentially through control over the movement of goods, people and capital.

Legend:

- Britain and overseas possessions
- France and overseas possessions
- Dutch colonial possessions (1795–1815 administered by Britain, mostly returned 1815/17)
- Portugal and overseas possessions
- Spain and overseas possessions
- Denmark and overseas possessions

Colonial Empires between 1800 and 1815

The map shows a transitional situation in world politics: Spain is still a powerful empire on the basis of its spatial reach; Britain, which has just lost its colonies on the American east coast, will in the course of the century expand

Russia and its spheres of influence in Siberia and Alaska

United States of America after 1783

Louisiana *(1763 Span, 1800 French, sold to the United States 1803)*

0   1000   2000   3000   4000 km

its sphere of power; the African continent has still not attracted the interest of European powers, and its colonization is confined to coastal strips.

Colonial Empires of the European powers *c.* 1914
The world is essentially divided between Russia, which dominates large parts of Asia, and Britain, whose power reaches from Canada to Australia and whose African colonial empire stretches from Cairo to Cape Town.

By comparison, the other European colonial empires hardly count, perhaps with the exception of the French.

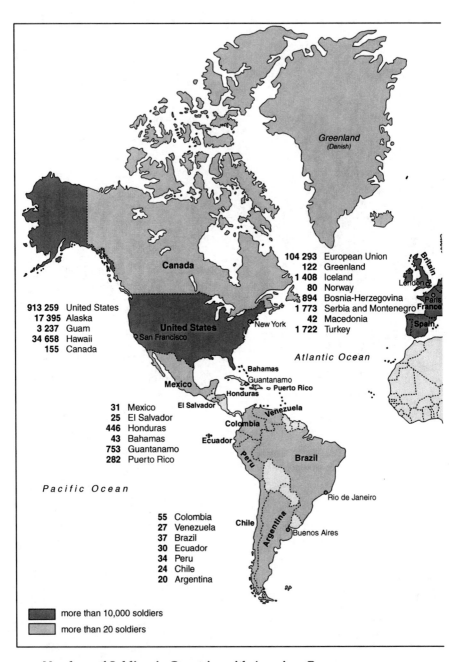

913 259 United States
17 395 Alaska
3 237 Guam
34 658 Hawaii
155 Canada

104 293 European Union
122 Greenland
1 408 Iceland
80 Norway
894 Bosnia-Herzegovina
1 773 Serbia and Montenegro
42 Macedonia
1 722 Turkey

31 Mexico
25 El Salvador
446 Honduras
43 Bahamas
753 Guantanamo
282 Puerto Rico

55 Colombia
27 Venezuela
37 Brazil
30 Ecuador
34 Peru
24 Chile
20 Argentina

more than 10,000 soldiers

more than 20 soldiers

Numbers of Soldiers in Countries with American Bases
(as of 31 December 2004)

The American military presence has been literally globalized since the end of
the East–West conflict. It constitutes a dense network of worldwide control, in

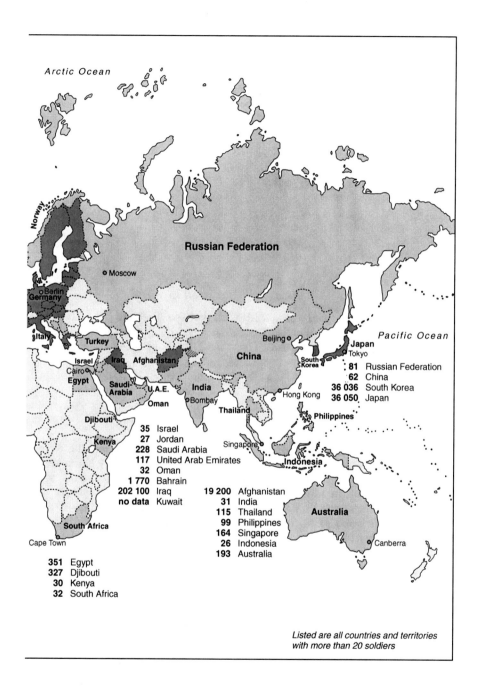

which the stress points of the Cold War are still recognizable but which is
increasingly expanding into the southern hemisphere.

NOTES

Chapter 1 What is an Empire?

1 On the prehistory of the third Gulf war see Aust and Schnibben, *Irak*, esp. pp. 39ff.; Tilgner, *Der inszenierte Krieg*, pp. 17ff.; Kubbig, *Brandherd Irak*, esp. pp. 9–20; Sofsky, *Operation Freiheit*, pp. 66–74; and Münkler, *Der neue Golfkrieg*, pp. 19–28.

2 On the history of NATO's eastward enlargement and the aims of those involved, see Asmus, *Opening NATO's Door*.

3 Mann, *Incoherent Empire*, p. 252. See also Czempiel, 'Pax Americana oder Imperium Americanum?' The term clearly refers back to an article by Robert Kagan, 'The Benevolent Empire'.

4 A consistent drawing of parallels between the USA and the Roman empire may be found in Bender, *Weltmacht Amerika*. The characterization of the USA as the 'New Rome' in world politics goes back to the middle of the nineteenth century: see Gollwitzer, *Geschichte des weltpolitischen Denkens*, vol. 1, pp. 489ff.; a less explicit comparison with the effectiveness of British forms of imperial rule runs through Mann's argument in *Incoherent Empire*; a fall similar to that of the Soviet Union is presented as the likely fate of the USA in Todd, *After the Empire*; and Ferguson also makes a number of evaluative comparisons between the USA and the British and Roman empires, in *Colossus*, pp. 19ff., 34, 44ff.

5 See Wood, *The Creation*, esp. pp. 48ff., and Richard, *The Founders and the Classics*. Right from the beginning, the proud claim to have taken over and developed Rome's republican tradition underlay the critical appraisal of Rome's passage from Republic to Empire, in which the assumption of a related decline in morals – derived from Roman historiography – was transposed to the contemporary British empire. The hard-won independence of the USA from Britain was thus also seen as a saving of the republic from imperiality. See Bailyn, *The Ideological Origin*, pp. 131ff., and Wood, *The Creation*, pp. 35f.

6 For a detailed discussion, see Daschitschew, *Moskaus Griff nach der Weltmacht*, pp. 41ff. and 511ff.

7 For a comparison of the British and Mongol empires, see Göckenjan, 'Weltherrschaft oder Desintegration?'; and, on the expansion of the Mongol empire, Weiers, 'Geschichte der Mongolen', pp. 45f.

8 The significance of the Achaemenid empire and its Hellenistic successors as links between the Mediterranean and Asia is well brought out in Breuer, *Imperien*, pp. 122–58. On Portugal's initial role in European empire-building, see Abernethy, *Dynamics of Global Dominance*, pp. 45ff., and Reinhard, *Kleine Geschichte des Kolonialismus*, pp. 25ff.

9 See the survey in Mommsen, *Imperialismustheorien*.

10 The comparison of imperial power with the sun and its satellites refers, as I see it, not to military but to economic imperiality. In the early nineteenth century the banker Nathan Rothschild explained to the House of Commons 'that London is the capital of the financial world, and that even major business deals are more or less necessarily concluded under the influence of this centre of the financial system, around which less prosperous countries move like the small heavenly bodies of the solar system and from which they must be content to derive their radiance and nourishment.' Quoted (and retranslated) from Gollwitzer, *Geschichte des weltpolitischen Denkens*, vol. 1, p. 505.

11 See Schuller, *Die Herrschaft der Athener*, pp. 54ff.

12 Heinrich Triepel (*Die Hegemonie*, pp. 146f.) has also called this 'absorptive hegemony'.

13 See Breuer, *Imperien*, pp. 140–7; the detailed discussion in Welwei, *Das klassische Athen*, pp. 77–139; on the replacement of *hegemonia* with *archē* as the political designation of Athenian rule, Triepel, *Die Hegemonie*, pp. 343ff.; and, on the alliance change, ibid., pp. 377ff. A detailed account of Athenian rule may be found in Schuller, *Die Herrschaft der Athener*, esp. pp. 153–65.

14 Quoted in Ferguson, *Empire*, p. 246.

15 Lundestad, *The United States and Western Europe since 1945: From Empire by Invitation to Transatlantic Drift*. See also Maier, *Among Empires*.

16 For the sake of completeness, it should be mentioned that one variant – the so-called periphery-oriented theories of imperialism – are well aware of the significance of the periphery in the formation of empires. In fact, they assume that 'the imperialist actions of the great powers are usually triggered by crises in the third world'. Mommsen, *Imperialismustheorien*, p. 81, and more generally pp. 80–90.

17 On the problem of conceptualizing long cycles in the rise and decline of great powers, see Modelski, *Long Cycles in World Politics*, pp. 7–38.

18 Doyle, *Empires*, pp. 306ff., 319ff. Admittedly Doyle has in mind French and German *imperialism* rather than successful *empire-building*.

19 See Kann, *A History of the Habsburg Empire*. On Charles's imperial ambitions, see Kohler, *Karl V.*, and Kohler, Haider and Otter, *Karl V.*

20 The quotations have been modified to conform to conventional usage. Trans.

21 The point here about the Habsburg monarchy also applies to
   Byzantium, which after the Islamic onslaught and the loss of large areas
   in the Middle East had the status of only a regional power – although
   this in no way put a stop to Byzantium's claim to rule the world. See
   Lilie, *Byzanz*, pp. 75–141, and Beck, *Das byzantinische Jahrtausend*,
   pp. 78–86.

22 Osterhammel (*Colonialism*, p. 17) draws a distinction between colonies
   as objects of political rule and as bases; these should be seen as starting
   points for two different kinds of empire-building.

23 In his social history of the fifteenth to eighteenth centuries, Fernand
   Braudel shows that the shift of Europe's main banking location from
   Italy (where Venice and Genoa had long been rivals for leadership) to
   the Low Countries (with Antwerp and later Amsterdam as the centre)
   and then finally to London had considerably more consequences for
   power relations in Europe than did the numerous battles over territory.
   Braudel, *Civilization and Capitalism*, vol. 2, pp. 394ff., and vol. 3,
   pp. 175ff., 239ff. Cf. Wallerstein, *The Modern World-System*, pp. 81f. and
   218ff.

24 See Nef, *Western Civilization*, pp. 84ff.; Parker, *The Military Revolution*,
   pp. 89ff.; and Cipolla, *Guns and Sails*, p. 89.

25 This was already apparent in the Soviet Union, which for a long time
   was a step ahead of the United States in the conquest of space.

26 On the concept of the *ecumene*, see Voegelin, *Das ökumenische Zeitalter*,
   pp. 58–62. One of the major errors of Carl Schmitt is to have overlooked the significance of cultural and technological factors. He started
   by criticizing the extension of the Monroe Doctrine, which had originally been limited to the American continent, but himself later drew
   up an outline for a 'German Monroe Doctrine' in Europe (Schmitt,
   'Völkerrechtliche Formen des modernen Imperialismus' and
   'Großraum gegen Universalismus'; see also Diner, 'Imperialismus').
   All these reflections remain tied to telluric ideas of space and therefore
   fail to see the dynamic of imperial 'global' ideas, which did not begin
   with capitalist expansion but certainly gained strength from it.

27 Breuer, *Imperien*, pp. 12ff. and 158ff.

28 See Lilie, *Byzanz*, pp. 143ff.

29 The only conflicts between Russia and Britain in the nineteenth century
   followed this dividing line: the dispute over control of the Bosphorus,
   which eventually led to the Crimean War, and the confrontation over
   Persia and Afghanistan. This does not mean that there were not
   repeated surges of Russophobic feelings among English intellectuals,
   which called into question the possibility of 'peaceful coexistence'
   between the two empires. See Gollwitzer, *Geschichte des weltpolitischen
   Denkens*, vol. 2, pp. 28ff., 71f.

30 In *The Pity of War*, Niall Ferguson recently sparked off a debate on the
   extent to which British policy misunderstood what was necessary for
   the empire's preservation in the early twentieth century, when Britain
   entered the First World War to prevent the formation of a German-led

continental empire. In fact, British politicians – most notably, foreign secretary Edward Grey – were basing themselves on the logic of their imperial 'world'. It is conceivable that, as Ferguson argues, a 'global shift' would have been in the long-term interests of the British empire. But it was scarcely a real possibility.

31 It may be, however, that references to the multi-ethnic or multinational character of empires are meant only to underline their difference from the nation-state, which is characterized by a tendency for political space and national identity to converge. See Münkler, *Reich, Nation, Europa*, pp. 61ff.

32 The figures are taken from Osterhammel, 'China', p. 122.

33 Thucydides, *The Peloponnesian War*, V: 84–116.

34 See the excellent interpretation of the Melian dialogue in Volkmann-Schluck, *Politische Philosophie*, pp. 39–58. In *Thucydides*, by contrast, Romilly attributes the conflict not to imperial factors (which the Melians would not have understood) but to the power politics of Athenian imperialism.

35 Which interpretation of Thucydides is preferred will naturally have something to do with the collective memory of a political community. Thus, a scenario of downfall in which large-scale power politics occupies the central position tends to be found mainly in the German literature.

36 Thucydides, *The Peloponnesian War*, I: 144.1 and II: 65.7.

37 Fulbright, *The Arrogance of Power*.

38 Habermas, 'Was bedeutet der Denkmalsturz?', and idem, 'Wege aus der Weltunordnung'.

39 Habermas, 'Wege aus der Weltunordnung', p. 34.

40 See, for example, Heinrichs, *Die gekränkte Supermacht*.

Chapter 2 Empire, Imperialism and Hegemony

1 For an excellent survey of debates at the time in Britain, Russia, the United States, France and Germany, see Gollwitzer, *Geschichte des weltpolitischen Denkens*, vol. 2. Critical references to them in imperialism theory are briefly presented in Mommsen, *Imperialismustheorien*, and Schröder, *Sozialistische Imperialismusdeutung*. On the history of the concept of imperialism, see Koebner and Schmidt, *Imperialism*.

2 It is amazing how similar this is to the present-day argument of large corporations that they can survive only by becoming 'global players'.

3 This state of excitement has been talked about mainly in relation to Germany: see, for example, Ullrich, *Die nervöse Großmacht*, or Radkau, *Das Zeitalter der Nervosität*. It was by no means confined to Germany, however, but manifested itself also in France and Britain, where a hysterical Germanophobia was quite widespread. See Gollwitzer, *Geschichte des weltpolitischen Denkens*, vol. 2, pp. 71f.

4 See Doyle, *Empires*, pp. 344ff.

5 On the imperial expansion of the United States in the late nineteenth century, see Wehler, *Der Aufstieg des amerikanischen Imperialismus*. The

wars associated with this are the subject of Boot, *The Savage Wars of Peace*: see esp. the section on the Philippines, pp. 99–128.

6 The chief representatives of the Marxist theory of imperialism are Rudolf Hilferding, Rosa Luxemburg, Karl Kautsky and Vladimir Ilich Lenin. The issue in the debates among them – whether imperialist expansion was attributable mainly to underconsumption or to overaccumulation – has no significance for what interests us here.

A remarkably positive account of traditional attitudes to the spirit of trade and change may be found in Werner Sombart's war book *Händler und Helden* (1915), which is not a 'patriotic aberration' on his part in the tumult of war but an application of his theory that capitalism, through its very successes, becomes immoderately fat and loses strength and dynamism; it therefore has to import attitudes foreign to its nature in order to survive. Schumpeter held an opposite view of the relationship between imperialism and capitalism: 'Imperialism thus is atavistic in character. [. . .] It is an atavism in the social structure, in individual, psychological habits of emotional reaction. Since the vital needs that created it have passed away for good, it too must gradually disappear, even though every warlike involvement, no matter how non-imperialist in character, tends to revive it.' Schumpeter, 'The Sociology of Imperialism', p. 65.

7 'Aggressive imperialism, which costs the taxpayer so dear, which is of so little value to the manufacturer and trader, which is fraught with such grave incalculable peril to the citizen, is a source of great gain to the investor who cannot find at home the profitable use he seeks for his capital, and insists that his Government should help him to profitable and secure investments abroad.' Hobson, *Imperialism*, p. 55.

8 Most of these attempts took place in the period after 1892, when Sergei Witte took over as finance minister. He had come to the view that the empire of the Russian tsars would become an exploited colony unless it too managed to move forward to a policy of economic imperialism, and that this would prove most feasible in East Asia. See Geyer, *Russian Imperialism*, pp. 147ff., 186ff.

9 A still impressive examination of this problem may be found in Aron, *The Century of Total War*, esp. the chapter on 'The Leninist Myth of Imperialism', pp. 56–73.

10 On the economic underpinning of Russia's change of alliances in the late 1880s, see Geyer, *Russian Imperialism*, pp. 169ff.

11 On the pumping dry of the peasantry, see Hosking, *Russia: People and Empire*, pp. 198–224.

12 Between 1887 and 1913 alone, 5.4 million people either emigrated or were deported to Siberia. Reinhard, *Kleine Geschichte des Kolonialismus*, pp. 164f.

13 Cf. Geyer, *Russian Imperialism*, p. 128.

14 Hosking, *Russia: People and Empire*, p. 36.

15 This is not to deny that the rise of certain merchant families was closely bound up with imperial expansion. One example was the Stroganovs,

who essentially propelled and directed the expansion into Siberia: Hosking, *Russia: People and Empire*, p. 13, and Reinhard, *Kleine Geschichte*, pp. 161f.

16 Similarly, the recurrent periods of disintegration within the Chinese empire, though separated by longer intervals than those in the Roman empire, uniformly originated in peripheral regions. See Schmidt-Glintzer, *China*, pp. 64ff., 113ff., 193ff.

17 See Lehmann, 'Das Ende der römischen Herrschaft'.

18 On the organization and recruitment of the janissary corps through the so-called blood tax, see Matuz, *Das Osmanische Reich*, pp. 98ff., and, on the decline of the janissaries as symptomatic of the weakening of the Ottoman empire, Jorga, *Geschichte des Osmanischen Reichs*, vol. 3, pp. 220ff. A succinct overview of the matter may be found in Ursinus, 'Byzanz, Osmanisches Reich, türkischer Nationalstaat', pp. 155f.

19 Pieper, 'Das Ende des spanischen Kolonialreiches', and Bernecker, *Spanische Geschichte*, pp. 107ff.

20 See below, p. 105

21 Quoted in Schell, *Unconquerable World*, p. 36.

22 See Robinson, *Africa and the Victorians*.

23 Schell, *Unconquerable World*, pp. 35–8.

24 The different British and American responses to instability in the periphery had more to do with specific political traditions than with normative differences of principle. For the British, the establishment of protectorates and colonies seemed to follow from their previous policies, but this did not come naturally to the Americans, whose war of independence against Britain was part of their country's founding myth. In reality, however, the way in which the Americans handled Panama or the Philippines led to the establishment of a protectorate. On the various phases of globalization as a compression of space and time, see Menzel, 'Die Globalisierung'.

25 To be sure, this transition should be seen more as the covering of a stretch of road than as the crossing of a threshold.

26 See, for example, Robinson, 'Non-European Foundations', and Fieldhouse, *Economics and Empire*.

27 For a critical assessment of this renaissance of imperialism theory and associated historical research in Germany, see Geiss, 'Kontinuitäten des Imperialismus'.

28 Marx's theory of Bonapartism was taken up by a number of authors in the twentieth century and used for the analysis of Italian fascism and National Socialism. See Jaschke, *Soziale Basis*.

29 Marx, 'The Eighteenth Brumaire', p. 236.

30 Ibid., p. 184.

31 Marx, 'First Address of the General Council', pp. 172–3.

32 On the concept of prestige, the key text remains, now as then, Kluth, *Sozialprestige*.

33 The model of different kinds of capital, which stems essentially from Pierre Bourdieu, was not current in the nineteenth century and

therefore not available to contemporary political theories of imperialism. But the fact, if not the reality, has a firm mooring within them.

34 See Koebner and Schmidt, *Imperialism*, pp. 1–26.

35 See Münkler, 'Das Reich als politische Macht'.

36 On the importance of prestige in international politics, see Gilpin, *War and Change*, pp. 30ff.

37 See below, pp. 111f.

38 For a brief overview, see Mommsen, *Imperialismustheorien*, pp. 7–11.

39 In *Myths of Empire* (pp. 21–6), Snyder goes through the incentive structures and sanction mechanisms of multipolar and bipolar systems with reference to hegemonic and imperial aspirations.

40 As far as the 'striving for prestige in the second rank' is concerned, it is of no consequence whether the prevailing conditions in international politics are defined as unipolar or multipolar. In either case, there is dramatically increased pressure on the hegemon to ensure that the allies recognize its hegemonic position. Following Mearsheimer (*The Tragedy of Great Power Politics*, pp. 12f.), we may describe both constellations as multipolarity with one potential hegemon – a system that he considers the most likely to produce conflict.

41 A carefully developed and richly documented argument along these lines may be found in Verenkotte, *Die Herren der Welt*, pp. 82ff.

42 See Koebner, *Imperialism*, pp. 135ff.

43 On the history of European power struggles and the failure of attempts to establish lasting hegemony, see Dehio, *The Precarious Balance*, and on the European balance and Britain's role, Vagts, 'Die Chimäre des europäischen Gleichgewichts'.

44 On the concept of a hegemonial war, see Gilpin, *War and Change*, pp. 186–210.

45 In the case of Spain, we need to distinguish between the extra-European empire, which lasted into the nineteenth century, and the attempt to build a European empire, which collapsed in the face of (partly concerted) action by France and the Ottoman empire. Here and in what follows, see Dehio, *The Precarious Balance*.

46 Such small wars should not be confused with the modern form of partisan warfare, although the two do have certain similarities. (See below, pp. 128ff.) The extremely brutal methods that can characterize them, flying in the face of all international law, may be illustrated by the crushing of the Herero resistance in German Southwest Africa in 1904: see Zimmerer and Zeller, *Völkermord*.

47 Bender (*Weltmacht Amerika*, pp. 170–6) has discussed the significance of a peripheral location for the rise of Rome and the United States.

48 On England's economic development since the eighteenth century and its lead over European rivals, see Landes, *The Wealth and Poverty of Nations*, pp. 213ff., and esp. the table on p. 232.

49 On the assumptions of imperialism theory, an imperialist world war between Britain and the United States would have been unavoidable – and an occasion for one came with British interference in the American

Civil War. According to the realist school of international politics, a British declaration of war on the Union would have been expected at that time, but of course nothing of the kind ever happened. See McPherson, *Battle Cry of Freedom*, pp. 384–90.

50 See Hosking, *Russia: People and Empire*, pp. 7ff.

51 In the Russo-Japanese war of 1904–5, Russia was punished for having grossly underestimated this opponent as one more pushover on the road of eastward expansion.

52 See Mao Tse-tung, 'On Protracted War' (May 1938).

53 In his inaugural lecture at Freiburg in 1895, Max Weber expressed as follows this shortening of the imperial time horizon: 'We must understand that the unification of Germany was a youthful prank committed by the nation at an advanced age, and should rather have been avoided on grounds of excessive cost if it was to form the conclusion instead of the point of departure for a policy of German world power' (Weber, 'The National State and Economic Policy', pp. 206–7). Having joined late the circle of imperial powers, Germany had to hurry if it was not to end up empty-handed.

54 In addition to Ullrich's *Die nervöse Großmacht* and Radkau's *Das Zeitalter der Nervosität*, the idea of narrower time horizons as a key element in imperial policy is discussed in Fenske, 'Ungeduldige Zuschauer'.

55 This account of international rivalry in terms of a zero-sum distribution of power within a pluriverse of states tending towards equality is the great strength of the so-called realist school of international politics, and especially of the key texts by Morgenthau (*Politics among Nations*) and Waltz (*Theory of International Politics*).

56 Mearsheimer, *The Tragedy of Great Power Politics*, esp. pp. 29ff.

57 Daase (in *Kleine Kriege – Große Wirkung*) argues that great wars stabilize the international order, and small wars call it into question.

58 See Münkler, *The New Wars*, pp. 70ff.

59 See Judt, *A Grand Illusion?* pp. 15–50.

60 See Junker, *Power and Mission*, pp. 51ff. and 73ff. See also pp. 142f. below.

61 Mann, *Incoherent Empire*, p. 265.

62 Johnson, *The Sorrows of Empire*, p. 30. Ferguson (*Colossus*, pp. 8–12), though himself a supporter of empire, has also described the distinction between empire and hegemony as more misleading than helpful.

63 Kissinger, *Does America Need a Foreign Policy?*, pp. 325ff.

64 A brief survey may be found in Verenkotte, *Die Herren der Welt*, pp. 68ff.

65 Triepel, *Die Hegemonie*, p. 189.

66 'One main effect . . . of our law is the growing replacement of rule over foreign countries and peoples with the weaker power of *hegemony*. The beginning of this trend may be dated to the time when Sparta ended its policy of conquest and annexation and concluded the first of its numerous hegemonial symmachy treaties, the one with Tegea. The degree to which direct rule has been replaced with hegemony in international life

may be seen on every page of the history of modern "imperialism".' Ibid., p. 147.
67 Ibid., p. 283.
68 Ibid., p. 176.
69 Ibid., p. 187.
70 Ibid., p. 343. Of course, the political context in which these concepts were defined and applied strongly suggests that it was a question not so much of making them clearer and tighter as of influencing decisions by means of political rhetoric – especially if, as Isocrates explains in his speech 'On the Peace', the Spartans' *hegemonia* on land eventually allowed them to gain *dynamis* at sea, although they soon lost it again as a result of various abuses (Isocrates, 'On the Peace', §§ 101–4). On the political background to this speech and Isocrates' position between imperialism and a politics of hegemony, see Ottmann, *Geschichte des politischen Denkens*, vol. 1/2, pp. 241f.
71 Doyle, *Empires*, pp. 54ff.
72 Ibid., p. 40.
73 Ibid., pp. 58ff.
74 Ibid., pp. 55ff. A detailed account of Athenian intervention in the internal affairs of its allies may be found in Schuller, *Die Herrschaft der Athener*, pp. 11ff. (on direct forms of rule) and pp. 80ff. (on indirect forms).
75 To be sure, such a way of contrasting the two alliance systems is likely to reproduce the war propaganda of the Corinthians within the Peloponnesian League, according to which the expansion of Athenian power had become a menace to the freedom of Greece, and a war against Athens was necessary to defeat the Delian–Attic League. Thucydides (*The Peloponnesian War*, I: 88) already warned of such a view and treated it as mere propaganda. The true reason for the war, as he saw it, was Corinthian and Spartan fears of the further peaceful growth of Athens.
76 Doyle, *Empires*, pp. 70ff.
77 'A lust for expansion was always alien to this Peloponnesian power [Sparta] after it solidly established its pre-eminence in the peninsula. Territorially sated, defensively inclined by character, anxious to secure its own "cosmos", Sparta had everything to lose and nothing to gain from a policy of expansion. Athens, however, being turned to the sea, was actually predetermined for such a policy; it relied for economic reasons on mastery of the sea, and therefore of the Aegean islands and the coast of Asia Minor, and it was being pushed in the same direction not least by the development of its own political and social conditions, the growth of its tradesmen and the thirst for plunder of its mobile population. It was therefore quite natural that Athenian hegemony took on an *imperialist* character, very similar, only not in form [*sic!*], to England's hegemony in today's British Commonwealth. However, the nakedly hegemonic character of British power is the result of later developments. In Athens, on the contrary, hegemony actually came before "rule".' Triepel, *Die Hegemonie*, p. 382.
78 Doyle, *Empires*, p. 81.

Chapter 3 Steppe Empires, Sea Empires and Global Economies

1   Mann, *The Sources of Social Power*, vol. 1: *A History of Power from the Beginning to AD 1760*, pp. 22ff.
2   See below, pp. 111ff.
3   Doyle, *Empires*, pp. 93–7. And see below, pp. 70ff.
4   See Heuss, *Römische Geschichte*, pp. 272–320, esp. pp. 289ff.
5   On the connection between 'world economies' and 'world empires', see Wallerstein, 'The Rise and Coming Demise of the World Capitalist System', esp. pp. 5ff.
6   See Kulischer, *Allgemeine Wirtschaftsgeschichte*, vol. 1, pp.78ff.
7   See the synthetic account in Reinhard, *Kleine Geschichte des Kolonialismus*, pp. 25–43.
8   'Aware of the physical impossibility of conquering too much territory, and actually uninterested in a political empire so far from Europe, the Portuguese aimed only at efficient sea control coupled with political hegemony in the form of areas of influence.' Oliveira Marques, *History of Portugal*, p. 233.
9   Ibid., pp. 243ff.
10   On the debate between the Dutch and British over whether the ocean should be treated as open (*mare liberum*) or closed (*mare clausum*), see Diner, 'Imperialismus und Universalismus', p. 24, and Boxer, *The Dutch Seaborne Empire*, pp. 84–112.
11   Oliveira Marques, *History of Portugal*, p. 232.
12   Oliveira Marques, *Geschichte Portugals*, p. 252.
13   Boxer, *The Dutch Seaborne Empire*, pp. 132ff. On the clear ways in which Dutch economic attitudes differed from those of the Portuguese, see Schama, *The Embarrassment of Riches*, pp. 252ff.
14   Maier, 'Die Grenzen des Empire', pp. 128f.
15   See below, pp. 157ff.
16   The relevant figures may be found in Nye, *The Paradox of American Power*, 37ff. On the greater importance of the finance sector, as against shares in world output, for the production of world economic dominance, see Mann, *Incoherent Empire*, pp. 50ff.
17   See Landes, *Wealth and Poverty of Nations*, pp. 256f., and especially Fischer, 'Internationale Wirtschaftsbeziehungen und Währungsordnung'.
18   Thucydides, *History of the Peloponnesian War*, I: 10.2. On the construction project and the imagery of the Acropolis, see Welwei, *Das klassische Athen*, pp. 120ff.; and, on Augustus' building programme and use of images, Zanker, *Power of Images in the Age of Augustus*.
19   On the construction of a war machine as the equivalent of a functioning administration in the Mesopotamian empires, see Edzard, *Geschichte Mesopotamiens*, pp. 170f. and 208f., although there is no mistaking his scepticism about the royal claims of victory and might. Michael Mann makes numerous references to the importance of the

military apparatus in early empire-building: see *The Sources of Social Power*, vol. 1, pp. 130–78 and 231–49.

20 Here and on what follows, see Göckenjan, 'Die Welt der frühen Reiternomaden'; and, on the significance of the early steppe empires for the progress of European society, Schieder, *Handbuch der europäischen Geschichte*, vol. 1, pp. 215f. and 357–70.

21 For a full account, see Grousset, *The Empire of the Steppes*; Altheim, *Geschichte der Hunnen*; and Maenchen-Helfen, *The World of the Huns*.

22 Weber, *Economy and Society*, vol. 1, p. 215.

23 The most fruitful applications of the concept of charisma have been to ethnogenesis in the Germanic world: see, for example, Wenskus, *Stammesbildung und Verfassung*, and Wolfram, *History of the Goths*. The military superiority of the Mongol cavalry armies, which gained their victories without the use of infantry, is explained in Liddell Hart, *Great Captains Unveiled*, pp. 3–34.

24 Here and on what follows, see Weiers, 'Geschichte der Mongolen'. Cf. Kämpfe, 'Činggis Khan'; Weiers, 'Von Ögödei bis Möngke'; and Morgan, *The Mongols*, esp. pp. 84–103. The source for all the works on the Mongols is a text in Mongolian from the first half of the thirteenth century: *The Secret History of the Mongols*.

25 Quoted from Weiers, 'Geschichte der Mongolen', p. 72.

26 On the development of the Ilkhanate, see Weiers, 'Geschichte der Mongolen', pp. 92–6, and Nagel, *Timur der Eroberer*, pp. 134ff. On Mongol rule in China, see Franke, *Geschichte des chinesischen Reiches*, vol. 4, pp. 424–959.

27 See Lewis, 'The Arabs in Eclipse', esp. pp. 110f.

28 See Nagel, *Timur der Eroberer*, pp. 151ff., and Irwin, 'The Emergence of the Islamic World System', pp. 71–6.

29 This explains why there can be no objective measure of imperial overstretch. Neither the greatest distance between centre and periphery nor the overall length of the imperial frontiers tells us anything at all if the forms of imperial expansion and integration are not taken into consideration. (See below, pp. 116ff.)

30 On the rise and structure of the European overseas empires, see especially Abernethy, *The Dynamics of Global Dominance*. Cf. Boxer, *The Portuguese Seaborne Empire* and *The Dutch Seaborne Empire*, and the summary account in Reinhard, *Kleine Geschichte des Kolonialismus*, pp. 25–52.

31 See below, p. 74.

32 See Vance, 'Vom mare nostrum zu Kiplings "The Seven Seas"'.

33 This development is described in detail in Heuss, *Römische Geschichte*, pp. 168ff., and Syme, *The Roman Revolution*, pp. 15ff.

34 We are here following the account in Schulz, 'Roms Eroberung des Mittelmeers'. It is remarkable that, in his search for parallels between the Roman and American empires, Peter Bender compares the period between the first and the third Punic War to that between the First World War and the Cold War: see his *Weltmacht Amerika*, pp. 60ff., and his summary in *Historische Zeitschrift* 279 (2004), pp. 430–2.

35 In the eighteenth and nineteenth centuries, however, Britain was spared a civil war like the one in Rome during the first century before Christ – perhaps partly because one had already taken place in the seventeenth century.

36 For a more detailed discussion, see Triepel, *Die Hegemonie*, 464ff.

37 On the reorganization of the state under Emperor Diocletian, see Bellen, *Grundzüge der Römischen Geschichte*, vol. 2, pp. 110ff. Estimates of tax revenue and troop strengths in the Eastern and Western empire may be found in Breuer, *Imperien der Alten Welt*, pp. 186ff.

38 On Russia's claim to be civilizing Central Asia, see Hosking, *Russia: People and Empire*, pp. 38f., and Geyer, *Russian Imperialism*, pp. 187ff. And, on Russia's being torn between West and East in the formation of its political-cultural identity, Figes, *Natasha's Dance*, esp. pp. 282ff.

39 See the various writings of Isaiah Berlin, especially 'Herzen and his Memoirs', and *Russian Thinkers*.

40 Hosking, *Russia: People and Empire*, p. 153.

41 'In the end, it proved impossible to bind together in a hegemonial association highly diverse historical regions, ranging from the republics marked by the Latin West, through the Eastern Slav/Orthodox parts to the lands forming part of Islamic culture.' Simon, 'Die Desintegration der Sowjetunion', p. 205.

42 The cultivation of political-cultural identity as the basis of the nation-state has recently been the object of intensive research, especially in Germany. See, for example, the volumes edited by Bernhard Giesen and Helmut Berding: *Nationale und kulturelle Identität*, *Nationales Bewusstsein und kollektive Identität* and *Mythos und Nation*.

43 See Rauchensteiner, 'Verlust der Mitte', and Kann, *A History of the Habsburg Empire*.

44 See Matuz, *Das Osmanische Reich*, p. 141.

45 Another link was the Confucian ethic of Chinese officialdom, for which deep trust in the civilizing effect of culture was opposed to the barbarian threat pressing in from the periphery. See below, pp. 78f.?

46 See Ebrey, *The Cambridge Illustrated History of China*, pp. 209f., and Merson, *Roads to Xanadu*, pp. 73ff. China is not the only country to have withdrawn from maritime trade for reasons of internal stability. The Ottoman empire, though deploying a considerable navy in the confrontation with Venice and Spain, handed over maritime trade almost entirely to foreign merchants: see Matuz, *Das Osmanische Reich*, p. 111.

47 The decision to end maritime expansion was not, however, uniformly followed through. (See Menzel, 'Eurozentrismus', esp. pp. 76f., which also gives additional bibliographical references.) Whether a continuing naval commitment would have blocked the European advance in the Indian Ocean, as representatives of so-called Asianism were recently arguing (ibid., pp. 74ff.), is highly doubtful. At least as likely was the disintegration and fragmentation of the Chinese empire in the wake of maritime expansion.

48   Here and on what follows, see Doyle, *Empires*, pp. 108ff., and Reinhard, *Kleine Geschichte des Kolonialismus*, pp. 24ff. On cultural contact between Europe and South or East Asia, see Osterhammel's fundamental work *Die Entzauberung Asiens*, and, on the various types of colonial relationship, Osterhammel, *Colonialism*, pp. 17ff.

49   The literature speaks mostly of *forms* of power, as does Michael Mann, whose typology is largely taken up here. But, following Pierre Bourdieu's theory of types of capital, I prefer to speak of *types* of power, to develop by analogy the idea of an exchange of types of power or a reciprocal compensation.

50   Tacitus, *Annals*, II: 9.

51   Bernecker, *Spanische Geschichte*, p. 35. Of course, the lack of merchants and bankers in Spain was also due to the expulsion of Jews and Moors. See also Elliott, 'The Decline of Spain'.

52   Bernecker, *Spanische Geschichte*, p. 34; Bennassar and Vincent, *Le Temps de l'Espagne*, pp. 103ff.; and esp. Cipolla, *Die Odysee des spanischen Silbers*, pp. 53ff.

53   Bennassar and Vincent, *Le Temps de l'Espagne*, pp. 86ff.

54   The significance of these peace treaties, involving sizeable concessions on Spain's part, was underlined by a number of events: the state bankruptcies of 1627, 1647 and 1652; the naval defeat at the hands of the Dutch in 1639; and the defeat at the battle of Rocroi in 1643, which shattered the myth of the invincibility of the Spanish infantry. On the Dutch push into Portuguese trading areas, see Reinhard, *Kleine Geschichte des Kolonialismus*, pp. 35–43.

55   See Roberts, *The Military Revolution*; Parker, *The Military Revolution*; and Parker, *The Army of Flanders*.

56   See Pollmann, 'Eine natürliche Feindschaft'.

57   See Pagden, *Spanish Imperialism*, esp. pp. 37ff.

58   For Gibbon (*Decline and Fall of the Roman Empire*, vol. 1, ch. 4), the decline began with the end of the Antonine age, whereas Otto Seeck's *Geschichte des Untergangs der antiken Welt* opens with the Diocletian reforms.

59   A subtly differentiated account of these reforms may be found in Bleicken, *Verfassungs- und Sozialgeschichte des Römischen Kaiserreichs*.

60   See Münkler, *Machiavelli*, pp. 121ff. and 374ff.

61   In the theory of economic conjunctures, long waves are known as Kondratiev cycles: they represent, as it were, the pendant in economic history to the political cycles that are being considered here.

62   On the debate concerning right and wrong measures, see Cipolla in his editor's introduction to *The Economic Decline of Empires*, pp. 5ff.

63   See, for example, Modelski and Thompson, *Leading Sectors and World Powers*; Modelski, *Long Cycles in World Politics*; Modelski and Thompson, *Seapower in Global Politics*; Thompson, *On Global War*.

64   This is evidently the supposition behind Joseph Nye's advice that the United States should bank more on 'soft power' than 'hard power', since it breeds less hostility and is more cost-effective. Nye, *The Paradox of American Power*, pp. 170–1.

65 Doyle, *Empires*, pp. 93ff.

66 After the victory at Actium, Octavian reduced the number of legions to twenty-six or twenty-five, which meant that 120,000 soldiers were discharged and provided with land in Italy or the provinces, or else given a monetary settlement in lieu. The parallel military reforms, which established a definite length of service and regular pay for legionaries, praetorians and members of auxiliary units, helped to strengthen the loyalty of the troops to army headquarters and to make them less dependent on their respective commanders. This was the core of the internal pacification of the empire. For a more detailed discussion, see König, *Der Römische Staat*, vol. 2, p. 35; Bellen, *Grundzüge der Römischen Geschichte*, vol. 1, pp. 163, 171 and 179; and Heuss, *Römische Geschichte*, pp. 298ff.

67 By plundering the Ptolemy treasure in Egypt and distributing the proceeds to the urban population in Rome, Octavian managed to reduce the interest on loans from 12 per cent to 4 per cent. The state treasury could thus repay the war loans and refrain from the collection of outstanding debts. The general remission of debts led to a sharp rise in prosperity, especially in the Eastern provinces. See Bellen, *Grundzüge der Römischen Geschichte*, vol. 1, p. 162; and Heuss, *Römische Geschichte*, pp. 294ff.

68 In the concluding sentence of his great work on the civil war period, Ronald Syme succinctly expresses the dialectical interplay of intention and function in the life of Augustus: 'For power he had sacrificed everything; he had achieved the height of mortal ambition and in his ambition he had saved and regenerated the Roman People.' *The Roman Revolution*, p. 524.

69 Syme (ibid.) draws an impressive picture of the moral corruption among the republican elite.

70 König, *Der Römische Staat*, vol. 2, p. 45.

71 See König, *Der Römische Staat*, vol. 2; Bellen, *Grundzüge der Römischen Geschichte*, vol. 1, p. 183; and Heuss, *Römische Geschichte*, p. 285.

72 In the *Res gestae Divi Augusti*, Octavian presented the conversion of *potestas* into *auctoritas* as the guiding principle of his rule: see Syme, *The Roman Revolution*, pp. 518ff.

73 See below, pp. 86f.

74 The figures are taken from Bellen, *Grundzüge der Römischen Geschichte*, vol. 1, pp. 107, 163 and 174.

75 On the *Consitiutio Antoniana*, see Bellen, *Grundzüge der Römischen Geschichte*, vol. 3, pp. 177ff.

76 See Potter, *Roman Italy*, pp. 60ff.

77 Bellen, *Grundzüge der Römischen Geschichte*, vol. 2, pp. 251ff.

78 See Bernecker, *Spanische Geschichte*, pp. 7ff.; and Doyle, *Empires*, pp. 111f.

79 I am therefore unable to accept Doyle's idea (*Empires*, pp. 118f.) that Spain, unlike England, crossed the Augustan threshold in relation to its colonies. What led him to this view is the fact that Spanish rule in the Americas lasted twice as long as English rule.

80   See Parker, *The Military Revolution*, pp. 12ff.; and Pepper and Adams, *Firearms and Fortifications*.
81   Bernecker, *Spanische Geschichte*, p. 36.
82   Ibid., p. 50.
83   Here and for what follows, see Hosking, *Russia: People and Empire*, pp. 76ff.
84   For an impressive account of this project and the problems associated with it, see Figes, *Natasha's Dance*, pp. 4–10.
85   See below, p. 90.
86   See Matuz, *Das Osmanische Reich*, pp. 69ff.
87   See Ursinus, 'Byzanz, Osmanisches Reich, türkischer Nationalstaat', p. 165.
88   Matuz, *Das Osmanische Reich*, pp. 141f.
89   Ibid., pp. 110f.
90   Ibid., pp. 45ff. Cf. Nagel, *Timur der Eroberer*, pp. 354ff.
91   Jorga, *Geschichte des Osmanischen Reichs*, vol. 1, pp. 325ff.
92   Matuz, *Das Osmanische Reich*, pp. 84f. and 98.
93   Here, and on what follows, see Ebrey, *The Cambridge Illustrated History of China*, and Schmidt-Glintzer, *China*.
94   See the detailed account in Franke, *Geschichte des chinesischen Reiches*, vol. 1, pp. 268–320.
95   Comparisons with the Roman empire occur repeatedly in accounts of Chinese history. See, for example, Ebrey, *The Cambridge Illustrated History of China*, p. 85.
96   Franke, *Geschichte des chinesischen Reiches*, vol. 1, pp. 388–431.
97   Ibid., vol. 2, pp. 350–529.
98   Ibid., vol. 4, pp. 101–24.
99   Ibid., vol. 4, pp. 351–423.

Chapter 4 Civilization and Barbarian Frontiers

1   In his *The European Miracle*, Eric Lionel Jones explains Europe's gain on Asia since early modern times by the small scale of its political order. On the beginnings of the multi-state pluriverse in Europe, see Fueter, *Geschichte des europäischen Staatensystems*; and, for a sceptical view of the quality of its political order, Vagts, 'Die Chimäre des europäischen Gleichgewichts', pp. 131ff.
2   Quoted from Fuhrmann, *Deutsche Geschichte im hohen Mittelalter*, p. 174.
3   Livius, *The History of Rome*, XXI: 44.
4   Virgil, *Aeneid*, I: 291–6, pp. 260–1.
5   Dante, *Monarchy*, p. 13.
6   See Botero's *Discorso dell'eccelenza della monarchia*, and Campanella's *Della monarchia di Spagna*. Cf. Bosbach, *Monarchia Universalis*, pp. 64ff., and Pagden, 'Instruments of Empire'.
7   See the detailed account in Fetscher, *Modelle der Friedenssicherung*, and Fischbach, *Krieg und Frieden in der französischen Aufklärung*. And, on the

significance of Kant's text on peace for contemporary debate on the world order, see Habermas, 'Das Kantische Projekt'.

8 Montesquieu, 'Réflexions sur la monarchie universelle', pp. 192ff.; cf. Böhlke, 'Esprit de nation', pp. 219ff.

9 One of the sharpest critics of the Spanish empire and its colonial policy was Abbé Raynal (Histoire philosophique et politique des établissements et du commerce des Européens dans les deux Indes, 1774): see Gollwitzer, Geschichte des weltpolitischen Denkens, vol. 1, pp. 262–85. And, on the concept of 'commercial society', see Bohlender, 'Government, Commerce and Civil Society'.

10 See Brown, Debating the Democratic Peace. And, for a critique of the basic assumptions of this theory, Münkler, 'Ist der Krieg abschaffbar?', esp. pp. 367ff.

11 Cooper, The Breaking of Nations, pp. 55ff. Similarly, Röhrich ('Problemfelder der Weltinnenpolitik') proposes to divide the OECD from the rest of the world, where 'condensed economic areas' have not taken shape.

12 Mearsheimer, The Tragedy of Great Power Politics, pp. 2f.

13 Kagan, 'Power and Weakness', and idem, On Paradise and Power.

14 Marx, 'The Eighteenth Brumaire', pp. 180ff. On the complexity of the concept of ideology, see the historical introduction in Lenk, Ideologie, pp. 17–59.

15 In any case, as soon as the concept goes outside the limited circle of ideology theorists.

16 On the links between commerce and piracy, as well as on the cooperation between regional powers and pirates in the Mediterranean in the first century BC, see Christ, Pompeius, pp. 56ff.

17 See Bleicken, Verfassungs- und Sozialgeschichte des Römischen Kaiserreichs, vol. 1, pp. 93f.

18 Augustine, City of God, XIX: 26.

19 On the political content of Virgil's poetry, see Rilinger, 'Das politische Denken der Römer', pp. 531ff., and Ottmann, Geschichte des politischen Denkens, vol. 2/1, pp. 183ff.

20 Virgil, Aeneid, I: 278–82, pp. 260–1.

21 On the political content of Horace's poetry, see Rilinger, 'Das politische Denken der Römer', pp. 534f., and Ottmann, Geschichte des politischen Denkens, vol. 2/1, pp. 168ff.

22 Horace, Carmina, III: 2, 13.

23 See Fuhrmann, Deutsche Geschichte im hohen Mittelalter, pp. 170ff.

24 The figure of the katechon, which played such a major role in the political imagination of the Hohenstaufens (especially Otto von Freising), regained a certain prominence in the political theory of Carl Schmitt: see Blindow, Carl Schmitts Reichsordnung, pp. 144ff.; and Nichtweiß, 'Apokalyptische Verfassungslehren', pp. 60ff.

25 Bernecker, Spanische Geschichte, pp. 57ff.; Pagden, Spanish Imperialism, pp. 13–36; and Otto, Conquista, Kultur und Ketzerwahn, pp. 45ff.

26 The view of religious plurality as central to imperial policy is represented by Adanir, 'Der Zerfall des Osmanischen Reiches', pp. 112ff.,

while the conception of its basically Islamic-expansionist character is defended in Philipp, 'Der aufhaltsame Abstieg des Osmanischen Reiches'.

27 See Lewis, *The Arabs in History*, pp. 56ff., and Hourani, *A History of the Arab Peoples*, pp. 22–38.

28 Jorga, *Geschichte des Osmanischen Reiches*, vol. 2, pp. 196ff.

29 Hosking, *Russia: People and Empire*, pp. 5ff. On the idea of the Third Rome, see Barudio, 'Die Macht des Hegemonialismus'.

30 Figes, *Natasha's Dance*, p. 152. On the imperial foreign policy of Ivan IV, see Stökl, *Russische Geschichte*, pp. 237–46.

31 Figes, *Natasha's Dance*, pp. 306ff.

32 Hosking, *Russia: People and Empire*, pp. 138ff.; Stökl, *Russische Geschichte*, pp. 450ff.

33 Quoted (and translated) from Lorenz, 'Das Ende der Sowjetunion', p. 259.

34 See Simon, 'Die Desintegration der Sowjetunion', esp. pp. 186ff.

35 On Britain's imperial mission, see Ferguson, *Empire*, pp. 115ff. A succinct account of its idea of civilizing the world may be found in Reifeld, 'Imperialismus', pp. 29ff.

36 Kipling, *Complete Verse*, pp. 321–3. Kipling's poem was also intended for the United States, which was beginning to face up to its imperial obligations.

37 Marx, 'The British Rule in India', pp. 580–2.

38 See Reinhard, *Kleine Geschichte des Kolonialismus*, pp. 97ff.

39 For a more detailed discussion, see Ferguson, *Empire*, pp. 117ff.

40 On American foreign policy since the late 1950s, see Hacke, *Zur Weltmacht verdammt*.

41 On the concept of aristocratic empires and the role of the aristocracy as a ruling class, see Kautsky, *The Politics of Aristocratic Empires*, esp. pp. 79ff. Kautsky is mainly concerned with empires in which power and influence rested on landed property, and whose defining feature was a lack of social change.

42 On the corollary to the Monroe Doctrine, see Johnson, *The Sorrows of Empire*, p. 192; and, on the pursuit of equilibrium in the Pacific, Junker, *Power and Mission*, pp. 34ff.

43 See Junker, *Power and Mission*, pp. 42ff.; Kissinger, *Does America Need a Foreign Policy?*, pp. 242ff.; and Mead, *Special Providence*, pp. 132–73.

44 In keeping with a long tradition, the ideology critique of the American empire sees all its major plans and decisions as determined by economic and political interests. The most important representative of this critique in the United States is Noam Chomsky, who subjects the various forms of empire-building to fundamental scrutiny in such works as *American Power and the New Mandarins* and *Hegemony or Survival*.

45 This religious thematic runs through the whole of US foreign policy, regardless of its fundamental posture or its underlying doctrine: see Mead, *Special Providence*, and Prätorius, *In God We Trust*.

46 On the identification of the four empires and the later extension to the Roman empire, see Koch, *Das Buch Daniel*, pp. 182ff., and Mosès, *Eros und Gesetz*, pp. 111–26.

47 See below, pp. 123f.

48 For an overview of the discourse of barbarism, see Schneider, *Der Barbar*, and Nippel, *Griechen, Barbaren und 'Wilde'*; and, on its structure and function in the transition from imperial reminiscence to a pluriverse of national identities, Münkler, Grünberger and Mayer, *Nationenbildung*, pp. 130ff. On the reactions of the discursively barbarized, see ibid., pp. 210ff., and von See, *Barbar, Germane, Arier*, pp. 31–60.

49 The following considerations owe much to Reinhart Koselleck's brilliant essay 'The Historical-Political Semantics of Asymmetric Counterconcepts'.

50 See Nippel, 'Griechische Kolonisation', and, on Francisco de Vitoria's legitimation of Spanish conquest policy as an ending of human sacrifice, Marina Münkler, 'Entdecker und Eroberer', pp. 173f.

51 In China, between the Song dynasty in the South and the Mongol Jin in the North, stories of the fate of Chinese women influenced the development of an especially intense image of the barbarian. See Ebrey, *Cambridge Illustrated History of China*, pp. 150ff.

52 See Münkler, *The New Wars*, pp. 83ff.

53 On the 'barbarization' of the Roman army, see Heuss, *Römische Geschichte*, pp. 484ff., and Goldsworthy, *The Complete Roman Army*, pp. 208ff.

54 See Schmidt-Glinzer, *China*, pp. 165ff.

55 Ebrey, *Cambridge Illustrated History of China*, p. 172.

56 Ibid., p. 173.

57 In his *De indis recenter inventis*, first published in 1538, Vitoria had still argued that the Spaniards' only legal claim in relation to the Indians was the *ius peregrinandi* and the *ius predicandi*: that is, the right to travel in their land, and the right to conduct missionary work among them. It would be permissible for the Spanish to use force only if the indigenous peoples opposed these rights with violence. On the top-level debate over the form and legitimacy of Spanish rule, see Pagden, *Spanish Imperialism*, pp. 13–36, and especially Marina Münkler, 'Entdecker und Eroberer', pp. 172ff.

58 Cf. Bitterli, *Die Entdeckung und Eroberung der Welt*, vol. 1, pp. 51ff.

59 Cf. Figes, *Natasha's Dance*, pp. 376ff.

60 On European steps to combat the Arab slave trade, see Albertini, *Europäische Kolonialherrschaft*, pp. 453 and 513f.

61 See Jeismann, 'Propaganda', and Hamann, *Der Erste Weltkrieg*, pp. 34ff., 42ff. In both cases, the image of barbarism was strongly coloured by charges of sexual violence against women.

62 On the refusal of suicide bombers to play by the rules, see Reuter, *Mein Leben ist eine Waffe*, pp. 9–31. And on the massacres in Rwanda, which could have been prevented if the international community had

intervened in time, see Des Forges, *Leave None to Tell the Story*, pp. 595ff.

63 Of course, the founders of maritime and commercial empires did not dispense entirely with military instruments, and Europe's superiority rested upon its caravels and galleons. See Cipolla, *Guns and Sails*, pp. 81ff.

64 See below pp. 151f.

65 See above pp. 47f., 70f.

66 See Potter, *Roman Italy*, pp. 182ff., and Doyle, *Empires*, pp. 102f.

67 Potter, *Roman Italy*, pp. 125ff., and, on the road network in the age of Diocletian, ibid., p. 132.

68 On the British railway system in India and the significance of the telegraph, see Ferguson, *Empire*, pp. 169ff.

69 A description of the Soviet Union's crumbling economic space may be found in Kapuściński, *Imperium*, pp. 107ff., and Kernig, *Lenins Reich in Trümmern*, pp. 333ff.

70 On Witte's imperial policy, see Hosking, *Russia: People and Empire*, p. 342; Geyer, *Russian Imperialism*, and Stökl, *Russische Geschichte*, pp. 610–18.

71 Hosking, *Russia: People and Empire*, pp. 315ff.

72 On the importance of the railway for an efficient transport system, see McNeill, *The Pursuit of Power*, pp. 242ff.

73 See Bernecker, *Spanische Geschichte*, pp. 62ff., and Cipolla, *Die Odysee des spanischen Silbers*, pp. 91ff.

74 Here and on what follows, see König, 'Der Zerfall des Spanischen Weltreichs in Amerika', pp. 128ff.

75 Ebrey, *Cambridge Illustrated History of China*, pp. 86ff.

76 Ibid., pp. 141f.

Chapter 5 The Defeat of Empires by the Power of the Weak

1 For Ludwig Dehio (*The Precarious Balance*), modern European history has been characterized by four successive attempts to achieve hegemony: the Spanish attempt, which already failed under Philip II; the first French attempt, which had exhausted itself by the end of the reign of Louis XIV; the second French attempt, which foundered with the fall of Napoleon; and the German attempt, which for Dehio began with Bismarck's unification of the Reich and ended in 1945.

2 See Gilpin, *War and Change*, pp. 186ff., and Mearsheimer, *The Tragedy of Great Power Politics*, pp. 32–54.

3 Keegan, *The First World War*, pp. 165ff., and Strachan, *The First World War*, pp. 24ff. The initially disastrous course of the war on the Serbian front was a result of the regroupment of Austro-Hungarian forces made necessary by Russia's entry into the war.

4 On the course of events and the autonomous logic of war, see Baumgart, *Die Julikrise*.

5 In the debate on war debts, German actions in July 1914 were interpreted in two conflicting ways: either as the result of extremely clumsy

German diplomacy; or as a deliberate push towards war, in which the new Balkan crisis was a mere pretext to break the Triple Alliance of France, Russia and Britain that encircled the Reich.

6 See Schley and Busse, *Die Kriege der USA*, pp. 58–63; and, on the small imperial wars of the United States, Boot, *The Savage Wars of Peace*.

7 The greatest concern over the Russian defeat was expressed in France, which saw it as a major weakening of its most important ally; sizeable loans were then granted for modernization of the Russian armed forces and the development of its railway network. This, in turn, led to considerable worries in Germany. See Howard, *The First World War*, pp. 24f.

8 For a detailed account of this crisis, see Lewis, *The Race to Fashoda*.

9 See Münkler, 'Staatengemeinschaft oder Imperium'.

10 See Modelski, *Seapower in Global Politics*, pp. 27ff.

11 See Massie, *Dreadnought*, pp. xxiv–xxv, 609ff.

12 See Heilbrunn, *Partisan Warfare*; Schulz, *Partisanen und Volkskrieg*; and Münkler, *Der Partisan*.

13 'Low intensity war' has come to stand as an umbrella term for such conflicts: see van Creveld, *On Future War*, pp. 57ff., 171ff., 207f.

14 David argues that these exceptions – which range from the battle in the Teutoburg Forest to Dien Bien Phu – were due to overconfidence on the part of the imperial players. *Military Blunders*, pp. 221–87.

15 Clausewitz, *On War*, p. 527.

16 Ibid., p. 528.

17 Ibid.

18 Clausewitz refers to this point in his chapter 'The People in Arms', which immediately follows the chapter 'Retreat to the Interior of the Country'. The two concepts are for him, as it were, functional equivalents: if the strategic depth for a retreat into the interior is lacking, it must be compensated for by an increased willingness for sacrifice on the part of the people. The political logic of guerrilla warfare is therefore as follows: 'A government must never assume that its country's fate, its whole existence, hangs on the outcome of a single battle, no matter how decisive. Even after a defeat, there is always the possibility that a turn of fortune can be brought about by developing new sources of internal strength or through the natural decimation all offensives suffer in the long run or by means of help from abroad. There will always be time enough to die; like a drowning man who will clutch instinctively at a straw, it is the natural law of the moral world that a nation that finds itself on the brink of an abyss will try to save itself by any means.' Ibid., p. 483.

19 Kissinger, 'The Vietnam Negotiations', p. 214. Raymond Aron had already made similar points in *Peace and War*, pp. 42, 56f.

20 Johnson, *Blowback*.

21 See above, pp. 41f.

22 Clausewitz, *On War*, p. 529.

23 Following Clausewitz, the military historian Hans Delbrück (*Die Strategie des Perikles*, pp. 27f.) distinguished between strategies

to defeat and to exhaust the enemy (*Niederwerfungsstrategie* and *Ermattungsstrategie*). The former he defined as unipolar, since it sought only to annihilate the enemy forces, whereas the latter was bipolar, since, according to the balance of forces and the political intent, it might result either in exhaustion of the enemy through military manoeuvres or in a decision on the battlefield. (For a more detailed discussion, see Lange, *Hans Delbrück und der 'Strategiestreit'*.) Of course, bearing in mind the more recent forms of guerrilla warfare, we would have to speak of the development of unipolarity within *Ermattungsstrategie*, since the possibility of a decisive battle lies in an unattainable future as soon as guerrillas have to face not just regional adversaries but an imperial war machine.

24 The year 1914 saw Britain enter the First World War essentially because of a perceived German threat to the empire (see Howard, *The First World War*, pp. 3, 9ff.); 1956 was the year of the Suez crisis (see below, p. 145).

25 Ferguson, *Empire*, pp. 346ff.

26 This self-deception is sympathetically described in Porter, *The Absent-Minded Imperialists*.

27 See Frey, 'Das Ende eines Kolonialreichs'.

28 See Rémond, *Le XXe Siècle*.

29 For a succinct yet brilliant analysis of the Algerian War, see Aron, *Clausewitz*, pp. 370f.

30 See below, pp. 138–9 ,141ff.

31 See Münkler, 'Kriegsszenarien des 21. Jahrhunderts', esp. pp. 84ff.

32 In the literature, symmetry and asymmetry are generally used as binary concepts, and on the whole this overlooks the fact that there are weaker and stronger asymmetries. The pair of concepts become analytically useful only if they are flexible enough to take this into account.

33 The kidnapping of craftsmen and engineers was widely practised by nomadic peoples in China's northwest frontier regions as a way of evening out the superiority of the empire. (See Merson, *Roads to Xanadu*, p. 54.) Similarly, the Ottomans regularly used 'Western' cannon founders, although in most cases they bought their services with money. (Cipolla, *Guns and Sails*, pp. 94ff.)

34 See Nef, *Western Civilization*, pp. 84ff., and Cipolla, *Guns and Sails*, pp. 101ff.

35 The figures are taken from De Schweinitz, *The Rise and Fall of British India*, p. 242. The fame of the battle of Omdurman was due not least to Winston Churchill's dazzling eye-witness report. That European colonial powers could not automatically count on such victories had been demonstrated two years earlier at Adna, when Ethiopian units inflicted a defeat on the Italians. (See Brogini Künzi, 'Der Sieg der Negus'.)

36 Here and on what follows, see Rosen, 'Ein Empire auf Probe', esp. pp. 92ff.

37 Carlo M. Cipolla (*Guns and Sails*, pp. 21–89) has demonstrated this with reference to the technological capabilities of the producers of cast-iron

cannons. When Britain and then Sweden succeeded in producing light, reliable and inexpensive cast-iron cannons, this technological advance gave them a decisive superiority over European rivals. But they exported cannons in great numbers and allowed craftsmen to emigrate together with the secrets of the trade, so that all the European powers were soon also in possession of high-quality cannons.

38 See Münkler, *Im Namen des Staates*, pp. 280ff.
39 See Rosen, 'Ein Empire auf Probe', p. 96.
40 On this concept, see Maier, 'Die Grenzen des Empire', p. 128.
41 The new 'National Security Strategy of the United States of America' may be consulted at http://www.whitehouse.gov/nsc/nss.pdf.
42 On the 'prehistory' of this new security doctrine, see Hacke, *Zur Weltmacht verdammt*, pp. 471ff. and 576ff.
43 See Johnson, *The Sorrows of Empire*, pp. 288–92, and Priest, *The Mission*, esp. pp. 121ff. The terms 'Shock and Awe' and 'Achieving Rapid Dominance', which bear the mark of Harlan Ullman, also describe strategies for the creation of imperial superiority at any time on the periphery.
44 Hobbes, *Leviathan*, Part I, ch. 13, p. 94.
45 Ibid., p. 97.
46 Political players which are not tied to a territory, and therefore not threatened with a nuclear counter-strike, might use nuclear weapons quite differently from states and, for example, create a long-term atmosphere of blackmail for territorially bound political players. (See Behr, *Entterritoriale Politik*, pp. 75ff. and 119ff.) Moreover, if nuclear weapons were to spread throughout the world, with inadequate controls and safeguards in many countries, they could be stolen by criminals and used to hold one or more states to ransom.
47 See Schröfl and Pankratz, *Asymmetrische Kriegführung*.
48 The following points are developed at greater length in Münkler, 'Ältere und jüngere Formen des Terrorismus'; 'Terrorismus heute'; and 'Wandel der Weltordnung'.
49 This point follows Clausewitz's triad of object, aim and means, according to which the object is what war is meant to achieve, and the aim is what must be achieved *in* war. See Clausewitz, *On War*, pp. 75ff.
50 See above, pp. 47ff.
51 See above, pp. 95f.
52 See Anderson, *Imagined Communities*, pp. 50ff., and Hobsbawm, *Nations and Nationalism*, pp. 136ff.
53 See Münkler, 'Partisanen der Tradition'.
54 See Olshausen, 'Das politische Denken der Römer', pp. 510f.
55 Cf. Pagden, 'Instruments of Empire'.
56 On the subject in general, see Steinweg, *Der gerechte Krieg*, and Walzer, *Just and Unjust Wars*. And, on the ways in which some Americans perceive themselves, see the manifesto 'What We Are Fighting For' (2002) published by a number of US intellectuals after the intervention in Afghanistan and in the run-up to the Iraq War: http://www.americanvalues. org/html/wwff.html.

57 Here and on what follows, see Steininger's synthetic account *Der Vietnamkrieg*.

58 On the distinction between instrumental and existential war, see Münkler, 'Instrumentelle und existentielle Auffassung des Krieges'.

59 'From 1988 on it became increasingly clear that, without massive military and economic disengagement, it would be impossible either to defuse the long-simmering regional conflicts or to give any significant relief to the Soviet budget. In 1990 the withdrawal from parts of the Third World then took on the characteristics of a flight, which with the end of the state led to the giving up of any policy to exercise influence in developing countries.' Simon and Simon, *Verfall und Untergang des sowjetischen Imperiums*, p. 199.

60 Cf. Schell, *Unconquerable World*, pp. 63ff.

61 See Ferguson, *Empire*, pp. 270–82.

62 See the trenchant account in Tuchman, *The March of Folly*.

63 For example, Hahlweg, *Guerilla*; von der Heydte, *Der moderne Kleinkrieg*; and Kitson, *Low Intensity Operations*.

64 See Kunisch, *Der kleine Krieg*, pp. 5–24.

65 For a survey of ethnic expulsions carried out by various empires in the twentieth century, and of ethnically motivated massacres in post-imperial spaces, see Naimark, *Fires of Hatred*.

66 Assyrian policy under Tighlatpileser III and Shalmaneser V involved deporting the upper layers through which a people was supposed to acquire the capacity for organization and action. On the Assyrian defeat of Israel, see Noth, *The History of Israel*, pp. 287ff. Nebuchadnezzar conducted a similar policy against Judah: see ibid., pp. 306ff.; and the contribution by Hayim Tadmor to Ben-Sasson, *A History of the Jewish People*, pp. 155ff.

67 The number who died as a result of the Armenian deportations is variously estimated between 200,000 and one million. The verdict on Turkish measures against the rebellious Armenians, who from the end of the nineteenth century had been trying to throw off Ottoman rule by means of terrorist attacks and a regular guerrilla war, are also not unanimous. Matuz (*Das Osmanische Reich*, p. 265) speaks of genocide (as do Majoros and Rill, *Das Osmanische Reich*, p. 360), while Kreiser and Neumann (*Kleine Geschichte der Türkei*, pp. 371–7) locate the 'resettlement law' of May 1915 more strongly in the context of military operations on the Caucasian front. Jorga reviews the position of Armenians in the Ottoman empire since the eighteenth century in *Geschichte des Osmanischen Reichs*, vol. 5, pp. 606–13.

68 See Noth, *The History of Israel*, pp. 438ff., and the contribution by Menahem Stern in Ben-Sasson, *A History of the Jewish People*, pp. 300–3.

69 See Angermann, *Die Vereinigten Staaten von Amerika*, pp. 313f., 400 and 426.

70 See Buruma, *Bad Elements*, pp. 299–315.

71 Fanon developed his idea of the therapeutic function of violence in the decolonization process in his two books: *The Wretched of the Earth* and

Black Skin, White Masks. On the psychopathology of guerrilla warfare, see Voss, 'Ich habe keine Stimme mehr, mein ganzes Leben flieht' (with an extensive bibliography).

72   A comparison between the anti-Napoleonic wars in Spain and Germany could have shown that, in the medium to long term, guerrilla warfare not only ruins the enemy but is associated with major and lasting destruction on one's own side. At the beginning of the nine-teenth century, both countries were occupied by Napoleonic troops and looked for ways of shaking off French rule. Whereas the Prussian polit-ical reforms should be seen as an attempt to offset inferiority (one result of the revolutionary changes in France) by restoring *symmetry*, the Spanish wagered on *asymmetry* by developing small war (*guerrilla*) into a largely independent form of warfare. In the end, both countries made a major contribution to the defeat of Napoleon. But, whereas Prussian society after 1814–15 entered a period of continual development, which the revolution of 1848–49 only accelerated, Spanish society in the nine-teenth century went through a long succession of crises and regime changes, and Spain became more and more disconnected from trends in the rest of Europe. See Bernecker, *Spanische Geschichte*, pp. 111–49.

73   This new influence, and the consequences it entailed, are discussed in Stiglitz, *Globalization and its Discontents*.

74   See Münkler, *The New Wars*, pp. 74ff., and 'Zur Charakterisierung der neuen Kriege'.

75   Nye, *The Paradox of American Power*, pp. 8ff., 99ff. Nye is well aware, of course, that soft power is considerably less amenable than hard power to political control.

76   Armstrong offers the most thorough examination of twentieth-century fundamentalism and its precursors, in *The Battle for God*.

77   Here and on what follows, see Noth, *The History of Israel*, pp. 367–85; Stern, in Ben-Sasson, *A History of the Jewish People*, pp. 201–23; and Soggin, *An Introduction to the History of Israel and Judah*.

78   It is true that issues of religion and identity alone were not decisive in triggering the revolt. The war of the Seleucids against the Ptolemaic rulers of Egypt cost a lot of money, more than Antiochus IV Epiphanes had at his disposal, and so he cast covetous eyes at the Temple treasures with the intention of appropriating them for his cause. The pillage of the Temple in Jerusalem made many Jews considerably more willing to join the rebels, or at least to give them support.

79   See Mosès, *Eros und Gesetz*, pp. 111ff.; and Koch, *Das Buch Daniel*, esp. pp. 127ff.

80   That the civil war also involved social issues, which found their cata-lyst in the religious-cultural conflict over the right way to live, is well brought out by Menahem Stern in his contribution to Ben-Sasson, *History of the Jewish People*, p. 205.

81   The defensive orientation of the partisan fighter is an important element in Carl Schmitt's character portrait: *Theorie des Partisanen*, p. 26. In the end Lenin did not convert 'defensive-indigenous defenders of

the fatherland' into 'globally aggressive revolutionary activists', as Schmitt thought that he would, but this change has been occurring as hard imperial power is increasingly replaced with soft power.

Chapter 6 The Surprising Return of Empire in the Post-Imperial Age

1   The return of the heroic problem-tackler in US cinema is a good indication of the mood change and the revival of self-confidence. Movies, of course, not only display such mood changes but also strengthen and accelerate them. Some evidence of General Schwarzkopf's therapeutic function in relation to the Vietnam trauma may be found in QRT, *Schwachtfelder der elektronischen Wüste*, pp. 10–39.

2   In the literature, the concept of asymmetry is generally used only for warfare by inferior forces: for example, to characterize guerrilla war or a campaign of terror. But there is also asymmetry on the side of the superior forces. See Münkler, 'Wandel der Weltordnung durch asymmetrische Kriege'.

3   Demandt, 'Die Weltreiche in der Geschichte', p. 223. In the 1990s, a number of books appeared in Germany which not only dealt with the more or less contingent end of particular empires but started from the idea of the end of all empire. See, for instance, Lorenz, *Das Verdämmern der Macht*; Altrichter and Neuhaus, *Das Ende von Großreichen*; and Demandt, *Das Ende der Weltreiche*.

4   Hobsbawm, *The Age of Extremes*, p. ix; cf. Hobsbawm, *The New Century*, pp. 2ff.

5   See Junker, *Power and Mission*, pp. 48ff.

6   Hobsbawm, *Age of Extremes*, pp. 31f.

7   See Dan Diner, *Das Jahrhundert verstehen*, pp. 85ff.; and, on the ethnic cleansing, ibid., esp. pp. 195ff.

8   This concept was first introduced by Carl Schmitt, in *Völkerrechtliche Großraumordnung mit Interventionsverbot für raumfremde Mächte*, and in 'Großraum gegen Universalismus', pp. 295–302. Of course, it is being used here differently from the way that Schmitt intended.

9   Ferguson, *Colossus*, p. 78.

10   It is an open question whether this was structurally bound up with the system of collectively organized lack of responsibility, or whether the reason for failure should rather be sought in the specific conditions of the interwar period (for example, a blockage resulting from mutual distrust among the great powers).

11   Hitler's alliance with the conservative elites in economic and military matters was based not least on the perspective of a spatially and temporally limited war to revise boundaries in Central Europe, in the course of which Germany's hegemonic position in the area would be restored. On the readiness to consider such a war, even among men who later became resolute opponents of Hitler, see Müller, 'Militärpolitik in der Krise'; and, on the significance of Southeastern

Europe for Hitler's decision to attack the Soviet Union, see Gorodetsky, *Grand Delusion*.

12 It is true that the briefly independent states of Georgia, Armenia and Azerbaijan were incorporated along with Ukraine into the Union of Soviet Socialist Republics, and that Moscow suppressed the strivings for independence in Belorussia and the Crimea and among the Bashkirs and Volga Tatars (see Motyl, *Sovietology, Rationality, Nationality*, pp. 105ff.). But Finland, the Baltic republics and Poland were able to escape the clutches of the Red Army, and in the Balkans and lower Danube the Soviet Union lost the influence that the Tsarist empire had previously enjoyed.

13 Where it was a question of restoring the lines of interest drawn by Bismarck's Reich and the empire of the Tsars, agreement was easily reached between Hitler and Stalin. But in areas that had belonged to the Austro-Hungarian and Ottoman empires, irresolvable conflicts emerged that eventually led to the end of the German–Soviet coalition. On the prehistory of the Hitler–Stalin Pact, see Besymenski, *Stalin und Hitler*, esp. pp. 111ff.; and, on the disputes concerning the lower reaches of the Danube and control of the Bosphorus, see Gorodetsky, *Grand Delusion*, pp. 95f., 102–5.

14 See Daschitschew, *Moskaus Griff nach der Weltmacht*, pp. 38ff.; and Simon, 'Die Desintegration der Sowjetunion', pp. 191f.

15 Quoted in Ferguson, *Colossus*, p. 111.

16 See above, p. 126.

17 See Mommsen, *Das Ende der Kolonialreiche*, and Abernethy, *The Dynamics of Global Dominance*, pp. 331ff.

18 A sophisticated explanation for this is offered in Jung, Schlichte and Siegelberg, *Kriege in der Weltgesellschaft*, pp. 56ff.

19 Kennedy, *The Rise and Fall*, p. 672. Cf. Kennedy, *Preparing for the Twenty-First Century*, pp. 291ff. A similar argument may be found in Nye (*The Paradox of American Power*), except that in his view the USA has offset its relative loss of hard power by the strengthening of its soft power.

20 Paul Kennedy describes as follows the risks of hastening decline: 'For it has been a common dilemma facing previous "number one" countries that even as their relative economic strength is ebbing, the growing foreign challenges to their position have compelled them to allocate more and more of their resources into the military sector, which in turn squeezes out productive investment and, over time, leads to the downward spiral of slower growth, heavier taxes, deepening domestic splits over spending priorities, and a weakening capacity to bear the burdens of defence.' *The Rise and Fall*, p. 689.

21 See, for example, Fieldhouse, *Economics and Empire*, and Robinson, *Africa and the Victorians*.

22 The strategic theorist Edward Luttwak has noted an extensive replacement of geopolitics by geo-economics, which ultimately suggests that the creation and safeguarding of imperial areas in the pursuit of power politics is no longer necessary (*The Endangered American Dream*,

pp. 307ff.). In this connection, Alexander Demandt writes: 'The universal empires combined with, and gave way to, economic empires. These are the great powers of the future. The struggle is no longer over state frontiers, but over markets, sources of raw materials and systems of rules. It is fought with trade boycotts, dumping prices and currency manipulation. These economic giants have their supporting leg in North America, Japan or Europe, but they also have a mobile free leg' ('Die Weltreiche in der Geschichte', p. 232).

23 On the creeping erosion of the state's capacity for control and management, see Reinhard, *Geschichte der Staatsgewalt*, pp. 509ff.; and, on the increasingly fictional nature of sovereignty, Badie, *Un monde sans souveraineté*.

24 Robert Cooper (*The Breaking of Nations*, pp. 16ff.) has identified such ideas as the structural model for the postmodern world or postmodern states. The problem with such a transfer, however, is the continued existence of modern, and *a fortiori* premodern, states – which is why the structure remains limited to the OSCE or EU area.

25 Saskia Sassen (*Losing Control?*) made the most radical predictions of a replacement of political-territorial with economic-global structures when she spoke of a comprehensive 'deterritorialization of space and time'. In her view, economic globalization and information technology are so closely intertwined that the state may come under pressure from a powerful capital regime and lose certain capacities for action as a result of fiscal shortfall.

26 The idea of the declining significance of states and the rise of NGOs also underlies the argument in Hardt and Negri, *Empire*.

27 Rorty, 'Ein Empire der Ungewissheit', p. 253. Walzer ('Is There an American Empire?') shows how difficult American liberals and leftists find it to grapple with the requirements of humanitarian interventions (which often show no consideration for state sovereignty), and therefore with imperial responsibilities and the avoidance of an imperial role.

28 See Fukuyama, *State-Building*; Hille, *State Building*; and Hippler, *Nation-Building*.

29 In their reflections on the order they call Empire, Michael Hardt and Antonio Negri certainly include attacks on its vulnerable lines of communication, but they conceive of such attacks as an element not of destruction but of the system's further development. By positing Empire in advance as all-inclusive, they define out of existence any threat from external attack. *Empire*, pp. 272ff. and 307ff.

30 On the new forms of warfare, see Münkler, *The New Wars*; 'Die Privatisierung des Krieges'; and 'The Wars of the 21st Century'. On the logistics and economics of the new wars, cf. Napoleoni, *Die Ökonomie des Terrors*.

31 Especially worthy of note here are Vidal, *Perpetual War for Perpetual Peace*, and Mailer, *Why Are We at War?* In Michael Mann too (*Incoherent Empire*, pp. 7f., 252 and 264f.), we find the view that the United States

under Clinton pursued a hegemonial policy, which then turned into an imperialist policy only under George W. Bush. Of course, Mann suspects that the hegemonial policy already produced more disorder than order.

32　See, for example, Boot, 'Plädoyer für ein Empire', p. 66, and Boot, *The Savage Wars of Peace*. Claus Leggewie ('Ein Empire der Demokratie', p. 205) also speaks of 'democratic imperialism'.

33　Ignatieff, *Empire Lite*.

34　Kennedy, *The Rise and Fall*. Similarly, Mearsheimer, *The Tragedy of Great Power Politics*.

35　For example, Doyle, *Empires*.

36　See Bacevich, 'New Rome, New Jerusalem'; and Maier, 'Die Grenzen des Empire'. By contrast, Joseph Nye ('Amerikas Macht', p. 160) stresses that US policy is still hegemonial, not at all imperial, as one can tell from such things as the US army's training and equipment for battle but not for police work. Mention should also be made here of Zbigniew Brzezinski's geostrategic study of the way in which the USA has safeguarded its leading role in world politics: *The Grand Chessboard*.

37　Ignatieff, 'Empire Amerika?', p. 30; Bacevich, 'New Rome, New Jerusalem', pp. 50ff.; Maier, 'Die Grenzen des Empire', pp. 126f.; Diner, 'Das Prinzip Amerika', p. 262.

38　This is true of Chalmers Johnson, in both *Blowback* and *The Sorrows of Empire*.

39　For Chalmers Johnson they have five functions: to safeguard US supremacy over the rest of the world; to eavesdrop on foreign residents and governments, and above all on companies (to acquire valuable information); to control oil reserves and routes used for the transportation of oil; to safeguard income and business for the petro-military complex; and to make life more pleasant for soldiers and their families, thereby boosting recruitment back home. *The Sorrows of Empire*, pp. 151ff.

40　Johnson, *The Sorrows of Empire*, p. 188. Brzezinski, a former presidential security adviser, scarcely differs from Johnson in identifying the ways in which America can safeguard its supremacy in the coming decades, although he places greater emphasis on what Nye calls 'soft power'. 'As the imitation of American ways gradually pervades the world, it creates a more congenial setting for the exercise of the indirect and seemingly consensual American hegemony. [. . .] American global supremacy is thus buttressed by an elaborate system of alliances and coalitions that literally span the globe.' Brzezinski, *The Grand Chessboard*, p. 27.

41　See Gallagher and Robinson, 'The Imperialism of Free Trade'. Cf. Mommsen, 'Wandlungen der liberalen Idee im Zeitalter des Imperialismus'.

42　See, for example, Mann, *Incoherent Empire*, pp. 58ff. Of course, this idea also appears among the intellectual supporters of empire. Bacevich, for example (*American Empire*, p. 3), writes of the open-door policy that underlies empire-building: 'Its ultimate objective is the creation of an open and integrated international order based on the principles of democratic capitalism, with the United States as the ultimate guarantor of order and enforcer of norms.' Here too there is a wide literature that regards US dominance as highly precarious on economic grounds. A good example is Soros, *The Bubble of American Supremacy.*

43 Diner, 'Das Prinzip Amerika', p. 273.

44 On the significance of peace-making wars conducted by the centre on the periphery, see Münkler, 'Kriege im 21. Jahrhundert', esp. pp. 93f.; and, on the wars occurring in the wake of (though not because of) globalization, Münkler, 'Politik und Krieg'.

45 Mann, *Incoherent Empire*, p. 13.

46 In this sense, Joseph Nye's insistence on 'soft power' (*The Paradox of American Power*) may also be seen as a way of exerting pressure for an imperial rather than an imperialist policy. Nor is it an accident that the harshest critics of US policy have regularly equated imperialism with militarism: e.g., Mann, *The Incoherent Empire*, pp. 252ff.; and Johnson, *Blowback*, pp. 29f., 93f. and 223f.

47 Johnson, *Blowback*, p. 220.

48 See James, *The End of Globalization*, and Fischer, 'Die Weltwirtschaft im 20. Jahrhundert'.

49 Ignatieff, *Empire Lite*, pp. 1–25. Samantha Power has gone even further, arguing that the spread of human rights is the condition for the maintenance of American power: see Power, 'Das Empire der Menschenrechte'. Cf. Beck, 'Über den postnationalen Krieg' and *Power in the Global Age.*

50 The concept goes back to Osterhammel, 'Kulturelle Grenzen bei der Expansion Europas', pp. 109ff.

51 This impression made itself felt again and again in the work of historians. In the twentieth century, no study was as influential in this respect as Syme's *The Roman Revolution* (1939), which used the mirror of Roman history to confirm and consolidate Anglo-American self-perceptions with reference to the destruction of democratic orders. The Roman analogy may be found in all authors who have concerned themselves with the formation of the American empire over the past century, regardless of whether they have treated it in a positive or a negative way. Most remarkable, perhaps, is the fact that even an author as sceptical of empire as Joseph Nye cannot escape the analogy. See his *The Paradox of American Power*, p. 169.

52 On the Roman orientation of the Napoleonic empire, see Lefebvre, *Napoleon*, pp. 160–204 *passim*. A particularly striking example of the way in which America's political self-perception took shape in relation to the Roman Republic is the *Federalist Papers* (1781–8), which developed and defended the project of a federal state (Hamilton, Madison and Jay, *The Federalist Papers*).

53 See, in particular, Johnson, *The Sorrows of Empire*, pp. 28ff. and 283ff.; and Chomsky, *Hegemony or Survival*, pp. 11–49.

54 Ignatieff, 'Empire Amerika?', pp. 24 and 31.
55 A survey of the wars conducted by the USA may be found, with the expected gestures of accusation, in Schley and Busse, *Die Kriege der USA*.
56 On this general point, see Beham, *Kriegstrommeln*; on the Gulf War, MacArthur, *Second Front*; on the Kosovo intervention, Lampe, 'Medienfiktionen beim NATO-Einsatz im Kosovo-Krieg 1999'; and, on the Iraq War, Tilgner, *Der inszenierte Krieg*, esp. pp. 17ff.
57 Johnson, *The Sorrows of Empire*, pp. 301f.
58 See Bröckers, *Verschwörungen, Verschwörungenstheorien und die Geheimnisse des 11.9.*, and Bröckers and Hauß, *Fakten, Fälschungen und die unterdrückten Beweise des 11.9.* Similarly, the Japanese attack on the US Pacific fleet at Pearl Harbor has been repeatedly 'decoded' as a conspiracy by President Roosevelt against the American people, by means of which he wrung its support for America's entry into the war. See, for example, Stinnett, *Day of Deceit*.
59 On the costs and losses of the First World War for Europeans, see Kolko, *Century of War*, pp. 88ff., 102ff. Junker (*Power and Mission*, p. 52) sums up the results for the USA: 'The United States, which through the First World War became the world's leading economic and trading power, further built up this position in the 1920s. [. . .] Its share of the world's output of industrial goods rose from 35.8 per cent in 1913 to an average of 46 per cent in the years from 1925 to 1929. The national income of the US, in dollar terms, was as high as that of the next 23 nations together, including Great Britain, Germany, France, Japan and Canada. New York became the world's second financial centre after London, and the world economic system became bicentric if not actually America-centric.' On the balance sheet of the Second World War, see Kolko, *Century of War*, pp. 205ff., and Overy, *Why the Allies Won*, pp. 326ff.
60 Bacevich, 'New Rome, New Jerusalem', p. 56.
61 In his analysis of the US empire, whose existence he does not for a moment doubt, Niall Ferguson comes to a similar conclusion (*Colossus*, p. 29), although he sees the Achilles heel as less the costs of imperium than the deficient 'will to power' of the American people.
62 See Münkler and Fischer, 'Nothing To Kill or Die For . . .'.
63 On America's imperialism of trade, see Wehler, *Der Aufstieg des amerikanischen Imperialismus*, pp. 259ff.; and, on Russian military imperialism and the failed attempt to supplement it with 'ruble imperialism', Geyer, *Russian Imperialism*, pp. 186ff.
64 Direct recruitment was preceded by the loaning of troops from other countries. Thus, during the American War of Independence, the British attempted to maintain their rule chiefly with the help of Hessian troops.
65 Johnson, *The Sorrows of Empire*, pp. 103f.
66 A survey of the well-known phenomenon of PMCs may be found in Ruf, *Politische Ökonomie der Gewalt*, pp. 317–45.
67 See Ferguson, *Colossus*, p. 18.
68 Nye, *The Paradox of American Power*, pp. 37ff.

69 Bacevich, 'New Rome, New Jerusalem', p. 57.
70 It is no accident that such critics of empire as Emmanuel Todd (*After the Empire*) and Charles Kupchan (*The End of the American Era*) lay the greatest stress on US domination of the world economy. See also Rifkin, *The European Dream*, chs. 7 and 8.
71 See above, p. 47.
72 On the political weight of a newly self-confident Europe, see Sloterdijk, *Falls Europa erwacht*, and Schmierer, *Mein Name sei Europa*, esp. pp. 174ff.; and, on the eastward expansion of NATO, Asmus, *Opening NATO's Door*, pp. 134ff.
73 Particularly worthy of note here are Todd (*After the Empire*, esp. pp. 191ff.) and Rifkin (*The European Dream*, esp. pp. 16ff., 64ff.). Kupchan (*The End of the American Era*, pp. 119ff.) starts from the assumption that the real challenge to the USA comes from Europe.
74 The debate on European identity has gained fresh momentum from the question of Turkish membership of the EU. See Leggewie, *Die Türkei und Europa*, and more generally, on the different facets of European identity, Hoffmann and Kramer, *Europa – Kontinent im Abseits?*
75 See Brague, *Eccentric Culture*, and Pomian, *L'Europe et ses nations*, pp. 14ff.
76 Valéry, 'The Crisis of Mind' (1919). See Lützeler, *Die Schriftsteller und Europa*, pp. 308f.
77 See Figes, *Natasha's Dance*, pp. 377ff.

REFERENCES AND BIBLIOGRAPHY

Abernethy, David B., *The Dynamics of Global Dominance: European Overseas Empires, 1415–1980*, New Haven, CT, and London 2000.

Adanir, Fikret, 'Der Zerfall des Osmanischen Reiches', in Alexander Demandt (ed.), *Das Ende der Weltreiche*, Munich 1977, pp. 108–28.

Albertini, Rudolf von, *Europäische Kolonialherrschaft: Die Expansion in Übersee von 1880–1940*, Zurich and Freiburg 1976.

Altheim, Franz, *Geschichte der Hunnen*, 5 vols, Berlin 1959–62.

Altrichter, Helmut, and Helmut Neuhaus (eds), *Das Ende von Großreichen*, Erlangen and Jena 1996.

Altvater, Elmar, and Birgit Mahnkopf, *Grenzen der Globalisierung: Ökonomie, Ökologie und Politik in der Weltgesellschaft*, 6th edn, Münster 2004.

Anderson, Benedict, *Imagined Communities*, London 1983.

Angermann, Erich, *Die Vereinigten Staaten von Amerika seit 1917*, 9th enlarged edn, Munich 1995.

Armstrong, Karen, *The Battle for God: Fundamentalism in Judaism, Christianity and Islam*, London 2000.

Aron, Raymond, *The Century of Total War*, Boston 1959.

Aron, Raymond, *Clausewitz: The Philosopher of War*, London 1982.

Aron, Raymond, *Peace and War: A Theory of International Relations*, Malabar 1981.

Asmus, Ronald D., *Opening NATO's Door: How the Alliance Remade itself for a New Era*, New York and Chichester 2002.

Augustine, Saint, *The City of God*, trans. Marcus Dods, New York 1950.

Aust, Stefan, and Cordt Schnibben (eds), *Irak: Geschichte eines modernen Krieges*, Munich 2003.

Bacevich, Andrew J., *American Empire: The Realities and Consequences of U.S. Diplomacy*, Cambridge, MA, and London 2003.

Bacevich, Andrew J., 'New Rome, New Jerusalem', *Wilson Quarterly*, 26, Summer 2002, pp. 50–8.

Badie, Bertrand, *Un monde sans souveraineté: les États entre ruse et responsabilité*, Paris 1999.

Bailyn, Bernard, *The Ideological Origins of the American Revolution*, Cambridge, MA, and London 1967.

Barudio, Günter, 'Die Macht des Hegemonialismus – das Moskauer Zarentum', in *Pipers Handbuch der politischen Ideen*, ed. Iring Fetscher and Herfried Münkler, vol. 3, Munich 1985, pp. 189–98.

Baumgart, Winfried (ed.), *Die Julikrise und der Ausbruch des Ersten Weltkriegs*, Darmstadt 1983.

Beck, Hans-Georg, *Das byzantinische Jahrtausend*, 2nd edn, Munich 1994.

Beck, Ulrich, *Power in the Global Age: A New Global Political Economy*, Cambridge 2005.

Beck, Ulrich, 'Über den postnationalen Krieg', *Blätter für deutsche und internationale Politik*, 8/1999, pp. 984–90.

Beham, Mira, *Kriegstrommeln: Medien, Krieg und Politik*, Munich 1996.

Behr, Hartmut, *Entterritoriale Politik: Von den internationalen Beziehungen zur Netzwerkanalyse*, Wiesbaden 2004.

Bellen, Heinz, *Grundzüge der Römischen Geschichte*, 3 vols, Darmstadt 1994–2003.

Bender, Peter, *Weltmacht Amerika: Das Neue Rom*, Stuttgart 2003.

Bennassar, Bartolomé, and Bernard Vincent, *Le Temps de l'Espagne: XVIe–XVIIe siècles: les siècles d'or*, Paris 1999.

Ben-Sasson, Haim Hillel (ed.), *A History of the Jewish People*, London 1976.

Berlin, Isaiah, 'Herzen and his Memoirs', in *Against the Current: Essays in the History of Ideas*, London 1979, pp. 188–212.

Berlin, Isaiah, *Russian Thinkers*, Harmondsworth 1979.

Bernecker, Walter L., *Spanische Geschichte: Von der Reconquista bis heute*, Darmstadt 2002.

Besymenski, Lew, *Stalin und Hitler: Das Pokerspiel der Diktatoren*, Berlin 2002.

Bitterli, Urs (ed.), *Die Entdeckung und Eroberung der Welt*, Munich 1980.

Bleicken, Jochen, *Verfassungs- und Sozialgeschichte des Römischen Kaiserreichs*, 2nd edn, 2 vols, Paderborn 1981.

Blindow, Felix, *Carl Schmitts Reichsordnung: Strategie für einen europäischen Großraum*, Berlin 1999.

Bohlender, Matthias, 'Government, Commerce und Civil Society: Zur Genealogie der schottischen politischen Ökonomie', in Hartmut Kaelble and Jürgen Schriewer (eds), *Gesellschaften im Vergleich*, Frankfurt am Main 1998, pp. 115–47.

Böhlke, Effi, *'Esprit de nation': Montesquieus politische Philosophie*, Berlin 1999.

Boot, Max, 'Plädoyer für ein Empire', in Ulrich Speck and Natan Sznaider (eds), *Empire Amerika: Perspektiven einer neuen Weltordnung*, Munich 2003, pp. 60–70.

Boot, Max, *The Savage Wars of Peace: Small Wars and the Rise of American Power*, New York 2002.

Bosbach, Franz, *Monarchia Universalis: Ein politischer Leitbegriff der frühen Neuzeit*, Göttingen 1986.

Boxer, Charles R., *The Dutch Seaborne Empire, 1600–1800*, London 1992.

Boxer, Charles R., *The Portuguese Seaborne Empire, 1415–1825*, Manchester 1991.

Brague, Rémi, *Eccentric Culture: A Theory of Western Civilization*, South Bend, IN, 2002.

Braudel, Fernand, *Civilization and Capitalism 15th–18th Century*, 3 vols, London 1981–4.

Breuer, Stefan, *Imperien der Alten Welt*, Stuttgart 1987.

Bröckers, Mathias, *Verschwörungen, Verschwörungstheorien und die Geheimnisse des 11.9.*, Frankfurt am Main 2002.

Bröckers, Mathias, and Andres Hauß, *Fakten, Fälschungen und die unterdrückten Beweise des 11.9.*, Frankfurt am Main 2003.

Brogini Künzi, Giulia, 'Der Sieg des Negus: Adna, 1. März 1896', in Stig Förster et al. (eds), *Schlachten der Weltgeschichte*, Munich 2001, pp. 248–63.

Brown, Michael E. et al. (eds), *Debating the Democratic Peace*, Cambridge, MA, and London 1996.

Brzezinski, Zbigniew, *The Grand Chessboard: American Primacy and its Geostrategic Imperatives*, New York 1997.

Buruma, Ian, *Bad Elements: Chinese Rebels from Los Angeles to Beijing*, London 2001.

Chomsky, Noam, *American Power and the New Mandarins*, New York and London 1969.

Chomsky, Noam, *Hegemony or Survival: America's Quest for Global Dominance*, London 2004.

Chomsky, Noam, *Year 501: The Conquest Continues*, Boston 1993.

Christ, Karl, *Pompeius: Der Feldherr Roms*, Munich 2004.

Cipolla, Carlo M. (ed.), *The Economic Decline of Empires*, London 1972.

Cipolla, Carlo M., *Guns and Sails in the Early Phase of European Expansion*, London 1965.

Cipolla, Carlo M., *Die Odysee des spanischen Silbers*, Berlin 1998.

Clausewitz, Carl von, *On War*, ed. and trans. Michael Howard and Peter Paret, Princeton, NJ, 1984.

Clauss, Manfred (ed.), *Die römischen Kaiser*, Munich 1997.

Cooper, Robert, *The Breaking of Nations: Order and Chaos in the Twenty-First Century*, London 2003.

Creveld, Martin L. van, *On Future War*, London 1991.

Czempiel, Ernst-Otto, 'Pax Americana oder Imperium Americanum?', *Merkur*, 2003/11, pp. 1003–14.

Daase, Christoph, *Kleine Kriege – Große Wirkung*, Baden-Baden 1999.

Dante Alighieri, *Monarchy, and Three Political Letters*, London 1954.

Daschitschew, Wjatscheslaw, *Moskaus Griff nach der Weltmacht: Die bitteren Früchte hegemonialer Politik*, Hamburg 2002.

David, Saul, *Military Blunders: The How and Why of Military Failure*, London 1997.

De Schweinitz, Karl, Jr, *The Rise and Fall of British India*, London 1983.

Dehio, Ludwig, *The Precarious Balance: The Politics of Power in Europe, 1494–1945*, London 1963.

Delbrück, Hans, *Die Strategie des Perikles erläutert durch die Strategie Freidrichs des Großen*, Berlin 1890.

Demandt, Alexander (ed.), *Das Ende der Weltreiche*, Munich 1997.

Demandt, Alexander, 'Die Weltreiche in der Geschichte', in Demandt (ed.), *Das Ende der Weltreiche*, Munich 1997, pp. 221–33.

Des Forges, Alison, *Leave None to Tell the Story: Genocide in Rwanda*, London 1999.

Diner, Dan, 'Imperialismus und Universalismus: Versuch einer Begriffsgeschichte', in Diner, *Weltordnungen: Über Geschichte und Wirkung von Recht und Macht*, Frankfurt am Main 1993, pp. 17–59.

Diner, Dan, *Das Jahrhundert verstehen: Eine universalgeschichtliche Deutung*, Munich 1999.

Diner, Dan, 'Das Prinzip Amerika', in Ulrich Speck and Natan Sznaider (eds), *Empire Amerika: Perspektiven einer neuen Weltordnung*, Munich 2003, pp. 256–74.

Dippel, Horst, 'Die Auflösung des britischen Empire oder die Suche nach einem Rechtersatz für formale Herrschaft', in Richard Lorenz (ed.), *Das Verdämmern der Macht*, Frankfurt am Main 2000, pp. 236–55.

Doyle, Michael W., *Empires*, Ithaca, NY, and London 1984.

Ebrey, Patricia Buckley, *The Cambridge Illustrated History of China*, Cambridge 1999.

Edzard, Dietz Otto, *Geschichte Mesopotamiens: Von den Sumeren bis zu Alexander dem Großen*, Munich 2004.

Elliott, John H., 'The Decline of Spain', in Carlo M. Cipolla (ed.), *The Economic Decline of Empires*, London 1972, pp. 168–95.

Fanon, Frantz, *Black Skin, White Masks*, London 1968.

Fanon, Frantz, *The Wretched of the Earth*, Harmondsworth 1967.

Fenske, Hans, 'Ungeduldige Zuschauer: Die Deutschen und die europäische Expansion 1815–1880', in Wolfgang Reinhard (ed.), *Imperialistische Kontinuität und nationale Ungeduld im 19. Jahrhundert*, Frankfurt am Main 1991, pp. 87–123.

Ferguson, Niall, *Colossus: The Price of America's Empire*, New York 2004.

Ferguson, Niall, *Empire: The Rise and Demise of the British World Order and the Lessons for Global Power*, London 2002.

Ferguson, Niall, *The Pity of War*, London 1998.

Ferguson, Niall, 'Das verleugnete Empire', in Ulrich Speck and Natan Sznaider (eds), *Empire Amerika: Perspektiven einer neuen Weltordnung*, Munich 2003, pp. 15–37.

Ferro, Marc, *The Great War, 1914–1918*, London 1973.

Fetscher, Iring, *Modelle der Friedenssicherung*, Munich 1972.

Fieldhouse, David, *Economics and Empire, 1830–1914*, London 1973.

Figes, Orlando, *Natasha's Dance: A Cultural History of Russia*, London 2002.

Fischbach, Claudius R., *Krieg und Frieden in der französischen Aufklärung*, Münster and New York 1990.

Fischer, Wolfram, 'Internationale Wirtschaftsbeziehungen und Währungsordnung vor dem Ersten Weltkrieg', in Wolfram, *Expansion, Integration,*

Globalisierung: Studien zur Geschichte der Weltwirtschaft, Göttingen 1998, pp. 79–86.

Fischer, Wolfram, 'Die Weltwirtschaft im 20. Jahrhundert', in Wolfram, *Expansion, Integration, Globalisierung: Studien zur Geschichte der Weltwirtschaft*, Göttingen 1998, pp. 140–65.

Franke, Otto, *Geschichte des chinesischen Reiches: Eine Darstellung seiner Entstehung, seines Wesens und seiner Entwicklung bis zur neuesten Zeit*, 5 vols, Berlin 1930–52.

Frey, Marc, 'Das Ende eines Kolonialreichs: Dien Bien Phu, 13. März bis 7. Mai 1954', in Stig Förster et al. (eds), *Schlachten der Weltgeschichte*, Munich 2001, pp. 358–73.

Fueter, Eduard, *Geschichte des europäischen Staatensystems von 1492–1559*, Munich 1919.

Fuhrmann, Horst, *Deutsche Geschichte im hohen Mittelalter* (vol. 2 of Joachim Leuschner, ed., *Deutsche Geschichte*), Göttingen 1978.

Fukuyama, Francis, *State-Building: Governance and World Order in the 21st Century*, Ithaca, NY, 2003.

Fulbright, William, *The Arrogance of Power*, Harmondsworth 1970.

Gallagher, John, *The Decline, Revival and Fall of the British Empire*, Cambridge 1982.

Gallagher, John, and Ronald Robinson, 'The Imperialism of Free Trade', *Economic History Review*, 6/1, 1953.

Geiss, Imanuel, 'Kontinuitäten des Imperialismus', in Wolfgang Reinhard (ed.), *Imperialistische Kontinuität und nationale Ungeduld im 19. Jahrhundert*, Frankfurt am Main 1991, pp. 12–30.

Geyer, Dietrich, *Russian Imperialism: The Interaction of Domestic and Foreign Policy 1860–1914*, Leamington Spa 1987.

Gibbon, Edward, *Decline and Fall of the Roman Empire*, 3 vols, London 1993.

Giesen, Bernhard, and Helmut Berding (eds), *Mythos und Nation*, Frankfurt am Main 1996.

Giesen, Bernhard, and Helmut Berding (eds), *Nationale und kulturelle Identität*, Frankfurt am Main 1991.

Giesen, Bernhard, and Helmut Berding (eds), *Nationales Bewusstsein und kollektive Identität*, Frankfurt am Main 1994.

Gilpin, Robert, *War and Change in World Politics*, Cambridge 1981.

Göckenjan, Hansgerd, 'Die Welt der frühen Reiternomaden', in Arne Eggebrecht (ed.), *Die Mongolen und ihr Weltreich*, Mainz 1989, pp. 7–43.

Göckenjan, Hansgerd, 'Weltherrschaft oder Desintegration? Krise und Zerfall des Mongolischen Großreichs', in Richard Lorenz (ed.), *Das Verdämmern der Macht: Vom Untergang großer Reiche*, Frankfurt am Main 2000, pp. 82–103.

Goldsworthy, Adrian, *The Complete Roman Army*, London 2003.

Gollwitzer, Heinz, *Geschichte des weltpolitischen Denkens*, 2 vols, Göttingen 1972–82.

Gorodetsky, Gabriel, *Grand Delusion: Stalin and the German Invasion of Russia*, New York 1999.

Grousset, René, *The Empire of the Steppes*, New Brunswick, NJ, 1970.

Habermas, Jürgen, 'Das Kantische Projekt und der gespaltene Westen', in Habermas, *Der gespaltene Westen*, Frankfurt am Main 2004, pp. 111–93.

Habermas, Jürgen, 'Was bedeutet der Denkmalsturz? Verschließen wir nicht die Augen vor der Revolution der Weltordnung: Die normative Autorität Amerikas liegt in Trümmern', *Frankfurter Allgemeine Zeitung*, 17 April 2003.

Habermas, Jürgen, 'Wege aus der Weltunordnung: Ein Interview mit Jürgen Habermas', *Blätter für deutsche und internationale Politik*, 1/2004, pp. 27–45.

Hacke, Christian, *Zur Weltmacht verdammt: Die amerikanische Außenpolitik von J. F. Kennedy bis G. W. Bush*, Munich 2001.

Hahlweg, Werner, *Guerilla: Krieg ohne Fronten*, Stuttgart 1968.

Hamann, Brigitte, *Der Erste Weltkrieg: Wahrheit und Lüge in Bildern und Texten*, Munich 2004.

Hamilton, Alexander, James Madison and John Jay, *The Federalist Papers*, New York 1961.

Hardt, Michael, and Antonio Negri, *Empire*, Cambridge, MA, 2000.

Heilbrunn, Otto, *Partisan Warfare*, New York 1962.

Heinrichs, Hans-Jürgen, *Die gekränkte Supermacht: Amerika auf der Couch*, Dusseldorf 2003.

Heuss, Alfred, *Römische Geschichte*, ed. J. Bleicken, 9th edn, Paderborn 2003.

Heydte, August von der, *Der moderne Kleinkrieg als wehrpolitisches und militärisches Phänomen*, Würzburg 1972.

Hille, Charlotte (ed.), *State Building: Challenges between Theoretical Necessity and Political Reality*, Leiden 2003.

Hippler, Jochen (ed.), *Nation-Building: Ein Schlüsselkonzept für friedliche Konfliktbearbeitung?*, Bonn 2004.

Hobbes, Thomas, *Leviathan, or the Matter, Forme, and Power of a Commonwealth Ecclesiastical and Civil*, London 1962.

Hobsbawm, Eric, *The Age of Empire 1875–1914*, London 1987.

Hobsbawm, Eric, *The Age of Extremes: The Short Twentieth Century, 1914–1991*, London 1994.

Hobsbawm, Eric, *Nations and Nationalism since 1780: Programme, Myth and Reality*, Cambridge 1990.

Hobsbawm, Eric, *The New Century: Eric Hobsbawm in Conversation with Antonio Polito*, London 2000.

Hobson, John Atkinson, *Imperialism*, London 1905.

Hoffmann, Hilmar, and Dieter Kramer (eds), *Europa – Kontinent im Abseits?*, Reinbek bei Hamburg 1998.

Horace, *Carmina, The Complete Odes and Epodes*, trans. David West, Oxford 1997.

Hosking, Geoffrey, *Russia: People and Empire, 1552–1917*, Cambridge, MA, 1997.

Hourani, Albert, *A History of the Arab Peoples*, London 1991.

Howard, Michael, *The First World War*, Oxford 2002.

Ignatieff, Michael, 'Empire Amerika?', in Ulrich Speck and Natan Sznaider (eds), *Empire Amerika: Perspektiven einer neuen Weltordnung*, Munich 2003, pp. 15–37.

Ignatieff, Michael, *Empire Lite: Nation Building in Bosnia, Kosovo and Afghanistan*, London 2003.

Irwin, Robert, 'The Emergence of the Islamic World System 1000–1500', in Francis Robinson (ed.), *The Cambridge Illustrated History of the Islamic World*, Cambridge 1996, pp. 56–85.

Isocrates, 'On the Peace', in *Speeches and Letters*, ed. George Norlin, vol. 2, London 1928.

James, Harold, *The End of Globalization: Lessons from the Great Depression*, Cambridge, MA, 2001.

Jaschke, Hans-Gerd, *Soziale Basis und soziale Funktion des Nationalsozialismus: Studien zur Bonapartismustheorie*, Opladen 1982.

Jeismann, Michael, 'Propaganda', in Gerhard Hirschfeld et al. (eds), *Enzyklopädie Erster Weltkrieg*, Paderborn 2003, pp. 198–209.

Jerabék, Rudolf, 'Conrad von Hötzendorf, Franz Freiherr', in Gerhard Hirschfeld et al. (eds), *Enzyklopädie Erster Weltkrieg*, Paderborn 2003, pp. 419–21.

Johnson, Chalmers, *Blowback: The Costs and Consequences of the American Empire*, New York 2000.

Johnson, Chalmers, *The Sorrows of Empire*, New York 2004.

Jones, Eric Lionel, *The European Miracle: Environments, Economies and Geopolitics in the History of Europe and Asia*, Cambridge 2003.

Jorga, Nicolae, *Geschichte des Osmanischen Reiches*, 5 vols, Gotha 1908–13; new edn, Darmstadt 1990.

Judt, Tony, *A Grand Illusion? An Essay on Europe*, New York 1996.

Jung, Dietrich, Klaus Schlichte and Jens Siegelberg, *Kriege in der Weltgesellschaft: Strukturgeschichtliche Erklärung kriegerischer Gewalt (1945–2002)*, Wiesbaden 2003.

Junker, Detlef, *Power and Mission: Was Amerika antreibt*, Freiburg 2003.

Kagan, Frederick W., 'War and Aftermath', *Policy Review* 108, August–September 2003, pp. 3–27.

Kagan, Robert, *Of Paradise and Power: America and Europe in the New World Order*, London 2003.

Kagan, Robert, 'The Benevolent Empire', *Foreign Affairs*, 111, 1998, pp. 24–33.

Kagan, Robert, 'Power and Weakness', *Policy Review*, 113, June–July 2002, pp. 3–28.

Kaldor, Mary, 'Das ohnmächtige Empire', in Ulrich Speck and Natan Sznaider (eds), *Empire Amerika: Perspektiven einer neuen Weltordnung*, Munich 2003, pp. 173–98.

Kämpfe, Hans-Rainer, 'Cinggis Khan', in Michael Weiers (ed.), *Die Mongolen: Beiträge zu ihrer Geschichte und Kultur*, Darmstadt 1986, pp. 183–91.

Kann, Robert A., *A History of the Habsburg Empire*, Berkeley, CA, 1974.

Kant, Immanuel, *On Perpetual Peace*, Indianapolis 1957.

Kapuściński, Ryszard, *Imperium*, London 1998.

Kautsky, John H., *The Politics of Aristocratic Empires*, Chapel Hill, NC, 1982.

Keegan, John, *The First World War*, London 1999.

Keegan, John, *A History of Warfare*, London 1993.

Kennedy, Paul, *Preparing for the Twenty-First Century*, London 1993.

Kennedy, Paul, *The Rise and Fall of the Great Powers: Economic Change and Military Conflict from 1500–2000*, London 1989.

Kernig, Claus D., *Lenins Reich in Trümmern: Schatten über Russlands Zukunft*, Stuttgart 2000.

Kipling, Rudyard, *Complete Verse*, Cambridge 1989.

Kissinger, Henry, *Does America Need a Foreign Policy? Towards a Diplomacy for the 21st Century*, New York 2002.

Kissinger, Henry, 'The Vietnam Negotiations', *Foreign Affairs*, 2/1969, pp. 211–34.

Kitson, Frank, *Low Intensity Operations: Subversion, Insurgency, Peace-Keeping*, London 1971.

Kluth, Heinz, *Sozialprestige und sozialer Status*, Stuttgart 1957.

Koch, Klaus, *Das Buch Daniel*, Darmstadt 1980.

Koebner, Richard, and Helmut Dan Schmidt, *Imperialism: The Story and Significance of a Political World, 1840–1960*, Cambridge 1964.

Kohler, Alfred, *Karl V: Eine Biographie*, Munich 1999.

Kohler, Alfred, Barbara Haider and Christine Otter (eds), *Karl V, 1500–1558: Neue Perspektiven seiner Herrschaft in Europa und Übersee*, Vienna 2002.

Kolko, Gabriel, *Century of War: Politics, Conflicts and Society since 1914*, New York 1994.

König, Hans-Joachim, 'Der Zerfall des Spanischen Weltreichs in Amerika', in Richard Lorenz (ed.), *Das Verdämmern der Macht: Vom Untergang großer Reiche*, Frankfurt am Main 2000, pp. 126–52.

König, Ingemar, *Der Römischer Staat II: Die Kaiserzeit*, Stuttgart 1997.

Koselleck, Reinhart, 'The Historical-Political Semantics of Asymmetric Counterconcepts', in Koselleck, *Futures Past: On the Semantics of Historical Time*, New York 2004, pp. 155–91.

Kreiser, Klaus, and Christoph K. Neumann, *Kleine Geschichte der Türkei*, Stuttgart 2003.

Kubbig, Bernd W. (ed.), *Brandherd Irak: US-Hegemonieanspruch, die UNO und die Rolle Europas*, Frankfurt am Main 2003.

Kulischer, Josef, *Allgemeine Wirtschaftsgeschichte des Mittelalters und der Neuzeit*, 2 vols, Berlin 1954.

Kunisch, Johannes, *Der kleine Krieg: Studien zum Heerwesen des Absolutismus*, Wiesbaden 1973.

Kupchan, Charles A., *The End of the American Era: US Foreign Policy and the Geopolitics of the Twenty-First Century*, New York 2002.

Lampe, Gerhard, 'Medienfiktionen beim NATO-Einsatz im Kosovo-Krieg 1999', in Michael Strübel (ed.), *Film und Krieg: Die Inszenierung von Politik zwischen Apologetik und Apokalypse*, Opladen 2002, pp. 127–34.

Landes, David, *The Wealth and Poverty of Nations: Why Some Are So Rich and Some So Poor*, New York 1998.

Lange, Sven, *Hans Delbrück und der 'Strategiestreit': Kriegsführung und Kriegsgeschichte in der Kontroverse 1879–1914*, Freiburg 1995.

Lefebvre, Georges, *Napoleon: From Tilsit to Waterloo*, New York 1969.

Leggewie, Claus, 'Ein Empire der Demokratie', in Ulrich Speck and Natan Sznaider (eds), *Empire Amerika: Perspektiven einer neuen Weltordnung*, Munich 2003, pp. 199–218.

Leggewie, Claus, *Die Türkei und Europa: Die Positionen*, Frankfurt am Main 2004.

Lehmann, Gustav Adolf, 'Das Ende der römischen Herrschaft über das 'westelbische' Germanien', in Rainer Wiegels and Winfried Woesler (eds), *Arminius und die Varusschlacht*, Paderborn 1995, pp. 123–41.

Lenk, Kurt (ed.), *Ideologie, Ideologiekritik und Wissenssoziologie*, Darmstadt 1972.

Lewis, Bernard, 'The Arabs in Eclipse', in Carlo M. Cipolla (ed.), *The Economic Decline of Empires*, London 1972, pp. 102–20.

Lewis, Bernard, *The Arabs in History*, London 1950.

Lewis, David Levering, *The Race to Fashoda*, New York 1987.

Liddell Hart, Basil H., *Great Captains Unveiled*, Edinburgh 1927.

Lilie, Ralph-Johannes, *Byzanz: Das zweite Rom*, Berlin 2003.

Livius, Titus, *The History of Rome*, vol. 3, London 1905.

Lorenz, Richard, 'Das Ende der Sowjetunion', in Lorenz (ed.), *Das Verdämmern der Macht: Vom Untergang großer Reiche*, Frankfurt am Main 2000.

Lorenz, Richard (ed.), *Das Verdämmern der Macht: Vom Untergang großer Reiche*, Frankfurt am Main 2000.

Lundestad, Geir, *The United States and Western Europe since 1945: From Empire by Invitation to Transatlantic Drift*, Oxford 1998.

Luttwak, Edward, *The Endangered American Dream*, New York 1993.

Lützeler, Paul Michael, *Die Schriftsteller und Europa: Von der Romantik bis zur Gegenwart*, Munich 1992.

MacArthur, John R., *Second Front: Censorship and Propaganda in the 1991 Gulf War*, rev. edn, Berkeley, CA, 2004.

McNeill, William, *The Pursuit of Power: Technology, Armed Force and Society since AD 1000*, Oxford 1983.

McPherson, James M., *Battle Cry of Freedom: The Civil War Era*, Oxford 1988.

Maenchen-Helfen, Otto, *The World of the Huns: Studies in their History and Culture*, Berkeley, CA, 1973.

Mahan, Alfred Thayer, *The Influence of Sea Power upon History 1660–1783*, New York 1957.

Mahnkopf, Birgit, 'Neoliberale Globalisierung und globaler Krieg', *Blätter für deutsche und internationale Politik*, 1/2004, pp. 47–57.

Maier, Charles S., *Among Empires: American Ascendancy and its Predecessors*, Cambridge, MA, 2006.

Maier, Charles S., 'Die Grenzen des Empire', in Ulrich Speck and Natan Sznaider (eds), *Empire Amerika: Perspektiven einer neuen Weltordnung*, Munich 2003, pp. 126–37.

Mailer, Norman, *Why Are We at War?*, New York 2003.

Majoros, Ferenc, and Bernd Rill, *Das Osmanische Reich 1300–1922*, Wiesbaden 2004.

Mann, Michael, *Incoherent Empire*, London 2003.

Mann, Michael, *The Sources of Social Power*, 2 vols, Cambridge 1986–93.

Mao Tse-tung, 'On Protracted War', in idem *Selected Works*, vol. 2, Peking 1965.

Marx, Karl, 'The British Rule in India', in *The Marx–Engels Reader*, ed. Robert Tucker, New York 1972, pp. 577–82.

Marx, Karl, 'The Eighteenth Brumaire of Louis Bonaparte', in Marx, *Surveys from Exile*, London 1973, pp. 143–249.

Marx, Karl, 'First Address of the General Council on the Franco-Prussian War', in Marx, *The First International and After*, London 1973, pp. 172–6.

Massie, Robert K., *Dreadnought: Britain, Germany and the Coming of the Great War*, New York 1992.

Matuz, Josef, *Das Osmanische Reich: Grundlinien seiner Geschichte*, Darmstadt 1994.

Mead, Walter Russell, *Special Providence: American Foreign Policy and How it Changed the World*, New York 2002.

Mearsheimer, John J., *The Tragedy of Great Power Politics*, New York 2001.

Melinz, Gerhard, 'Vom osmanischen Mosaik zur türkischen Staatsnation', in Ernst Bruckmüller et al. (eds), *Nationalismus: Wege der Staatenbildung in der außereuropäischen Welt*, Vienna 1994, pp. 51–75.

Menzel, Ulrich, 'Eurozentrismus versus ReOrientierung', in Menzel, *Paradoxien der neuen Weltordnung*, Frankfurt am Main 2004, pp. 64–90.

Menzel, Ulrich, 'Die Globalisierung vor der Globalisierung', in Menzel, *Paradoxien der neuen Weltordnung*, Frankfurt am Main 2004, pp. 31–50.

Menzel, Ulrich, 'Die neue Hegemonie der USA und die Krise des Multilateralismus', in Menzel, *Paradoxien der neuen Weltordnung*, Frankfurt am Main 2004, pp. 93–151.

Merson, John, *Roads to Xanadu: East and West in the Making of the Modern World*, London 1989.

Modelski, George, *Long Cycles in World Politics*, Seattle 1987.

Modelski, George, and William R. Thompson, *Leading Sectors and World Powers: The Coevolution of Global Politics and Economics*, Columbia, SC, 1986.

Modelski, George, and William R. Thompson, *Seapower in Global Politics, 1494–1993*, Basingstoke 1988.

Mommsen, Wolfgang J. (ed.), *Das Ende der Kolonialreiche: Dekolonisation und die Politik der Großmächte*, Frankfurt am Main 1990.

Mommsen, Wolfgang J., *Imperialismustheorien: Ein Überblick über die neueren Imperialismusinterpretationen*, Göttingen 1977.

Mommsen, Wolfgang J., 'Wandlungen der liberalen Idee im Zeitalter des Imperialismus', in Mommsen, *Der europäische Imperialismus*, Göttingen 1979, pp. 167–205.

Montesquieu, Charles de Secondat, 'Réflexions sur la monarchie universelle', in *Oeuvres complètes*, vol. 2, Paris 1964, pp. 192–7.

Morgan, David, *The Mongols*, London 1986.

Morgenthau, Hans, *Politics among Nations: The Struggle for Power and Peace (1948)*, New York 1973.

Mosès, Stéphane, *Eros und Gesetz: Zehn Lektüren der Bibel*, Munich 2004.

Motyl, Alexander J., *Sovietology, Rationality, Nationality: Coming to Grips with Nationalism in the USSR*, New York 1990.

Müller, Klaus-Jürgen, 'Militärpolitik in der Krise: Zur militärpolitischen Konzeption des deutschen Heeres-Generalstabs 1938', in Dirk Stegemann et al. (eds), *Deutscher Konservatismus im 19. und 20. Jahrhundert: Festschrift für Fritz Fischer*, Bonn 1983, pp. 333–45.

Münkler, Herfried, 'Ältere und jüngere Formen des Terrorismus: Strategie und Organisationsstruktur', in Werner Weidenfeld (ed.), *Herausforderung Terrorismus*, Wiesbaden 2004, pp. 29–43.

Münkler, Herfried, 'Analytiken der Macht: Nietzsche, Machiavelli, Thukydides', in Michael T. Greven (ed.), *Macht in der Demokratie*, Baden-Baden 1991, pp. 9–44.

Münkler, Herfried, 'Angriff als beste Verteidigung? Sicherheitsdoktrinen in der asymmetrischen Konstellation', *Internationale Politik und Gesellschaft*, 3/2004, pp. 22–37.

Münkler, Herfried, 'Gegensätzliche Kriegsursachenanalysen: Aristophanes, Thukydides, Platon und die Vernunft der Regierenden', in Münkler, *Über den Krieg: Stationen der Kriegsgeschichte im Spiegel ihrer theoretischen Reflexion*, Weilerswist 2002, pp. 19–33.

Münkler, Herfried, *Im Namen des Staates: Die Begründung der Staatsraison in der frühen Neuzeit*, Frankfurt am Main 1987.

Münkler, Herfried, 'Instrumentelle und existentielle Auffassung des Krieges bei Carl von Clausewitz', in Münkler, *Über den Krieg: Stationen der Kriegsgeschichte im Spiegel ihrer theoretischen Reflexion*, Weilerswist 2002, pp. 91–115.

Münkler, Herfried, 'Kriege im 21. Jahrhundert', in Erich Reiter (ed.), *Jahrbuch für internationale Sicherheitspolitik 2003*, Hamburg 2003, pp. 83–97.

Münkler, Herfried, 'Ist der Krieg abschaffbar? Ein Blick auf die Herausforderungen und Möglichkeiten des 20. Jahrhunderts', in Bernd Wegner (ed.), *Wie Kriege enden: Wege zum Frieden von der Antike bis zur Gegenwart*, Paderborn 2002, pp. 347–75.

Münkler, Herfried, 'Kriegsszenarien des 21. Jahrhunderts', in Karl Acham (ed.), *Faktizitäten der Macht*, Vienna 2004, pp. 79–94.

Münkler, Herfried, *Machiavelli: Die Begründung des politischen Denkens der Neuzeit aus der Krise der Republik Florenz*, Frankfurt am Main 1982.

Münkler, Herfried, *Der neue Golfkrieg*, Reinbek bei Hamburg 2003.

Münkler, Herfried, *The New Wars*, trans. Patrick Camiller, Cambridge 2005.

Münkler, Herfried (ed.), *Der Partisan: Theorie, Strategie, Gestalt*, Opladen 1990.

Münkler, Herfried, 'Partisanen der Tradition', in Münkler, *Gewalt und Ordnung: Das Bild des Krieges im politischen Denken*, Frankfurt am Main 1992, pp. 127–41.

Münkler, Herfried, 'Perspektiven der Befreiung: Die Philosophie der Gewalt in der Revolutionstheorie Frantz Fanons', *Kölner Zeitschrift für Soziologie und Sozialpsychologie*, 3/1981, pp. 437–68.

Münkler, Herfried, 'Politik und Krieg: Die neuen Herausforderungen durch Staatszerfall, Terror und Bürgerkriegsökonomien', in Armin Nassehi and Markus Schroer (eds), *Der Begriff des Politischen*, Baden-Baden 2003, pp. 471–90.

Münkler, Herfried, 'Die Privatisierung des Krieges: Warlords, Terrornetzwerke und die Reaktion des Westens', *Zeitschrift für Politikwissenschaft*, 1/2003, pp. 7–22.

Münkler, Herfried, 'Das Reich als politische Macht und politischer Mythos', in Münkler, *Reich, Nation, Europa: Modelle politischer Ordnung*, Weinheim 1996, pp. 11–59.

Münkler, Herfried, *Reich, Nation, Europa: Modelle politischer Ordnung*, Weinheim 1996.

Münkler, Herfried, 'Rezension zu Benders *Weltmacht Amerika*', *Historische Zeitschrift*, 279, 2004, pp. 430–2.

Münkler, Herfried, 'Staatengemeinschaft oder Imperium: Zur Gestaltung der "Weltinnenpolitik"', *Merkur*, 2/2004, pp. 93–105.

Münkler, Herfried, 'Terrorismus heute: Die Asymmetrisierung des Krieges', *Internationale Politik*, 2/2004, pp. 1–11.

Münkler, Herfried, 'Wandel der Weltordnung durch asymmetrische Kriege', in Josef Schröfl and Thomas Pankratz (eds), *Asymmetrische Kriegführung – ein neues Phänomen in der internationalen Politik?*, Baden-Baden 2004, pp. 85–93.

Münkler, Herfried, 'The Wars of the 21st Century', *International Review of the Red Cross*, 85, March 2003, pp. 7–21.

Münkler, Herfried, 'Zur Charakterisierung der neuen Kriege', in *Krieg der Gegenwart – eine Beurteilung*, MiLAK Schrift No. 4, 2004, pp. 21–32.

Münkler, Herfried, and Karsten Fischer, '"Nothing to Kill or Die for . . .": Überlegungen zu einer politischen Theorie des Opfers', *Leviathan*, 3/2000, pp. 343–62.

Münkler, Herfried, Hans Grünberger and Kathrin Mayer, *Nationenbildung: Die Nationalisierung Europas im Diskurs humanistischer Intellektueller*, Berlin 1998.

Münkler, Marina, 'Entdecker und Eroberer', in Eva Horn et al. (eds), *Grenzverletzer*, Berlin 2002, pp. 156–75.

Nagel, Tilman, *Timur der Eroberer und die islamische Welt des späten Mittelalters*, Munich 1993.

Naimark, Norman, *Fires of Hatred: Ethnic Cleansing in 20th Century Europe*, Cambridge, MA, 2001.

Napoleoni, Loretta, *Die Ökonomie des Terrors*, Munich 2004.

'National Security Strategy of the United States of America', at http://www.whitehouse.gov/nsc/nss.pdf.

Nef, John U., *Western Civilization Since the Renaissance: Peace, War, Industry and the Arts*, New York 1963.

Nichtweiß, Barbara, 'Apokalyptische Verfassungslehren: Carl Schmitt im Horizont der Theologie Erik Petersons', in Bernd Wacker (ed.), *Die eigentlich katholische Verschärfung: Konfession, Theologie und Politik im Werk Carl Schmitts*, Munich 1994, pp. 37–64.

Niedhart, Gottfried, 'Der Erste Weltkrieg: Von der Gewalt im Krieg zu den Konflikten im Frieden', in Bernd Wegner (ed.), *Wie Kriege enden: Wege zum Frieden von der Antike bis zur Gegenwart*, Paderborn 2002, pp. 187–211.

Nippel, Wilfried, *Griechen, Barbaren und 'Wilde': Alte Geschichte und Sozialanthropologie*, Frankfurt am Main 1990.

Nippel, Wilfried, 'Griechische Kolonisation: Kontakte mit indigenen Kulturen, Rechtfertigung von Eroberung, Rückwirkungen auf das Mutterland', in Raimund Schulz (ed.), *Aufbruch in neuen Welten und neue Zeiten: Die großen maritimen Expansionsbewegungen der Antike und Frühen Neuzeit im Vergleich der europäischen Geschichte*, Munich 2003 (supplement of the journal *Historische Zeitschrift*, vol. 34), pp. 13–27.

Noth, Martin, *The History of Israel*, London 1983.

Nye, Joseph, 'Amerikas Macht', in Ulrich Speck and Natan Sznaider (eds), *Empire Amerika: Perspektiven einer neuen Weltordnung*, Munich 2003, pp. 156–72.

Nye, Joseph, *The Paradox of American Power: Why the World's Only Superpower Can't Go it Alone*, New York 2002.

Nye, Joseph, *Soft Power: The Means to Success in World Power*, New York 2004.

Oliveira Marques, A. H. de, *Geschichte Portugals und des portugiesischen Weltreichs*, Stuttgart 2001.

Oliveira Marques, A. H. de, *History of Portugal*, New York 1976.

Olshausen, Eckart, 'Das politische Denken der Römer zur Zeit der Republik', in *Pipers Handbuch der politischen Ideen*, ed. Iring Fetscher and Herfried Münkler, vol. 1, Munich 1988, pp. 485–519.

Osterhammel, Jürgen, 'China, Niedergang und Neubildung eines Vielvölkerreiches', in Richard Lorenz (ed.), *Das Verdämmern der Macht: Vom Untergang großer Reiche*, Frankfurt am Main 2000, pp. 104–25.

Osterhammel, Jürgen, *Colonialism: A Theoretical Overview*, Princeton, NJ, 1997.

Osterhammel, Jürgen, *Die Entzauberung Asiens: Europa und die asiatischen Reiche im 18. Jahrhundert*, Munich 1998.

Osterhammel, Jürgen, 'Kulturelle Grenzen bei der Expansion Europas', *Saeculum*, 46, 1995, pp. 101–38.

Ottmann, Henning, *Geschichte des politischen Denkens*, 2 vols, Stuttgart 2001-2.

Otto, Wolfgang, *Conquista, Kultur und Ketzerwahn: Spanien im Jahrhundert seiner Weltherrschaft*, Göttingen 1992.

Overy, Richard, *Why the Allies Won*, New York 1995.

Pagden, Anthony, 'Instruments of Empire: Tommaso Campanella and the Universal Monarchy of Spain', in Pagden, *Spanish Imperialism and Political Imagination*, New Haven, CT, 1990, pp. 37–63.

Pagden, Anthony, *Spanish Imperialism and Political Imagination*, New Haven, CT, 1990.

Parker, Geoffrey, *The Army of Flanders and the Spanish Road, 1567–1659*, Cambridge 1972.

Parker, Geoffrey, *The Military Revolution: Military Innovations and the Rise of the West, 1500–1800*, 2nd edn, Cambridge 1996.

Pepper, Simon, and Nicholas Adams, *Firearms and Fortifications: Military Architecture and Siege Warfare in Sixteenth-Century Siena*, Chicago 1986.

Philipp, Thomas, 'Der aufhaltsame Abstieg des Osmanischen Reiches', in Helmut Altrichter and Helmut Neuhaus (eds), *Das Ende von Großreichen*, Erlangen and Jena 1996, pp. 211–23.

Pieper, Renate, 'Das Ende des spanischen Kolonialreiches in Amerika', in Alexander Demandt (ed.), *Das Ende der Weltreichen*, Munich 1997, pp. 74–88.

Pipes, Richard, *The Russian Revolution*, London 1990.

Pollmann, Judith, 'Eine natürliche Feindschaft: Ursprung und Funktion der Schwarzen Legende über Spanien in den Niederländen, 1560–1581', in Franz Bosbach (ed.), *Feindbilder: Die Darstellung des Gegners in der politischen Pulizistik des Mittelalters und der Neuzeit*, Cologne 1992, pp. 73–93.

Pomian, Krzysztof, *L'Europe et ses nations*, Paris 1990.

Porter, Bernard, *The Absent-Minded Imperialists: Empire, Society and Culture in Britain*, Oxford 2004.

Porter, Bernard, 'Die Transformation des *British Empire*', in Alexander Demandt (ed.), *Das Ende der Weltreichen*, Munich 1997, pp. 155–73.

Potter, Timothy, *Roman Italy*, London 1987.

Power, Samantha, 'Das Empire der Menschenrechte', in Ulrich Speck and Natan Sznaider (eds), *Empire Amerika: Perspektiven einer neuen Weltordnung*, Munich 2003, pp. 138–53.

Prätorius, Rainer, *In God We Trust: Religion und Politik in den USA*, Munich 2003.

Priest, Dana, *The Mission: Waging War and Keeping Peace with America's Military*, New York 2003.

QRT [Markus Konradin Leiner], *Schlachtfelder der elektronischen Wüste: Schwarzkopz, Schwarzenegger, Black Magic Johnson*, Berlin 1999.

Radkau, Joachim, *Das Zeitalter der Nervosität: Deutschland zwischen Bismarck und Hitler*, Munich 1998.

Rauchensteiner, Manfried, 'Österreich-Ungarn', in Gerhard Hirschfeld et al. (eds), *Enzyklopädie Erster Weltkrieg*, Paderborn 2003, pp. 64–86.

Rauchensteiner, Manfried, 'Verlust der Mitte: Der Zerfall des habsburger Reiches', in Helmut Altrichter and Helmut Neuhaus (eds), *Das Ende von Großreichen*, Erlangen and Jena 1996, pp. 225–46.

Reifeld, Helmut, 'Imperialismus', in *Pipers Handbuch der politischen Ideen*, ed. Iring Fetscher and Herfried Münkler, vol. 5, Munich 1987, pp. 23–53.

Reinhard, Wolfgang, *Geschichte der Staatsgewalt*, Munich 1999.

Reinhard, Wolfgang, *Kleine Geschichte des Kolonialismus*, Stuttgart 1996.

Rémond, René, *Le XXe Siècle*, rev. edn, Paris 2002.

Reuter, Christoph, *Mein Leben ist eine Waffe: Selbstmordattentäter – Psychogramm eines Phänomens*, Munich 2002.

Richard, Carl J., *The Founders and the Classics: Greece, Rome, and the American Enlightenment*, Cambridge, MA, 1994.

Rifkin, Jeremy, *The European Dream: How Europe's Vision of the Future is Quietly Eclipsing the American Dream*, Cambridge 2004.

Rilinger, Rolf, 'Das politische Denken der Römer: Vom Prinzipat zum Dominat', in *Pipers Handbuch der politischen Ideen*, ed. Iring Fetscher and Herfried Münkler, vol. 1, Munich 1987, pp. 521–93.

Roberts, Michael, *The Military Revolution, 1550–1660*, Belfast 1956.

Robinson, Ronald, *Africa and the Victorians: The Official Mind of Imperialism*, London 1968.

Robinson, Ronald, 'Non-European Foundations of European Imperialism: Sketch for a Theory of Collaboration', in Roger Owen and Bob Sutcliff (eds), *Studies in a Theory of Imperialism*, London 1972, pp. 117–42.

Röhrich, Winfried, 'Problemfelder der Weltinnenpolitik', in Astrid Sahm et al. (eds), *Die Zukunft des Friedens*, Wiesbaden 2000, pp. 257–67.

Romilly, Jacqueline de, *Thucydides and Athenian Imperialism*, Oxford 1953.

Rorty, Richard, 'Ein Empire der Ungewissheit', in Ulrich Speck and Natan Sznaider (eds), *Empire Amerika: Perspektiven einer neuen Weltordnung*, Munich 2003, pp. 240–55.

Rosen, Stephen Peter, 'Ein Empire auf Probe', in Ulrich Speck and Natan Sznaider (eds), *Empire Amerika: Perspektiven einer neuen Weltordnung*, Munich 2003, pp. 83–103.

Ruf, Werner (ed.), *Politische Ökonomie der Gewalt: Staatsverfall und die Privatisierung von Gewalt und Krieg*, Opladen 2003.

Sassen, Saskia, *Losing Control? Sovereignty in the Age of Globalization*, New York 1996.

Schama, Simon, *The Embarrassment of Riches: An Interpretation of Dutch Culture in the Golden Age*, London 1987.

Schell, Jonathan, *Unconquerable World: Power, Nonviolence and the Will of the People*, London 2004.

Schieder, Theodor (ed.), *Handbuch der europäischen Geschichte*, Stuttgart 1968–87.

Schieder, Theodor, 'Typologie und Erscheinungsformen des Nationalstaats in Europa', in Schieder, *Nationalstaat: Studien zum nationalen Problem und modernen Europa*, Göttingen 1991, pp. 65–86.

Schley, Nicole, and Sabine Busse, *Die Kriege der USA: Chronik einer aggressiven Nation*, Kreuzlingen and Munich 2003.

Schmidt-Glintzer, Helwig, *China: Vielvölkerreich und Einheitsstaat*, Munich 1997.

Schmierer, Joscha, *Mein Name sei Europa: Einigung ohne Mythos und Utopie*, Frankfurt am Main 1996.

Schmitt, Carl, 'Großraum gegen Universalismus: Der völkerrechtliche Kampf um die Monroedoktrin', in Schmitt, *Positionen und Begriffe*, Berlin 1988, pp. 295–302.

Schmitt, Carl, *Theorie des Partisanen*, Berlin 1963.

Schmitt, Carl, 'Völkerrechtliche Formen des modernen Imperialismus', in Schmitt, *Positionen und Begriffe*, Berlin 1988, pp. 162–80.

Schmitt, Carl, *Völkerrechtliche Großraumordnung mit Interventionsverbot für raumfremde Mächte*, Berlin and Vienna 1939.

Schneider, Manfred, *Der Barbar: Endzeitstimmung und Kulturrecycling*, Munich 1997.

Schröder, Hans-Christoph, *Sozialistische Imperialismusdeutung: Studien zu ihrer Geschichte*, Göttingen 1973.

Schröfl, Josef, and Thomas Pankratz (eds), *Asymmetrische Kriegführung – ein neues Phänomen in der internationalen Politik?*, Baden-Baden 2004.

Schuller, Wolfgang, *Die Herrschaft der Athener im Ersten Attischen Seebund*, Berlin 1974.

Schulz, Gerhard (ed.), *Partisanen und Volkskrieg: Zur Revolutionierung des Krieges im 20. Jahrhundert*, Göttingen 1985.

Schulz, Raimund, 'Roms Eroberung des Mittelmeers und der Vorstoß in den Atlantik: Reaktion und Rückwirkungen auf die Ideologie, Geographie, Ethnographie und Anthropologie der späten Republik und frühen Kaiserzeit', in Schulz (ed.), *Aufbruch in neuen Welten und neue Zeiten: Die großen maritimen Expansionsbewegungen der Antike und Frühen Neuzeit im Vergleich*, Munich 2003, pp. 29–50.

Schumpeter, Joseph, 'The Sociology of Imperialism', in Schumpeter: *Imperialism and Social Classes: Two Essays*, New York 1955.

See, Klaus von, *Barbar, Germane, Arier: Die Suche nach der Identität der Deutschen*, Heidelberg 1994.

Seeck, Otto, *Geschichte des Untergangs der antiken Welt*, 6 vols, Berlin 1895–1920; Darmstadt 2000.

Simon, Gerhard, 'Die Desintegration der Sowjetunion', in Alexander Demandt (ed.), *Das Ende der Weltreichen*, Munich 1997, pp. 174–210.

Simon, Gerhard, and Nadja Simon, *Verfall und Untergang des sowjetischen Imperiums*, Munich 1993.

Sloterdijk, Peter, *Falls Europa erwacht: Gedanken zum Programm einer Weltmacht am Ende des Zeitalters ihrer politischen Absence*, Frankfurt am Main 1994.

Snyder, Jack, *Myths of Empire: Domestic Politics and International Ambition*, Ithaca, NY, 1991.

Sofsky, Wolfgang, *Operation Freiheit: Der Krieg im Irak*, Frankfurt am Main 2003.

Soggin, J. Alberto, *An Introduction to the History of Israel and Judah*, London 1993.

Sombart, Werner, *Händler und Helden: Patriotische Besinnungen*, Munich 1915.

Soros, George, *The Bubble of American Supremacy: Correcting the Misuse of American Power*, New York 2004.

Steininger, Rolf, *Der Vietnamkrieg*, Frankfurt am Main 2004.

Steinweg, Rainer (ed.), *Der gerechte Krieg: Christentum, Islam, Marxismus*, Frankfurt am Main 1980.

Stiglitz, Joseph, *Globalization and its Discontents*, New York 2002.

Stinnett, Robert B., *Day of Deceit: The Truth about FDR and Pearl Harbor*, New York 2000.

Stökl, Günther, *Russische Geschichte*, Stuttgart 1997.

Strachan, Hew, *The First World War*, Oxford 2001.

Syme, Ronald, *The Roman Revolution: On Political and Social Change between 60 BC and 14 AD*, Oxford 1939.

Tacitus, *Annals*, trans. Alfred John Church and W. Jackson Brodribb, New York 2003.

Taube, Manfred (ed.), *Die Geheime Geschichte der Mongolen*, Munich 1989.

Thompson, William R., *On Global War: Historical-Structural Approaches to World Politics*, Columbia, SC, 1988.

Thucydides, *History of the Peloponnesian War*, trans. Rex Warner, Harmondsworth 1954.

Tilgner, Ulrich, *Der inszenierte Krieg: Täuschung und Wahrheit beim Sturz Saddam Husseins*, Berlin 2003.

Todd, Emmanuel, *After the Empire: The Breakdown of the American Order*, New York 2003.

Triepel, Heinrich, *Die Hegemonie: Ein Buch von führenden Staaten*, Stuttgart 1938.

Tuchman, Barbara, *The March of Folly: From Troy to Vietnam*, New York 1984.

Ullrich, Volker, *Die nervöse Großmacht: Aufstieg und Untergang des deutschen Kaiserreichs 1871–1918*, Frankfurt am Main 1997.

Ursinus, Michael, 'Byzanz, Osmanisches Reich, türkischer Nationalstaat: Zur Gleichzeitigkeit des Ungleichzeitigen am Vorabend des Ersten Weltkriegs', in Richard Lorenz (ed.), *Das Verdämmern der Macht: Vom Untergang großer Reiche*, Frankfurt am Main 2000, pp. 153–72.

Vagts, Alfred, 'Die Chimäre des europäischen Gleichgewichts', in Vagts, *Bilanzen und Balancen: Aufsätze zur internationalen Finanz und internationalen Politik*, Frankfurt am Main 1979, pp. 131–60.

Valéry, Paul, 'The Crisis of Mind' (1919), second letter, http://www.historyguide.org/europe/valery.html.

Vance, Norman, 'Vom mare nostrum zu Kiplings "The Seven Seas": Das Römische Weltreich und Britanniens Wahrnehmung des Empire von 1600–1914', in Raimund Schulz (ed.), *Aufbruch in neuen Welten und neue Zeiten: Die großen maritimen Expansionsbewegungen der Antike und Frühen Neuzeit im Vergleich*, Munich 2003, pp. 79–108.

Verenkotte, Clemens, *Die Herren der Welt: Das amerikanische Imperium*, Munich 2003.

Vidal, Gore, *Perpetual War for Perpetual Peace: How We Got to Be So Hated*, New York 2002.

Virgil, *Aeneid*, in *Virgil in Two Volumes*, vol. 1, London 1974.

Voegelin, Eric, *Das ökumenische Zeitalter – Weltherrschaft und Philosophie*, Munich 2004.

Volkmann-Schluck, Karl-Heinz, *Politische Philosophie*, Frankfurt am Main 1974.

Voss, Tobias, '"Ich habe keine Stimme mehr, mein ganzes Leben flieht": Psychische Dimensionen des Guerilla-Krieges', in Herfried Münkler (ed.), *Der Partisan: Theorie, Strategie, Gestalt*, Opladen 1990.

Wallerstein, Immanuel, *The Modern World-System: Capitalist Agriculture and the Origins of the European World-Economy in the Sixteenth Century*, New York 1974.

Wallerstein, Immanuel, 'The Rise and Coming Demise of the World Capitalist System: Concepts for Comparative Analysis', in *The Capitalist World-Economy: Essays by Immanuel Wallerstein*, Cambridge 1979.

Waltz, Kenneth, *Theory of International Politics*, Reading, MA, 1979.

Walzer, Michael, 'Is There an American Empire?', *Dissent*, Fall 2003, pp. 27–31.

Walzer, Michael, *Just and Unjust Wars*, London 1978.

Weber, Max, *Economy and Society*, 2 vols, Berkeley, CA, 1968.

Weber, Max, 'The National State and Economic Policy', in K. Tribe (ed.), *Reading Weber*, London 1989, pp. 188–209.

Wehler, Hans-Ulrich, *Der Aufstieg des amerikanischen Imperialismus: Studien zur Entstehung des Imperium Americanum 1865–1900*, Göttingen 1974.

Weiers, Michael, 'Geschichte der Mongolen', in Arne Eggebrecht (ed.), *Die Mongolen und ihr Weltreich*, Mainz 1989, pp. 45–114.

Weiers, Michael, 'Von Ögödei bis Möngke: Das mongolische Großreich', in Weiers (ed.), *Die Mongolen: Beiträge zu ihrer Geschichte und Kultur*, Darmstadt 1986, pp. 192–216.

Welwei, Karl-Wilhelm, *Das klassische Athen: Demokratie und Machtpolitik im 5. und 4. Jahrhundert*, Darmstadt 1999.

Wenskus, Reinhard, *Stammesbildung und Verfassung: Das Werden der frühmittelalterischen Gentes*, Cologne 1961.

'What we're fighting for – wofür wir kämpfen', *Blätter für deutsche und internationale Politik*, 6/2002, pp. 756–60.

Wolfram, Herwig, *History of the Goths*, Berkeley, CA, 1988.

Wood, Gordon S., *The Creation of the American Republic, 1776–1787*, Chapel Hill, NC, 1969.

Zanker, Paul, *The Power of Images in the Age of Augustus*, Ann Arbor, MI, 1988.

Zimmerer, Jürgen, and Joachim Zeller (eds), *Völkermord in Deutsch-Südwestafrika: Der Kolonialkrieg (1904–1908) in Namibia und seine Folgen*, Berlin 2003.

INDEX

CPSIA information can be obtained at www.ICGtesting.com
Printed in the USA
BVOW02s2039260114

342971BV00010B/294/P